FACTA DUCIS VIVENT, OPEROSAQUE
GLORIA RERUM.——OVID, IN LIVIAM, 265.

THE HERO'S DEEDS AND HARD-WON
FAME SHALL LIVE.

CHARLES XII.

CHARLES XII.
FROM A PORTRAIT BY JULIUS KRONBERG.

Frontispiece.

CHARLES XII

AND THE COLLAPSE OF THE
SWEDISH EMPIRE

1682-1719

BY

ROBERT NISBET BAIN

Select Bibliographies Reprint Series

 BOOKS FOR LIBRARIES PRESS
FREEPORT, NEW YORK

First Published 1895
Reprinted 1969

STANDARD BOOK NUMBER:
8369-5064-X

LIBRARY OF CONGRESS CATALOG CARD NUMBER:
70-95062

PRINTED IN THE UNITED STATES OF AMERICA

PREFACE

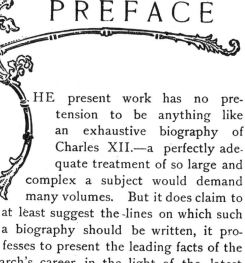

THE present work has no pretension to be anything like an exhaustive biography of Charles XII.—a perfectly adequate treatment of so large and complex a subject would demand many volumes. But it does claim to at least suggest the lines on which such a biography should be written, it professes to present the leading facts of the heroic monarch's career in the light of the latest investigations and it endeavours to dissipate the many erroneous notions concerning "The Lion of the North" for which Voltaire's brilliant and attractive work, I had almost said romance, *Histoire de Charles XII.* is mainly responsible.

It is a question, I think, how far original documents should be consulted in the compilation of a short sketch of this kind, or even whether they should be consulted at all. For the use of original documents necessitates, generally speaking, the addition of notes, appendices and other literary *impedimenta* which are almost out of place in a popular book of so small a compass as the present one. Nevertheless, I have endeavoured, somewhat reluctantly, to steer a middle course, by following the best available Swedish monographs in the purely historical and political portions of this book while going to original documents for the private conduct and personal character of my hero.—It now remains for me to set out my principal authorities.

I.

ORIGINAL DOCUMENTS.

1.—*Konung Karl XIIs. Egenhandiga Bref.* Ed. CARLSON.

2.—*Fragments tirés des chroniques moldaves pour servir a l'histoire de Pierre le Grand et Charles XII.* Ed. KOGALNICEANŬ.

3.—*Des Printzens Max Emanuels Herzog in Wurtemberg Riesen und Campagnen.*

4.—*Karl XI's Dagbok.*

5.—*Kurze Nachricht von Sr Konigliche Majt's Studien* (by Count POLUS).

6.—*Negociations de M. le Comte d'Avaux . . . a la cour de Suede* (No. 33 of the publications of the Historical Society at Utrecht, new series).

7.—*Letters and Despatches of John Duke of Marlborough.* Ed. MURRAY.

8.—*Correspondance diplomatique . . . du Duc de Marlborough.* Ed. VREEDE.

9.—*Historia Ablegationis Danielis Krmann . . . ad regem Sveciæ Carolum XII. 1708–9.* (Publication of the Hungarian Historical Society, 1894.)*

---

* Now used for the first time. So far as I am aware this document is quite unknown to Swedish historians.

II.

MONOGRAPHS, FOR THE MOST PART SWEDISH.

1.—CARLSON : *Sveriges Historia under Konungarne af Pfalziska Huset.*
2.—BESKOW : *Karl den Tolfte.*
3.—FRYXELL : *Berättelser ur Svenska Historien.**
4.—CARLSON : *Carl den Tolftes tåg mot Ryssland.*
5.—HAMILTON : *Minne af Grefve C. G. Rehnskjold.*
6.—SVEDELIUS : *Minne af Grefve Karl Piper.*
7.—CARLSON : *Om Fredsunderhandlingarne åren 1709–1718.*
8.—SVEDELIUS : *Minne af Grefve Arvid Horn.*
9.—LILLIESTRÅLE : *Magnus Stenbock och Slaget vid Helsingborg.*
10.—LAGERMARK : *Karl XIIs Krig i Norge.*
11.—HOLM : *Studier til den store nordiske Krigs Historie.*
12.—BESKOW : *Friherre G. H. von Görtz, statsman och statsoffer.*
13.—AXELSON : *Bidrag till Kännedomen om Sveriges tillstånd på Karl XIIs tid.*
14.—SARAUW : *Die Feldzüge Karls XII.*
15.—CARLEN : *Några blad om Carl XII.*
16.—BRÜCKNER : *Peter der Grosse.*

R. NISBET BAIN.

August, 1895.

---

* This entertaining but prejudiced and uncritical work should be used very cautiously.

CONTENTS.

CHAPTER VII.

CHAPTER VIII.

CHAPTER IX.

CHAPTER X.

CHAPTER XI.

Pultawa not an irreparable disaster—Anomalous position of
Sweden in 1709—The Danes invade Scania—Stenbock de-
feats them at the battle of Helsingborg—Total loss of
Sweden's Baltic provinces—Neutrality compact of The
Hague—Charles repudiates it—The Russo-Turkish war—
The King and the Senate—Arvid Bernard Horn—Growing
differences — Charles's reproaches — Dire distress of the
nation—Financial shifts—Stenbock sent to Germany with a
fresh army—Capture of Rostock—Desperate position of
Stenbock—King Stanislaus departs for Bender—Battle of
Gadebusch.

CHAPTER XII.

Necessity for Sweden to surrender something—Obstinacy of
Charles—Rejects the mediation of England—And the offer
of the alliance of Prussia—Movements of Stenbock after
Gadebusch—The burning of Altona—Surrender of the
Swedes at Tönning—Last sufferings and death of Stenbock
—Desperate position of Sweden—Finland lost—Stettin oc-
cupied—Charles refuses the mediation of Louis XIV.—
Despair of the Swedish Senate—A Riksdag summoned—
Condition of the finances—Dissatisfaction of the Estates—
Their revolutionary projects—Ambiguous conduct of the
Princess Ulrica—Energetic intervention of Chancellor Horn
—Return of Charles XII.—Enthusiasm in Sweden—Fresh
complications—Prussia and Hanover declare war against
Charles—The siege of Stralsund—Engagement of Stresow
—Fruitless heroism of the King—Fall of Stralsund.

CHAPTER XIII.

CHAPTER XIV.

ILLUSTRATIONS.

[1] From an engraving in Kronberg's Magazine.
[2] " Svenska Drottningar."
[3] Viebull's " Sveriges Storhetstid." Hiertas. Stockholm.
[4] Snoilsky, " Svenska Bilder."
[5] Fryxell, " Berättelser ur Svenska Historien."

[1] Fryxell, " Berättelser ur Svenska Historien."
[2] Viebull's " Sveriges Storhetstid." Hiertas. Stockholm.
[3] " Svenska Landtmarskalkar."
[4] Danmarks, Norges og Sverige Historien.
[5] Cartensen's " Tordenskiold."
[6] From a plate by Cederström.
[7] " Svenska Drottningar."

CHARLES XII.

CHARLES XII.

AND THE COLLAPSE OF THE SWEDISH EMPIRE.

CHAPTER I.

INTRODUCTORY.

1522–1697.

The history of Sweden the history of her kings—Sudden growth of the Swedish Empire—Gustavus Adolphus's genius mischievous to Sweden—Sweden as a great Power—Axel Oxenstjerna—Frivolity of Christina—Exploits of Charles X.—Position of Sweden at his death—Long and ruinous minority of Charles XI.—Magnus Gabriel de la Gardie—Outbreak of a general European war—Engagement of Fehrbellin lays bare the real weakness of Sweden—Heroism of youthful Charles XI.—His drastic remedies—Restoration of Sweden as a great Power—The monarchy made absolute.

HE history of Sweden, it has well been said, is the history of her kings. Till the reign of Gustavus Vasa there was no such thing as a Swedish State in the modern sense of the word. Sweden in those days was a name rather than a nation. Even so late as the third decade of the sixteenth century she cheerfully submitted to the humiliation of being

I

treated as little better than a trading colony by the Hansa League to avoid absorption by Denmark. Gustavus I. laid the foundations of her national existence as well as of her future greatness in the strong monarchy which he bequeathed to his sons, and so well did he do his work that even their follies and blunders could not seriously shake it. Gradually the young State began to feel her power and expand in every direction. The complications resulting from the collapse of the German Order first gave her a footing on the other side of the Baltic, and with the acquisition of Reval (1561) her dominion in the North may be said to have been founded. From Esthonia she advanced, step by step, into Livonia, though here the way was barred, for a time, by the valour of the Polish chivalry and the genius of the Grand Hetman of Lithuania, Jan Karol Chodkiewicz. Nevertheless, in Livonia also, Sweden, on the whole, stood her ground, and it was the tenacity of that cruel but eminently capable monarch, Charles IX., that prepared the way for the ultimate triumph of his illustrious son. Gustavus Adolphus inherited from his father a war with Russia as well as a war with Poland. Only two years before, Charles IX. had combined (1609) with Tsar Vasily Shuisky against their common foe Poland, but the swift and irresistible advance of the Poles upset all the calculations of the allies. Vasily was deposed and carried off to Warsaw; a Polish prince was placed on the Muscovite throne, and Russia was straightway plunged into such a horrible state of anarchy that her speedy and complete dissolution seemed inevi-

table. Unable to assist their ally, the Swedes had
now to look to themselves. Their plans alternated
between raising up a Swedish tsar against his Polish
competitor, or appropriating all Russia between
Great Novgorod and Archangel; but, ultimately,
the vastness of Russia's domains and the doggedness of her people saved her now as they had saved
her from the Tartars two centuries before. With
the election of the first Romanov, a new era began
for the distracted country, and after a glorious but
indecisive six years' struggle, Gustavus, recognising
the impossibility of obliterating his eastern neigh-
bour, dictated a peace that was to paralyse her for a
century. By the Peace of Stolbova (27 Feb., 1617)
Russia abandoned all her claims to Esthonia and
Livonia, ceded Carelia and Ingria to Sweden, and
paid besides a war indemnity of 200,000 rubles. By
this humiliating treaty the frontier of Russia was
thrust back beyond Lake Ladoga and she was totally
excluded from the Baltic.

The war with Poland (then at the height of her
short-lived power) proved a much more serious business. It took Gustavus nine years of hard fighting
to wrest Livonia from her grasp ; but the victory of
Wallhof (7 June, 1626) finally completed the work.
With Riga in his possession, he was now master of
the Dwina, and in 1626 he transferred the war to
West Prussia (then a fief of Poland) that he might
gain the command of the Vistula likewise and so de-
prive Poland also of her northern seaboard. Imperial indeed was the policy of the great Swede.
It was his secret but steadfast resolve to found a

Scandinavian empire with the Baltic for its Mediter-
ranean; nay, there is good reason to believe that,
had he lived to realise his ambition, he would have
transferred his capital from the shores of the remote
Mälare to a more central position on the very spot
where Peter the Great, a century later, with equal
prescience, was to erect Petersburg. Unfortunately
for Sweden, this magnificent project was postponed
to a nobler but less practical ambition—the heroic
monarch determined to champion the desperate
cause of his suffering co-religionists in Germany.
No vision of an imperial crown, as some have
thought, tempted him to draw his sword in their
behalf. There can now be no doubt that, in this matter, he consulted his conscience rather than his common-sense, and not without reason has grateful
Protestantism regarded him, ever since, as her ideal
hero and her typical saint, her Bayard and her St.
Louis in one.

Yet, although Gustavus's German crusade is his
fairest title to. fame, politically it was a serious
blunder, for glorious as were its immediate results,
its ultimate consequences proved mischievous and
even ruinous to his country. His original project
of establishing a compact, connected and, to a certain extent, homogeneous empire round the shores
of the Baltic was well within the reach of Sweden's
resources, and had he stopped short at the Dwina, or
even at the Vistula, it could easily have been accomplished and Sweden might, to this day, have remained the Mistress of the North. But every step
he took westward of the Vistula was a false step

because it removed him farther and farther from the
real centre of his power; he was now fighting other
peoples' battles instead of his own; his very
triumphs were illusory because they blinded his
country to her inherent weakness and, but for the
genius of the extraordinary man he left behind him
to sustain his empire during the minority of his
daughter, even the crowning victory of Breitenfeld
(7 Sept., 1631) had like to have been the grave of
Sweden's greatness.

For it was the unerring eye and steady hand of the
Swedish Chancellor, Axel Oxenstjerna ("that axle
on which the world turns," as the French diplomatists called him), that during the next twelve
anxious years steered Sweden safely through the
sea of troubles which threatened every moment to
engulph her. That she emerged from the Thirty
Years' war, not merely a great Power, but the
acknowledged head of Continental Protestantism,
was mainly due to the wisdom and courage of this
great statesman. It was he who, throughout the
crisis of the struggle, kept her wavering allies
together; skilfully hid her weakness from the watch-
fulness of her foes; gave fresh generals to her armies
and fresh armies to her generals; inspired the
Swedish Senate and the Swedish Estates with something of his own patriotism and withstood the Queen
herself at the Council Board when her levity seemed
likely to fritter away the fruits of so many costly
triumphs. Christina herself was obliged to respect
the veteran statesman who had been her father's
most cherished counsellor and her own faithful

guardian; but her vanity chafed against an authority which obscured while it protected the throne. Though she could not set aside she delighted to thwart the all-powerful Chancellor, and it was chiefly due to her interference that the Peace of Westphalia was not so advantageous to Sweden as Oxenstjerna tried to make it. Inadequate, almost paltry, was the reward which Sweden thereby obtained for the services and the sacrifices of eighteen years. Western Pomerania with the islands of Rügen and Usedom, a small strip of Eastern Pomerania with the towns of Stettin, Damin, Golbrow and the Isle of Wollin; Wismar and the district of Poel and Neukloster; the former Bishopric of Bremen and Verden with a seat and a vote in the German Reichstag and the direction of the Lower Saxon circle alternately with Brandenburg, was all that fell to her share. These new possessions, it will be seen, gave Sweden the control of the three chief rivers of Germany, the Oder, the Elbe and the Weser, and she had the exclusive right to all the tolls levied thereon. They were, indeed, her most lucrative possessions so long as she held them, but a single glance at the map of Europe will suggest, at once, the difficulty she would have in retaining these scattered, outlying possessions. Her former allies already began to regard her as an intruder, and it was not to be expected that Germany would tamely submit to a foreign Power having the practical control of her external trade. These German possessions, moreover, were mischievous to Sweden in another way. They gave her a false importance on the Continent which she was always endeavouring to increase and thus withdrew her from her natural policy, the consolidation of her northern dominions round the Baltic, a task now needing all her energies and resources. For so poor and thinly populated a country to attempt to dominate Germany and remain the Mistress of the North at the same time meant inevitable disaster, though favourable circumstances and an extraordinary succession of great rulers postponed the evil day for something more than half a century. Moreover, Christina's boundless extravagances during the last six years of her reign did not tend to improve matters. The resources of the State in those days were mainly derived from the vast crown-lands, and these Christina distributed so recklessly among her favourite courtiers that, at last, the permanent annual loss to the Crown was no less than £200,000, and when, in 1654, she voluntarily resigned the crown to her cousin Charles,* the new King found the realm not very far removed from bankruptcy. His first care was to summon the Estates to relieve his more pressing wants and, at his suggestion, and with their consent, it was resolved to *reduce*, or, as we should say, recover a certain proportion of the alienated crown-lands; and a fresh department of state was formed to carry out this very necessary reform. Then, after celebrating his marriage with the Princess Hedwig Eleanora of Holstein, the King embarked for the Continent to begin a war that he was never to finish.

---

* Charles X. was the son of Catherine, daughter of Gustavus Vasa, and John Casimir, Duke of Zweibrücken.

The marvellous exploits of Charles X., though
not nearly so well known as they should be, can,
nevertheless, only be hinted at here. Charles's policy was a continuation and extension of the original
policy of Gustavus Adolphus freely interpreted by
the extravagant imagination of a Prince, who, with
all his genius, was much more of a knight-errant than
a statesman or even a general. It was his intention,
primarily, to round off and weld together Sweden's
Baltic possessions by adding thereto all the Polish
territory intervening between Pomerania and Livonia. The wretched condition of Poland, engaged
as she then was in a mortal struggle with her own
rebellious Cossacks aided by Russia, seemed to
promise him an easy triumph, and, in fact, within
six months he had driven John Casimir, the Polish
King, into exile and taken possession of nearly the
whole of Poland proper. But he soon found that it
was easier to beat the Polish hosts than to subdue
the Polish nation. The tyranny of the northern invader led to a general rising and in Stephen Czar-
niecki (*vir molestissimus*, as Charles X. called him)
the Poles found at last a deliverer. Despite fresh
victories (notably the great three days' battle of
Warsaw, 18–20 July, 1656), Charles found himself
steadily losing ground and, to add to his troubles,
Russia now fell upon Livonia and Esthonia ; Denmark, instigated by the Emperor, invaded Bremen
and South Sweden simultaneously, while Brandenburg, his sole ally, suddenly went over to his enemies.
Then it was that Charles dissipated the league that
seemed about to overwhelm him by leading a host

of 13,000 men across the barely frozen waters of the
Belt, a feat absolutely without a parallel in history,
annihilating the Danish forces that barred the way to
Copenhagen, and dictating to the terrified Danish Government the humiliating Peace of Roskilde (26 Feb.,
1658). In pursuance of his Pan-Scandinavian policy,
Charles tried by this treaty to detach Denmark from
Holland, so as to "have his back free," as he expressed it, while dealing with his other foes. But
the Dutch, well aware of Charles's intention to ex-
clude them altogether from the Baltic, secretly encouraged the Danes to refuse to ratify the treaty
and, accordingly, after six months of diplomatic fen-
cing, a second war between the two northern Powers
began. Charles, thoroughly determined this time to
wipe out the Danish monarchy altogether, invaded
Zealand in August, 1658, captured the fortress of
Kronberg commanding the Sound, and proceeded to
invest Copenhagen. But a strong Dutch fleet under
Van Weisenaer, after six hours' hard fighting, forced
the passage of the Sound (29 October, 1658) and
threw supplies and reinforcements into the beleaguered city. Still Charles persisted, but the heroic resistance of the besieged, the destruction of a Swedish
army-corps in Funen and a general invasion of all
his continental possessions by his numerous foes inclined him, at last, to peace. Wisely trusting rather
in the support of his own subjects than to the mediation of interested foreign Powers, he summoned a
Riksdag, or Diet, to Gothenburg at the end of 1659.
He was now willing to come to terms with Denmark,
Holland and Poland so as to have his hands free to

deal with Russia and Brandenburg; but death over-
took him (13 February, 1660) at the very moment
when his country had most need of his genius to ex-
tricate her from the difficulties into which his ambition had plunged her. He left behind him an only
son, a child four years of age.

Had the enemies of Sweden only realised her utter
prostration they would not have listened so readily
to the pacific overtures that she now hastened to
make to them. But the victories of Charles X., if
they did nothing else, at least inspired Europe with
a wholesome fear and a respect of the Swedish arms,
and thus materially assisted the Swedish regency in
its endeavours to come to terms with the hostile
coalition. The ambitious dreams of Charles X. had
indeed to be abandoned; but, on the other hand,
Sweden lost nothing at all on the Continent, while in
the Scandinavian peninsula itself she gained at last
her natural frontiers by the acquisition of the provinces of Scania, Halland and Bleking, which had
belonged to Denmark time out of mind.

The regency appointed by Charles X. consisted of
the Queen Dowager and the five great officers of
state. The Queen herself was a nonentity, but as the
five magnates had grown grey in the public service
and each, in his own line, had already done notable
deeds, the dying monarch had good reason to believe that he had left his infant son in safe and strong
hands. As a matter of fact this regency was the
weakest and most mischievous Sweden ever had.
The most respectable of the five regents were Counts
Gustaf Bonde and Per Brahe, excellent types of the

old-fashioned conservative aristocracy at its best, and so long as the former was alive and the latter in health, things went fairly well; but, ultimately, the management of affairs fell entirely into the hands of the Chancellor, Magnus Gabriel de la Gardie, always the evil genius of the regency. The brilliant accomplishments, immense wealth and princely liberality of De la Gardie had made him the most conspicuous figure in Sweden during three successive reigns; but he had never shewn any particular aptitude for affairs and his boundless extravagance and frivolity were as ruinous to his country as to himself. Under his misrule Sweden sunk lower than she had ever sunk before. At home De la Gardie's administration was marked by the most criminal recklessness. The salutary *reduction* scheme, whereby Charles X. had hoped gradually to diminish the national debt and double the national revenue, was allowed to stand still because it was unpopular with the nobility; the prodigalities of Christina were renewed and the supporters of the Minister were enriched at the public expense while the soldiers of the frontier garrisons were starving and the salaries of half the civil service remained unpaid for lack of funds. Moreover, the financial difficulties of the country reacted injuriously on her foreign policy. Sweden now became what she had never been before, a mere mercenary of France. The continental complications resulting from the ambition of Louis XIV. led both France and the allies banded against her to bid against each other for the support of the great northern Power. De la Gardie was the friend of France,

but his opponents in the Senate were for a watchful
neutrality whose object should be to check the extravagant pretensions of *le grand Monarque* by drawing nearer to England and Holland. For a time, too
(1668–1672), they carried their point, and the Triple
Alliance which compelled Louis XIV. to accept the
terms of the allies was mainly their work. But, in
the long run, De la Gardie prevailed. By the Treaty
of Stockholm (14 April, 1672) Sweden virtually sold
herself to Louis XIV., by engaging to hold an army-
corps of 16,000 men in Germany at his disposal in
return for ample subsidies. At the same time De la
Gardie flattered himself that he would be able to steer
clear of a war and so get the indispensable subsidies
for nothing. But the course of events proved too
strong for him. Throughout 1673–4 Sweden tried,
in vain, to mediate between the belligerents. Then
Louis grew impatient and peremptorily demanded
that Sweden should give him the covenanted assistance for which he had already paid ; and so, at last,
in December, 1674, Marshal Wrangel invaded Brandenburg and went into winter quarters there.
There was a pause of suspense during which all
Germany looked for fresh proofs of Sweden's ancient
prowess, and then the seed sown by twelve years of
sloth and slackness was reaped in manifest disaster.
Anticipating attack by himself attacking, the Elector
of Brandenburg surprised a Swedish division at Fehrbellin (28 June, 1675) and defeated it with the loss of
600 men, whereupon the Swedes fell back at all points.

The so-called Battle of Fehrbellin was little more
than a sharp engagement, but its moral effect was

QUEEN HEDWIG ELEANORA, CHARLES XII'S GRANDMOTHER.

tremendous. The general belief in the invincibility of the Swedish arms was rudely shaken ; her German allies drew back, and Denmark, Brandenburg, Holland and the Emperor fell upon her simultaneously. By the end of 1676 nearly all her German possessions were lost, while her fleet was annihilated by the combined Dutch and Danish squadrons under Juel and Van Tromp at the great two days' battle of Öland. At this crisis it was the heroic energy of the young King that alone saved the country. Charles XI. was at this time a rough lad of twenty whose education had been shamefully neglected by his guardians ; but the bitter ordeal of the next six years was to ripen, or rather harden, him into a stern and precocious manhood. At first, indeed, it seemed as if the poor youth were absolutely stunted and stupefied by the disasters which crashed down upon him one after another ; but, hampered though he was at every step by craven counsellors and incompetent ministers, his unconquerable courage sustained him to the end, and his shrewd common-sense (always his strong point) divining that a victory obtained at any cost was now the sole remedy for the universal demoralisation, he led his army straight against the invading Danes and utterly routed them at the battle of Halmstad (17 August, 1676). At the end of the same year the young King again attacked the Danes at Lund, against the advice of all his generals, and won another victory which, relatively to the numbers engaged, was the bloodiest of the century, 8300 out of 16,000 combatants perishing on the field. The year 1677 was marked by two crushing

naval defeats of the Swedes at the hands of the
Danes and Dutch and the total loss of Pomerania;
but, in Sweden itself, Charles with only 9000 men
defeated 12,000 Danes at the battle of Landscrona
after a fierce struggle of eight hours. This crowning
victory enabled the Swedes in 1678 to recover all the
Scanian fortresses captured by the Danes; but an
invasion of Prussia from Livonia failed utterly—
thus, after seven years of incessant fighting, Sweden
had been barely able to keep the foe at bay at home
and had lost everything abroad. Fortunately, for
her, an uninterrupted series of victories had, in the
meantime, made her ally, Louis XIV., the arbiter of
Europe, and the terms which he condescended at
last to offer his antagonists, in the course of 1678, in-
cluded a full restitution of all the territory wrested
from Sweden. Protestations were in vain, on this
point *le grand Monarque* was inexorable. He needed
a strong power in the North devoted to his interests,
and by the treaties of Nijmegen, St. Germaine,
Celle and Lund, Sweden recovered all her German
possessions except a few trifling strips of territory
which her high-handed protector took upon himself
to cede to her more importunate creditors without
her knowledge or consent. Upon the proud and
sensitive mind of Charles XI., however, the dictatorial, almost contemptuous, tone of his magnificent
protector produced an ineffaceable impression.
Henceforth he was possessed by an inveterate dislike and distrust of everything French,* and we shall

---

* He would not even wear "a French knife" as he contemptuously
called the rapiers of the period.

see that in this, as in so many other respects, Charles XII. was his father's own son.

Charles XI. devoted the rest of his days to setting his house in order. The fiery ordeal through which he had just passed had opened his eyes to the real situation of his country ; his practical common-sense was convinced that only the most rigid economy could make her Government strong and stable once more, and he really seems to have believed himself divinely commissioned to reform her abuses and re-establish her greatness. His plan was a very simple one. He determined to thoroughly carry out his father's *reduction*, or land-recovery, scheme, well aware that in this he could count upon the support of his people; and he addressed himself to the task with an energy and a perseverance compared with which even the labours of a Frederick the Great or a Joseph II. seem insignificant. Never, indeed, was any Swedish monarch so popular as Charles XI. The nation at large thoroughly believed in him and contrasted his manifold energy and manifest honesty with the slackness and problematical probity of the aristocratic classes. Ever since the days of Gustavus Adolphus the nobility and gentry of Sweden had tended to become more and more of a dominating and exclusive military caste gradually appropriating the bulk of the crown-lands and, as a matter of fact, both impoverishing the State (which in those days was synonymous with the Crown) and gradually obliterating the yeomanry and peasant proprietors. So violent and vindictive, indeed, was class feeling in Sweden in those days, that the Riksdag or Diet was now inclined to give the King even more than he asked for; the noble and the non-noble orders bid repeatedly against each other to win his favour, and if at the end of his reign Charles XI. found himself one of the most absolute princes in Europe, it was far less the result of his own seeking than of his people's choosing. From the first the three lower Estates (Clergy, Burgesses and Peasants) warmly supported the King's land-redemption project, not so much because the State would gain as because the gentry would suffer by it. The Riksdags of 1682, 1686 and 1693 successively authorised Charles XI. to examine all the title-deeds of all the landed estates in the realm with a view to their ultimate recovery by the Crown; zealously interpreted all the fundamental laws in a non-natural, monarchical sense, and even revived long obsolete laws for the express benefit of the Crown. It is remarkable, too, that, in all these matters the Estates themselves took the initiative. The King, all along, kept discreetly in the background, skilfully taking advantage of the antagonism of the Estates; now and then putting leading questions to them as to the exact limits of his prerogatives and invariably using their invariably favourable responses as the starting-points for fresh pretensions. At last the Riksdag became little more than the obsequious mouth-piece of royalty, and the climax of self-surrender was reached when the Riksdag of 1693 by its so-called "*Suveränetets-förklaring*," or Declaration of Sovereignty, solemnly declared his Majesty to be "an all-commanding sovereign king responsible for his actions to none on earth, but with power and authority as a Christian King to rule and govern his realm as it seemeth him best." On the other hand, it is only fair to add that Charles XI. made excellent use of his practically unlimited power. His ordering, reforming hand was felt in every corner of the realm, and though the redemption of the crown-lands was frequently pressed on with a relentless sternness not easily distinguishable from cruelty, and though such an economical revolution could not fail, for a time, to depreciate all sorts of property and thus have a very unsettling effect generally, yet, in the long run, it was a distinct and lasting benefit to the State and the nation. The finances were regulated, the treasury was replenished, trade developed, agriculture improved and the national defences were strengthened and multiplied.

And the moral improvement of Sweden under Charles XI. was even more remarkable than her material improvement. It stands to reason that under an absolute monarch whose every action was determined by a stern sense of duty, and who was known to work all his days and half his nights in the public service, thrift and industry would be regarded as the cardinal virtues and none would have the slightest chance of preferment who was not prepared to work at least as hard as his master. The people naturally followed the example of their King and the wholesome influence of Charles XI. had a bracing, hardening effect upon the national character which was perhaps the real secret of that wonderful elasticity which enabled the nation to sustain a twenty years' war against the banded might of Europe beneath the banner of his heroic son.

The stability of Sweden at home corresponded with her renewed importance abroad. In the latter days of Charles XI. she once again became a great Power whose friendship was coveted and whose enmity was avoided. The King himself, who had no great liking for diplomacy (he seems to have regarded it as little else than lying on a large scale), left the department of foreign affairs almost entirely in the hands of his Chancellor, the aged Bengt Oxenstjerna, whose cautious circumspection managed, though not without some difficulty, to keep Sweden clear of all continental complications. Oxenstjerna shared his master's distrust of Louis XIV., and the guarantee treaty of The Hague which he concluded with Holland in September, 1681 (Spain and the Emperor acceding to it a year later), aimed at keeping France in her proper place. Louis retaliated by arming Denmark and Brandenburg against Sweden, and in 1683 a Franco-Danish fleet actually appeared in the Baltic; but Holland hastened to the assistance of her ally and the Peace of Regensburg ultimately restored the tranquillity of Europe for the next five years. In 1688, however, the ambition of Louis XIV. raised up a fresh coalition against him and led to another European war. Strenuous efforts were made on both sides to draw Sweden into it; but though Charles XI., mindful of his youthful exploits, was strongly tempted to draw his sword once more, his constant regard for the true welfare of his country prevailed. He waited, therefore, until the belligerents were exhausted and then (1697) offered his mediation which was accepted at the great peace congress at Rijswijk, the history of which belongs to the reign of his son.

Such, in short, prior to the accession of Charles XII., was the political history of Sweden, an outline of which was necessary to the right understanding of that monarch's reign. We have seen, to sum up briefly, how the modern Swedish State was, in the main, the creation of Gustavus Vasa; how its normal development was interrupted under his sons, and diverged eccentrically under his grandson ; how the weakness of Sweden's neighbours and the greatness of her own ,rulers enabled her, for a time, to persevere in her glorious but mistaken policy; how the slightest reverse (*e. g.* Fehrbellin) sufficed to shake the imposing but unsubstantial fabric of her greatness to its very base, and how, finally, only the casual assistance of a foreign potentate permitted that painstaking master-builder, Charles XI., to shore up again, though not for long, the subsiding political structure. But such an unnatural state of things could not last for ever. Indefensible historically and impossible geographically, the Swedish Empire was bound to fall sooner or later, and it is the heroic but hopeless struggle of Charles XII. to still uphold it when its time had come, which gives to his adventurous career its inexhaustible interest and its tragic pathos.

CHAPTER II.

CHARLES XI.

1682–1697.

Birth of Charles XII.—Character as a child—His mother Queen Ulrica Leonora—Her wise system of education—His first tutor, Nordenhjelm—A dialogue on courage—Sweden under Charles XI.—His genius for work—Dangerous pastimes—Hard riding—Bear-hunting—His piety—Charles XII.'s Governors, Lindskjöld, Gyldenstolpe—New tutors, Polus, Cronhjelm—The Prince's studies—Moral training—Death of the Queen—Strong influence of Charles XI. on the character of his son—"My son Carl's" hardy training—Last illness and death of Charles XI.

E find the following entry on June 17, 1682, in Charles XI.'s diary: "To-day, Saturday, at a quarter to eight in the morning, my consort was delivered of and bare me a son. Eternal praise and glory be to God who hath holpen her and may He likewise help her speedily to her former health again"—this child, the only one of Charles XI.'s five sons who survived babyhood, was named after his father and the world knows him now as Charles XII. During his early infancy, the boy was brought up

20

beneath the eye of his excellent mother, the prudent, amiable and pious Ulrica Leonora, whose virtues and charities endeared her as much to the land
of her adoption as to the land of her birth.*   " She
was," wrote the French ambassador D'Avaux at the
time of her death, "she was beloved and honoured
by all men, because to all she was kind and good."
Her son had more reason than anyone else to be
grateful to her.   He seems to have been one of
those lads who are full of rare promise, but need the
control of a firm and steady hand.   His strength of
character at a very early age considerably impressed
those about him, but must have tried them severely
too.   On one occasion, when his mother came to the
nursery to take him to church, he absolutely refused
to stir from the high chair in which he was perched.
The Queen, much astonished, asked the reason why,
when it appeared that he had promised his nurse
not to move till she came back and nothing could
prevail upon the child to depart from his given
word.   Naturally enough this commendable firmness of purpose became sheer obstinacy in nine
cases out of ten.   Thus, on another occasion, he
chose to maintain that blue was black, and stuck
to his opinion through thick and thin, and once he
got the idea into his head that the court-painter
Behn was exactly like a monkey, and nothing in the
world could get it out again.   His courage was
equally precocious.   How, when a little boy, his
hand was severely bitten by a ravenous dog to

---

* She was the youngest surviving daughter of Frederick III. of
Denmark.

which he had surreptitiously offered a crust of bread
under the dinner-table; how he tried to shield the
offending animal by secretly wrapping his napkin
about the wound, and how his sudden faintness
from loss of blood alone betrayed the accident, is a
well-known story; throughout his life, indeed, he
had a perfect horror of cowards and cowardice. It
was the constant aim of his wise and watchful
mother to tame and soften this essentially manly
but stubborn and masterful nature, and to her loving
care is mainly due the early development of the
nobler features of his character, such as his truthful-
ness, piety, self-control and love of justice, qualities
which were to distinguish him ever afterwards. She
taught him to say his prayers at her knee every
morning and evening; she accustomed him betimes
to the sobering sight of misery and the joy of re-
lieving it by making him her little almoner among
her poor, and she was particularly urgent with him
on the duty of guarding his tongue and temper and
respecting the feelings of others. Nor, a scholar
herself, was she unmindful of his mental training.
He was taught German as well as Swedish from his
very cradle; he learnt his first ideas of things from
Ulrica Leonora's magnificent collections of coins,
medallions and engravings; was encouraged to ask
questions about all he heard and saw, and soon took
a delight in repeating every evening to his mother
all that he had been taught during the day. When
he was four he had sufficiently advanced to need a
tutor, so his mother took him with her to the University of Upsala and, after very careful enquiries,

selected three of the professors there, leaving it to
the little Prince himself to choose which of the three
he liked best.   Without a moment's hesitation
Charles gave his hand to Andreas Norcopensis who,
in the following year, was made a Secretary of State
and ennobled under the name of Nordenhjelm, so as
to qualify him for his high office.   Nordenhjelm,
" the father of Swedish eloquence " and by far the
greatest Latin scholar that his country had yet produced, was a quiet, old-fashioned, god-fearing man
of simple tastes and habits, who would have been
considered an oddity at any other Court than that
of Charles XI.   Although nearly forty-nine years
older than his little pupil, he soon succeeded in winning the child's love and confidence.   His success as
a tutor was certainly remarkable, though his labours
were, no doubt, very much lightened by the Prince's
extraordinary quickness.   In a very short time and
" as if in sport," Charles had mastered the rudiments
of geography, arithmetic, history and the elements
of Latin grammar.   Some fragments of the conver-
sations which Nordenhjelm used to have with his
pupil have come down to us, and are interesting as
showing the bias of the child's mind even at that
early age.   Take for instance the following dialogue
on courage — Nordenhjelm : " Is it right, think
you, to expose one's self to danger? "—Charles :
" Yes, but not too much."—N. " When do you
think, then, that one is *too* venturesome ? "—C.
"When one cares for nothing at all."—N. " Now
would it not be better *never* to expose one's self to
danger ? "—C. " No, for then one would be called a

hare."—N. "But, surely, it is better to be called a
hare and live, than to be called a lion after one is
dead?"—C. "No, it would be shameful to live and
be called a hare. I would rather be dead and honoured." Another time Nordenhjelm asked the little
Prince for his definition of a gentleman. Charles
replied that a gentleman should be generous and
kindly but withal of a stout heart, rough as a lion to
his enemies but as gentle as a lamb to all at home.

The Queen continued to regularly examine her
son to see what progress he made and, to stimulate
him still further by a noble example, she had printed
for his special use a good German translation of the
diary in which his grandfather Charles X. had kept
a record of his own youthful studies and travels.
When, however, the boy had reached his seventh
year, his father considered him old enough to have
a room of his own, and "be put into the hands of
men-folk," so Count Erik Lindskjöld was appointed
his governor, though Nordenhjelm continued to be
his tutor.

The precocious manliness of Charles XII. was not
a little stimulated and developed by the rude but
bracing moral atmosphere to which he was accustomed from his infancy. Sweden under Charles XI.
has been compared to a vast, perfectly regulated
machine, the motive power of which was the ubiquitous, indefatigable King himself. It may be still
more appropriately described as a huge patriarchal
household where economy, frugality, punctuality,
industry and practical piety were not so much abstract principles as the hard concrete cardinal factors

of everyday life. In that ideal regime of common-
sense everybody's value was measured by the qual-
ity plus the quantity of the work he did, the King
in this, as in all other respects, setting the example.
Charles XI. rose every day, summer and winter, between three and four, and by breakfast time (six
o'clock) most of his Cabinet work was over. The
Ministers naturally imitated their master, and we
are told by eye-witnesses that their ante-chambers
were thronged as early as five o'clock. Of anything
like a Court in the modern, conventional sense of
the word there was no sign. The practical, hard-
headed, under-educated monarch despised the luxuries and the refinements of life and looked upon
sloth and frivolity as unpardonable offences. Besides,
there was nobody to keep a Court going. The
Queen Consort, especially in her later years, was so
great an invalid that she rarely quitted her rooms;
the Queen Dowager divided her time pretty equally
between her lap-dogs and her card-tables, while the
King, when he was not shut up with his secretaries,
was scouring the country, taking stock of everything,
seeing that everyone was doing his duty, snatching
a hasty, random meal here and there on his way and
grudging even the time he gave to sleep. Soldier-
ing, hunting and break-neck riding were his only
pastimes, and the more perilous they were, the more
he seemed to like them. His military exercises could
scarcely be called *sham* fights, for they were always
attended by loss of limb or life, Charles himself
breaking his thigh so seriously on one occasion,
while charging, that he was lame for the rest of his

days. His rapid rides and drives were scarcely less
dangerous. The French ambassador, D'Avaux, attributed Charles XI.'s last illness to his "terrible
gallops and frequent falls."—"For several years," * he
adds, "the King has delighted in riding fifty to sixty
Swedish leagues at a stretch with such prodigious
rapidity that a good courier could not do in two
days what he has done in one." As a bear-hunter
he was unmatched for skill and courage, frequently
attacking the animal at close quarters and single-
handed to save a comrade. On one such occasion
he exerted himself so violently as to burst a blood-
vessel, an accident which was very nearly the death
of him. On Sundays, however, he was always
"quiet," as he expressed it, attending divine service
twice and often thrice during the day and hearing a
sermon in his own room when he could not go to
church. His piety, indeed, was deep and unaffected
and coloured every action of his life. He read a
chapter in the Bible every morning and evening, took
the sacrament very regularly and never without careful preparation, kept the anniversary of the Battle of
Lund in his own chamber on his knees, and ordered
the titles "His Majesty" and "Our Most Gracious
King" to be struck out of the prayer for the Royal
Family in the Swedish Liturgy because, to use his
own words: "I am but a man and a sinner like other
men and Almighty God is appeased not by high-
sounding titles, but by the prayers of faithful and
humble hearts."—He would listen, moreover, with

---

* D'Avaux, xxxiv., 57. Charles in his *Dagbok*, frequently alludes
to these hard rides with evident satisfaction.

exemplary humility to remonstrances and even reproaches from the pulpit as coming from God, though
otherwise his almost ungovernable temper would rage
tempestuously on the slightest contradiction, to the
terror of those about him.   Under such a monarch,
who was only saved from being a downright Puritan
by a very strong if somewhat rough sense of humour,
the pleasures of the Court were always severely simple
and with an obviously practical end.   In Charles
XI.'s private diary, which extends over twenty years,
there is only one recorded instance of a masquerade.
Weddings, christenings, church-services, reviews,
sledging-parties, these were the ordinary relaxations
which Charles XI. allowed himself and his family.
More special occasions were the public receptions of
foreign princes (the only times when there was something like pomp and ceremony), the public recanta-
tions of Jews or papists which the royal family
always made a point of attending, and once a juggler
was admitted into the palace to perform tricks with
a magic wand.   The King was not, however, the
absolute boor he is sometimes represented to be.
The interest he took in church architecture and his
munificence to the great artist, Ehrenstrahl, whom
he ennobled, show that he had some taste for art
though, to be sure, the *chef-d'œuvres* he liked the
best were the pictures of the bear-hounds that had
saved his life and the hunters that he had ridden to
death which still adorn the walls of the Palace of
Gripsholm and attest the genius of the Swedish
Landseer.

Charles XI. gave the same minute attention to the

education of his son that he gave to everything
else and the happy knack with which he hit upon
the right men for his purpose says much for his
natural shrewdness. Count Erik Lindskjöld, the
Prince's first governor, was the son of a smith who
had risen to the highest offices in the State entirely
by his own exertions, and was equally famous in his
day as a poet, scholar, speaker and statesman. His
tact, cheerfulness and astonishing capacity for hard
work greatly endeared him to the King, and the
Danish minister at Stockholm has described him as
"the strongest spirit of them all who can twist all
men and all things as he will." Unfortunately the
young Prince had the benefit of his experience for
only two years, Lindskjöld dying somewhat suddenly at the beginning of 1690. He was succeeded
by the adroit and keen-witted Count Nils Gyldenstolpe, one of the most successful of Charles XI.'s
diplomatists, who, after spending most of his time
abroad in his country's service, had so many charges
thrust upon him on his return home that his super-
intendence of his illustrious pupil's studies must
have been very perfunctory. The lion's share of
the work therefore fell upon the tutor, Nordenhjelm, who also died in 1694. Thomas Polus, a
diplomatist of high standing and large experience,
took his place, but being at the same time indispensable elsewhere as one of the overworked Secretaries
of State, he received, eleven months later, the assistance of Gustavus Cronhjelm, also an official of great
experience whose Latin orations were much admired.
In theology the Prince was instructed by that model

prelate Erik Benzelius, Bishop of Strengnäs, afterwards Primate, who composed a *Breviarium Historiæ Ecclesiæ* for his special behoof.

Despite this constant change of teachers, most of whom could only have given him a very small portion of their precious time, the Prince made extraordinarily rapid progress in his studies. His natural parts were excellent, but a strong bias in the direction of abstract thought and mathematics in particular was noticeable from the first. For history and languages he had less liking, while the fine arts and *belles-lettres* scarcely interested him at all. He readily assimilated whatever was taught him and digested it with remarkable thoroughness. In a very short time he could translate Latin into Swedish and German, and German or Swedish into Latin at sight, and he learnt enough of Greek to be able to read his Testament in the original language. He was well acquainted with the works of Cæsar, Justin, Cornelius Nepos, Cicero and, perhaps, Curtius before he was twelve, and heroic lives, such as are to be found in the Latin classics and the Norse Sagas, had an attraction for him which his tutor considered absolutely mischievous. On one occasion Nordenhjelm is said to have asked him what he thought of Alexander the Great.—" I should love to be like him," replied the Prince.—" But he only lived till he was thirty-two," objected the tutor.—"When one has conquered a whole kingdom, one has lived quite long enough," said Charles. French he always disliked, no doubt copying his father in this respect. It was only on being told that the Kings of Poland

and Denmark knew it thoroughly and it would be a
shame for a King of Sweden to be inferior to them
in knowledge of any sort, that he was persuaded to
learn it at all, but he could very seldom be prevailed
upon to speak it. His first governor, Lindskjöld,
tried to arouse him out of this obstinacy by remarking what a graceful and useful accomplishment it
would be for a Swedish King to be able to address
a French ambassador in his own language.—"My
dear Lindskjöld," replied the Prince, "I know some
French already and mean to learn still more. Should
I ever meet the King of France, I will speak to him
in his own language; but, surely, it would be more
becoming for any French ambassador who comes
hither, to learn Swedish for my sake than for me to
learn French for his."

A German scholar * of the last century, comment-
ing upon Charles XII.'s studies and tutors, ignorant-
ly exclaims: "How extraordinary must have been
the genius of the hero since it happily resisted the
united efforts of a whole company of pedantic busy-
bodies who, with the best intentions in the world,
would fain have stifled it." Now, to say nothing of
the fact that most of Charles's preceptors, so far
from being mere pedants, were hard-headed men of
the world first and only scholars afterwards, we can
satisfy ourselves from the very careful directions
drawn up by Charles XI. for the guidance of his son's
governors and tutors, what a horror the boy's parents
had for anything like cramming. The tutorial staff
was strictly enjoined not to overload the pupil's

---

* A. L. Schlözer.

PALACE AT STOCKHOLM, AT END OF 17th CENTURY.

memory, nor disgust him with too many subjects at
a time ; but to lead him on insensibly, and as if
spontaneously, from one thing to another. His
studies were to be made pastimes. Moreover, as
might have been expected of such parents as Charles
XI. and Ulrica Leonora, far more care was given to
the lad's moral than to his mental training. The
following extract from the above mentioned directions speaks for itself : " The tutor must impress
upon his pupil, on all occasions, that although he is
a King's son and the heir to a great realm, nevertheless he ought always humbly to recognise this as
God's special grace and favour and be diligent in
acquiring those Christian virtues and necessary dispositions which can alone make him worthy of his
high birth and fit for his high calling. The Prince
must learn, betimes, to bear in mind that it is
Almighty God alone who sets kings up and puts
them down, and 't is He who will, one day, demand
a strict reckoning from all those who are born to
crowns and sceptres as to how they have made use
of what has been placed in their hands, wherefore it
becomes them especially to take heed lest they mis-
use the authority which God has given them to the
oppression of others and their own destruction."

The death of his mother in 1693 when he was only
eleven years old was an irreparable loss to Charles
XII., but his father now took him in hand and did
much to make of him the man he was to be. It is
true that Charles XI. has been severely blamed in
some quarters for interrupting his son's studies and
giving him, as it has been said, a wrong bias. I am

inclined to think, however, that the strong common-
sense of the father knew what was best for his own
son. The fact is often overlooked that, as a child,
Charles XII. was so delicate, that many, D'Avaux
among the number, never thought that he would
live to see manhood. Over-study would have been
very injurious to such a weakling. What the lad
wanted most was plenty of exercise and fresh air
and the father, who had outgrown his own somewhat
delicate infancy by means of the same vigorous regi-
men, determined that his son should do likewise.
So the little fellow was taught to ride before he was
four, and at eight he was quite at home in the saddle. He shot his first fox when he was seven, and
the sangfroid with which he brought down his first
bear, at a single shot, when only eleven, astonished
the most experienced huntsmen and delighted his
proud father. A few weeks later he shot his first
stag dead at ninety-six paces, a fact also noted in the
King's private diary with evident satisfaction. From
henceforth the companionship between father and
son became closer and closer and, in his later years,
it is always " with my son, Carl " * that Charles XI.
goes his rounds, drilling regiments, conducting
manœuvres, attending christenings, weddings, and
funerals, inspecting studs, foundries, churches, dock-
yards, factories, granaries, and in this way the boy
was gradually initiated into all the minutiæ of
administration. For the science of war he had
already a marked preference. His favourite pastime
at six years of age was to construct trenches and

---

* *Dagbok.*

bastions on scientific principles, and the Wednesday
and Friday lessons in fortification and strategy
given to him by Quartermaster-general Stuart (but
only as a treat after his other lessons had been done)
were his happiest moments. As he grew older he
took an active part, as often as possible, in the
reviews and skirmishes in which his father delighted
so much. He would be seen at these so-called *sham*
fights which were often such serious businesses,
plunging into the thickest of the *melée*, with a recklessness which would have endangered his life but
for his wariness and coolness. He was very proud
of the knocks and bruises he frequently received on
these occasions and learnt, betimes, from his father
to despise luxury and even comfort. The private
diary of Charles XI. shows how watchful he was over
his son and also how dearly he loved him, though,
stern hard man as he was, he shrank from any outward exhibition of feeling, save that of anger, as
weak and womanish. I am inclined to think, too,
that his influence over his son was far greater than
is commonly supposed and that this influence accounts for very much in Charles XII.'s character
which is otherwise inexplicable, such, for instance,
as his precocious reserve and taciturnity, his dislike
of everything French, and his self-assured and un-
hesitating choice or rejection of servants and ministers at the beginning of his reign when he was still a
mere boy. Unfortunately for the young Prince, and
for Sweden, that salutary influence was now to be
withdrawn at the very moment when it was most
needed.

3

Since the death of his consort, Charles XI. had been a changed man. This bereavement had suddenly and completely shattered the fortitude on which he prided himself so much—his sorrow was so violent that he had even to take to his bed. On the occasion of the Queen's funeral, some weeks later, we are told * that he wept all through the four hours that the ceremony lasted and long afterwards, when he was, seemingly, much the same as before; the pathetic entries in his private diary, † intended for no eye but his own, show that her loss was a wound which never really healed. In the course of 1694 the King was tormented by internal pains yet, with characteristic obstinacy, would take nothing for them but such simple domestic remedies as his mother could suggest, and he abated not a tittle of his rigorous labours and perilous pastimes. Throughout 1695 he grew slowly but steadily worse, and by the summer of 1696 was so seriously ill that the doctors were sent for, but their drugs benefited him but little. ‡ Still, though he could scarce hold himself upright, he persisted in going about as if nothing were the matter—it seemed as if that iron will which had never yet bent before the might of circumstances would now fain wrestle with the mortal foe within. In January, 1697, he undertook a long and fatiguing tour of inspection and returned to Stockholm a dying man, though none dare tell him so. Through-

---

* D'Avaux.

† *Dagbok*, 31 December, 1693.

‡ Characteristically enough there is nothing at all said about this in his diary.

out February and March he grew weaker and weaker, so that the Crown Prince had now to do the honours of the Court, though his father, as late as February 21st, was at a wolf hunt and three days later went on another tour of inspection. But it was to be his last. Immediately on his return he took to his bed and prayers were offered up for him in all the churches, a thing which he had hitherto sternly forbidden. By April 1st, which fell on Good Friday, all hope was abandoned, and the royal patient's sufferings were so terrible that his speedy release became the dearest wish of those who loved him best. The last sign of recognition he gave was on Easter Tuesday, a few moments before his death, when his aged equerry, Gustaf Hard, who had been the constant companion of all his adventurous rides and hunts, was brought to his bedside. The familiar sight of that faithful old servant revived, for an instant, the memory of the dying monarch. He stretched out his hands towards his comrade and cried : "Farewell, Gustaf Hard ! thanks for every day we have had together ! God grant we may meet again in the Kingdom of Heaven !" These were his last intelligible words. He expired at half-past nine on the evening of April 5, 1697, in the thirty-seventh year of his reign and the forty-second of his age. No other Swedish King had ever deserved so well of his country.

CHAPTER III.

THE BOY-KING.

1697–1700.

The Regency—Diligence of the King—Taciturnity—Abilities—The noiseless Revolution—Charles absolute—The Coronation—Alarming novelties thereat—Radical administrative changes—Polus and Piper—Fears of "a hard reign"—The King's character—His humanity—Application—"The Holstein frenzy"—Second visit of the Duke of Holstein—Charles beleaguered by Princesses—His martial temperament—Troubled state of European politics—The Holstein question—Marriage of the Duke of Holstein with Charles's sister—Formation of a coalition against Sweden—Johan Reinhold Patkul—His career and character—The Holstein question reaches an acute stage—Denmark begins hostilities—Charles quits his capital—Commencement of the Great Northern war.

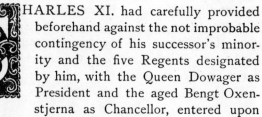

HARLES XI. had carefully provided beforehand against the not improbable contingency of his successor's minority and the five Regents designated by him, with the Queen Dowager as President and the aged Bengt Oxenstjerna as Chancellor, entered upon their functions immediately after the demise of the Crown. The members of this Regency (the third that Sweden had had within the last fifty years) if not exactly great statesmen were, at any rate, practical, hard-headed politicians who had not served under such a master as Charles XI. in vain, and during the seven months that they held sway no blunders were made and no national interests were injured which, considering the difficulties that confronted them both at home and abroad, is saying a good deal. The internal administration continued on much the same lines as during the late reign, while abroad the successful conclusion * of the great peace congress at Rijswijk, chiefly owing to the tact and patience of the President, Baron Lillieroth, the Swedish minister at The Hague, was justly regarded as a signal triumph of Sweden's pacific diplomacy. The young King (he was only fifteen) was present in the council every day and took a deep and growing interest in the discussions there. He spoke frequently and much to the point on all subjects except foreign affairs, and his utterances we are told argued a maturity of judgment far beyond his years. But other and less pleasing traits of character also came to light, chief among which was an occasional obstinate taciturnity unnatural in one so young. Thus, to give only one instance, during the long debates in the Senate as to the fitness of Colonel Maurice Vellingk for the post of envoy at the Luneberg Court, the King was repeatedly asked his opinion on the matter but, despite all the efforts of his grand-

---

* Peace between France and the maritime Powers was concluded on September 20, 1697, and between France and the Emperor a month later.

mother and his five guardians, not a syllable could
be got out of him.* Still, on the whole, Charles's
conduct impressed people very favourably. His
courage and sangfroid were remarkable. On the
occasion of the great fire, soon after his accession,
which utterly destroyed the palace at Stockholm
and, for a time, left the royal family houseless, he
displayed a truly astonishing presence of mind. The
ever-watchful D'Avaux was much struck by his application and ability and privately reports to Louis
XIV. that the young King of Sweden during the
whole period of his tutelage showed much good
sense and judgment. He adds that Charles has
ambition, large views, great designs and the noble
emulation of imitating the actions of great men.
There can, indeed, be little doubt that if only the
young Prince had been allowed the opportunity of
gradually gaining experience and developing his
naturally great talents for the next few years beneath
the guidance of his guardians, as Charles XI. had
intended, he would have made as good a king as
ever his father had been. Unfortunately it was not
to be. A sudden though noiseless revolution was
now to traverse all the wise precautions of Charles
XI. and place absolute power in the hands of a rash
lad of fifteen.

This calamity, for such it ultimately proved to

---

* That such occurrences were pretty frequent is obvious from such
entries in the protocols as these: " His majesty would give no
opinion"—" His majesty made no reply thereto." *Carlson.*—Compare *D'Avaux :* " A peine aucun sénateur lui peut-il arracher une
parole. Il écoute tout ce qu'on lui dit, mais il ne repond pas un
mot."

Sweden, was due to several causes. The death of
Charles XI. had, awakened many hopes and removed
many fears. The nobility and gentry, who had
trembled for twenty years beneath his iron sceptre,
breathed freely once more and already began schem-
ing for the recovery of their lost power and property.
From the Regents, who were mostly self-made men
and rigorous disciples of the late King, they had little
to expect; but they flattered themselves they would
be sure of the grateful liberality of the young Prince if
they succeeded in freeing him from the bonds of
tutelage. When we add that the members of the
Raad, or Senate, which under the will of the late
King had a part, though a subordinate part, in the
government, were jealous of the accidentally superior
authority of the Regents, who, only a few months
before, had been no more than their own colleagues;
when we recollect, moreover, that the Regency itself
was distracted by endless dissensions, especially in
relation to foreign affairs, the Chancellor, Oxenstjerna,
clinging tenaciously to the Maritime Powers while
his "contradictors," as he called them, advocated the
French alliance, the, at first sight, strange and start-
ling events of the short Riksdag of 1697, which was
summoned, ostensibly to bury the late King, are
easily intelligible.

The Estates assembled at Stockholm on Saturday,
November 6th, and on the following Monday the
nobility, who fancied they had most to gain by the
projected change, proceeded to carry it out forthwith. Taking advantage of the momentary absence
of the Secretary of the House, the Marshal of the

Diet, in a tone of voice " between chatting and de-
bating," turned to the gentleman nearest to him and
began eloquently expatiating on the King's precocious talents ; suggested what a delightful thing it
would be if the Estates could see their gracious
young King in the full possession of his rights before
they separated, and insinuated that his Majesty
might, perhaps, receive such a representation with
favour. He was interrupted by loud hurrahs from
the nobility and gentry, and all, with one voice, expressed the wish that the King might be immediately
invited to assume the government of the realm. A
formal motion to that effect was then made and carried almost by acclamation (what feeble opposition
there was being promptly suppressed) and a deputation instantly waited upon Charles, who received the
delegates graciously but prudently advised them,
first of all, to consult the Senate on so important a
matter. An hour later a delegation of seventy-four
noblemen and gentlemen, headed by their Marshal,
waited upon the Senate accordingly ; the Senate and
the Regents, determined not to be behindhand with
the nobility in their devotion to royalty, expressed
their hearty concurrence with the motion of the First
Estate and the Regents ; the Senate and the noble
deputation waited upon the King forthwith, when
Chancellor Oxenstjerna, acting as spokesman, begged
his Majesty to gladden the hearts of his subjects
by graciously assuming the reins of government.
Charles at once expressed his willingness to concur
with the desires of his faithful subjects, whereupon
the Queen Dowager, the Regents and the Senate

QUEEN ULRICA LEONORA I.
FROM AN OLD PRINT.

kissed the King's hand and congratulated him on his
assumption of the royal power. This speculation of
the nobility, for it was nothing else, had been carried
out without the consent or even the knowledge of
the three lower Estates, the clergy, burgesses, and
peasants ; but they were now formally acquainted
with and invited to co-operate in it. A few timid
warning voices were raised in the Estate of clergy,
but the bulk of the commoners showed an equal
alacrity in king-making, and a joint deputation from
all four Estates went helter-skelter up to the palace
to respectfully petition his Majesty, in the name of
the Riksdag, to take the government into his own
hands. The King's reply was brief but to the point.
He would not resist, he said, the urgent appeal of
the Estates of the realm, but would take over the
government of the kingdom in God's name. It was
characteristic of him that, immediately after the
deputation had withdrawn, he retired to his own
chamber and spent an hour there on his knees in
silent prayer. This noiseless revolution, whose consequences were to be so momentous both to Sweden
and to Europe, had been accomplished in less than
twelve hours.

A period of surprise and uncertainty ensued. The
impenetrable reserve and taciturnity of the young
King baffled all conjecture. The French ambassador, D'Avaux, was only expressing the opinion of
everyone else when he wrote home to his Court :
" We don't know where we are at present." The nobility, who hoped most from the change of government they had brought about, were the first to dis-

cover that their new master had a heavier hand than
the old one. The Riksdag had been dissolved after
a three weeks' session, but each of the four Estates
was allowed to sit separately for some weeks longer
to settle its particular affairs. The nobility had
interpreted this as a sign of the King's good-will, and
forthwith submitted to him sundry petitions in
which they humbly besought him to relieve their
burdens and especially to suspend or, at any rate,
restrict the operation of the land-redemption system. In a week the petitions were returned with
the curt and caustic reminder that his Majesty
considered himself the best judge of all personal
merit and would be gracious to whom he chose.
The novelties introduced by Charles at his coronation were still more portentous. In the first place
the Estates had to swear the oath of allegiance
before instead of after that function as heretofore.
The fact that the crown was not, according to time-
honoured custom, placed on the King's head *during*
the ceremony, but was worn by his Majesty on his
way to church, also caused considerable uneasiness.
The Senate too, instead of riding on horseback in
the royal procession, as usual, had to walk holding
the baldachin over the head of the King, who rode
to church in full regalia.* He was welcomed at the
church door by the archbishop and attendant prelates with the words: " Blessed is he that cometh
in the name of the Lord ! " and escorted to the sanc-
tuary, where he took his seat on a silver chair placed

---

* The crown fell from his head just as he was mounting his horse,
an accident naturally interpreted by many as of very evil omen.

on a throne draped with scarlet damask and cloth of gold. After listening to a sermon from Bishop Spegel and divesting himself of his crown and mantle, he knelt before the altar for his anointing, which was performed in the usual way, immediately after which he replaced the crown on his head and remounted his throne. But the most significant of all these changes was the King's omission to take the coronation oath, as all his ancestors had done since the foundation of the monarchy, an omission which was interpreted to mean that he considered himself under no obligation whatever to his subjects. A pang of dismay, we are told by a contemporary, went through the very bones and marrow of the spectators and many began to ask themselves where this young Prince who, at the very outset of his reign, did not hesitate to break the most venerable customs of the land would be likely to stop.

Equally radical were the administrative changes, though here it was not so much public opinion as private ambition that suffered. Only two days after the coronation, the aged Chancellor, Oxenstjerna, was sharply reminded that he was no longer a diplomatic oracle but simply the chief clerk of a department of State and was ordered to confine himself entirely to the duties of that department for the future. On the other hand proceedings were instituted against two of Oxenstjerna's most illustrious opponents, Fabian Wrede and Nils Bjelke, for alleged maladministration and even peculation. The Raad or Senate too, that venerable assembly of experienced councillors, lost most of its remaining authority

and was quite overshadowed by two new men of
lowly origin to whom the King now gave his entire
confidence. These new men, Thomas Polus and
Carl Piper, were made Senators (December 31, 1697)
and subsequently Counts (January 3, 1698) on the
same day and had the chief control of foreign and
domestic affairs respectively. Polus, whom we have
already learnt to know as one of Charles's tutors, is
described by the foreign ministers at Stockholm as
an able and honest statesman; but he seems to have
lacked initiative and was certainly nothing like so
prominent a person as his colleague Piper, who for
the next thirteen years was to be, as we shall see, the
right-hand man of the young King. The government
now took more and more of an autocratic shape
even in its outward forms. D'Avaux describes
Charles at this period as even more imperious in
public than his father. " The Senators," he tells us,
" used to enter the chamber of the late King whenever they chose, and when there would converse
freely and pretty loudly; but now they cannot enter
without permission and, while there, must stand in
respectful silence except when they whisper a word
in each other s ears." Anti-monarchical strictures,
however respectful or indirect, were promptly visited
with cruel rigour. Thus, for instance, a country
parson named Jacob Boethius, who had protested
from the pulpit against absolute power being placed
in the hands of a boy of fifteen, was arrested in his
bed, at midnight, dragged all the way to Stockholm
and condemned to death though the sentence was
commuted by the King to imprisonment for life in

a fortress.   No wonder then if many, like the French
ambassador, began to fear " a hard reign."   Nevertheless, so far as it could be discerned at all, the
character of the young King was, on the whole, en-
couraging, especially when it began to be evident
that his conduct was regulated by strict principle
and not by mere caprice.   His absolute refusal to
countenance torture as an instrument of judicial in-
vestigation on the ground that "confessions so
extorted give no sure criteria for basing a judgment
upon," showed him to be more humane as well as
more enlightened than the majority of his council
which had defended the contrary opinion.   His application to affairs was exemplary, to many it even
seemed excessive.   " The King," writes the English
minister, Robinson, to his Court, " has already begun
to take cognisance of affairs and give commands in
all matters with the same perseverance and unceas-
ing diligence as his father did.   He rises every
morning at five o'clock and is at work the greater
part of the day, so that if he is well served and does
not injure his health by too much work . . . .
there is every prospect here of a happy reign."

But for all his affectation of grown-up airs, for all
his really extraordinary precociousness, Charles was,
after all, but a boy, and his boyishness frequently
rebelled against the unnatural restraint imposed upon
it by breaking all bounds.   This is the real explanation of his extravagances during the two visits of his
kinsman, Frederick IV., Duke of Holstein, which so
disturbed and distressed his sober-minded subjects.
The Duke first arrived in Sweden in the middle of

April, 1698, stayed till the middle of August, and
was married on June 2d to the King's eldest and
favourite sister, the Princess Hedwig Sofia. Charles,
who inherited his father's affection for the House of
Holstein and his father's hatred of the rival monarchy of Denmark, entertained his cousin magnificently. The Duke's journey through the land resembled a triumphal progress. His entry into Stockholm was the most brilliant pageant within living
memory. The King, the Senate and a mob of lesser
notabilities met him at the north gate and escorted
him to the palace amidst the welcoming roar of hundreds of guns. The Duke very soon won the young
King's entire confidence and gained an extraordinary
influence over him by stimulating his natural liking
for dangerous sports and urging him on to the wild-
est escapades. It seemed as if the King, for the first
time in his life, had got a comrade after his own
heart and was determined to make the most of the
opportunity. This period of Charles's life has sometimes been called "the Holstein frenzy," and it well
deserves the name. To say nothing of the break-
neck rides, which were of every-day occurrence after
the Duke's arrival, the royal kinsmen frequently
amused themselves by smashing all the plates and
glasses on the dinner-table and flinging all the furni-
ture out of the palace windows. Sometimes they
varied their diversions by tearing off the wigs and
breaking the swords of their gentlemen-in-waiting,
and one evening the good Stockholmers were horrified
to see the King and the Duke come riding into town
on the same horse (the Duke sitting behind the King

with nothing on but his shirt) while they broke to
pieces with their drawn swords all the windows they
passed on their way.   On another occasion, the
French ambassador tells us, the King and the Duke
tested the sharpness of their swords by decapitating
calves, sheep and dogs in the royal apartments and
pitching the bleeding heads out of the window. This
engrossing pastime lasted a whole week, by the end
of which time the interior of the palace resembled a
shambles. Such conduct naturally excited universal
indignation and disgust, especially against the Duke,
who was even suspected of sinister designs upon the
King's life and crown, for Charles's health was known
to be anything but robust and his rooted objection
to matrimony left the unpleasant prospect of a dis-
puted succession by no means improbable. To the
general satisfaction, however, the King's manners
improved immediately after the Duke's departure
and he became the same taciturn, industrious, self-
contained youth he had been before. The Duke came
again in July, 1699, and on this occasion Charles's
conduct though just as boisterous was, certainly, a
little more decorous. An additional twelve months'
experience of affairs had somewhat sobered him, and
he was more mindful of his kingly dignity. During
the Duke's second stay, the ordinarily gloomy
Swedish Court seemed absolutely transformed. The
King spared no expense in honour of his guests, and
scattered what still remained of his father's hoard *

* Unlike his father he was naturally open-handed.   It is estimated
that from March 10 to August 13, 1698, he spent 835,000 dlr. in
presents and entertainments and his foreign guests cost him not less
than £300 a day.

with a lavish hand. Balls, plays and masquerades followed in rapid succession, Charles himself frequently dancing with such fire and vigour as to be obliged to change his clothes twice or thrice in the course of the evening. The best troupe of actors that money could procure was obtained from Paris, a theatre was erected for them in the palace and they played before the Court twice a week. The saturnine young King frolicking with maids of honour was an unwonted spectacle, and must have revived considerably the fainting hopes of the mob of matchmakers, who haunted his Court in those days with comical pertinacity. During the winter of 1698–9 these errant wooers were particularly active. Despite the unusual severity of the winter, one foreign princess after another forced her way up to Stockholm through interminable and ever-increasing snow-drifts. In the beginning of December the Dowager-Duchess of Holstein, who had an inkling of the nuptial negotiations then going on between .the Swedish and Danish Courts and was determined to prevent them if possible, came, dragging her youthful daughter along with her as an additional competitor for the hand of the young King. The Duchess, during her five days' journey through Sweden, suffered severely through stress of weather, but gallantly persisted in her design though it took no less than sixteen horses to drag her carriage along and, at last, she had to leave them in the snow and take to a peasant's sledge instead. The Danish minister arrived ten days later, for the express purpose of circumventing her, and began his visit by taking to his bed in consequence of exposure in the impassable snow-drifts. In February the Princess of Brunswick-Bevern and her daughter arrived at Stockholm on precisely the same errand as the Dowager-Duchess of Holstein. " What does *she* want?" Charles is reported to have said on being informed of her arrival; " surely we have enough of that sort here already!" The ministers of Wurtemberg and Brandenburg were also busily negotiating with the same object in view so that, as Carlson aptly expresses it, " the future great Captain found himself formally beleaguered by Princesses!"

But the fair besiegers soon found him to be impregnable. Charles was of a naturally frigid temperament and the only women whose society he ever cared for were his excellent mother and his eldest sister, Hedwig Sofia, now Duchess of Holstein. A quiet, comfortable domestic life had no charms for him, but in perils and hardships he had always delighted. Once, in midwinter, when quite a child, he left his bed and lay on the bare boards all night in order to " harden himself," and caught a cold in consequence which nearly killed him. Fighting was his true vocation, danger his native element and he was never so radiantly happy as when in the midst of a *melée.* The force of circumstances was now to give him his heart's desire and launch another hero upon the world.

For while Charles XII. was thus serving his apprenticeship at home in peace if not in quietness, abroad storms had already begun to darken the political horizon and the outbreak of the bloody war
4

which was to convulse all Europe for a whole generation could now only be a question of time. In the
South the question of the Spanish succession was
exercising the minds of statesmen, and all the Powers
concerned were anxiously awaiting the death of
Carlos II. of Spain sword in hand. In the North
the perpetual dispute between the House of Holstein and the Danish crown was an equally burning
question, and here Sweden was immediately, not to
say principally, concerned. After the death of Duke
Christian Albert in 1694, Christian V. of Denmark
had renewed all Denmark's ancient claims upon the
Gottorp possessions. Charles XI. had at once made
the cause of the new Duke, Frederick IV., his own
and a peace congress, under the mediation of Sweden,
was held at Pinneberg which, however, came to
nothing. After Charles XI.'s death the quarrel
blazed forth more violently than ever and the Danish troops invaded Holstein and destroyed the fortifications lately erected there. The eagerness, however, with which all the great Powers courted the
friendship of Sweden during the year 1698 (the year
of the many alliances, as it has been called) was not
without its effect upon Denmark and an attempt was
even made to bring about a marriage between
Charles XII. and the Danish Princess, Sofia Hedwig,
which was frustrated by the visit of the Duke of
Holstein to Sweden and his marriage to Charles's
sister. But the Duke, as we have seen, won even
more than this, he won Charles's friendship, a friendship always charily given, but, once given, irrevocable.
Indeed the Holstein match marks a turning-point in

Sweden's history and the subsequent appointment
of the Duke of Holstein as generalissimo of the
Swedish troops in Germany was its speedy and significant consequence. Now that Sweden had definitely thrown in her lot with Holstein, Denmark was
bound in self-defence to look out for allies, and these
were already to hand in the new King of Poland,
Augustus II., and the Tsar, Peter I. It was the
ruling ambition of the former to make his Saxon
Electorate a great Power and while ostensibly negotiating an alliance with Sweden and protesting, both
privately and publicly, his unalterable devotion to
the young Swedish King, he was all the time secretly
plotting against him. His chief counsellor at this
time was the Livonian, Johan Reinhold Patkul, that
political firebrand who was to set the whole North
in flames and whose career and character now
require a word of explanation.

Patkul was born at Stockholm in 1660, in a dungeon whither his mother had accompanied his father
who lay there under suspicion of having betrayed the
fortress of Wolmar to the Poles. He entered the
Swedish army at an early age and was already a
captain when, in 1689, at the head of a deputation
of Livonian gentry, he went to Stockholm to protest against the rigour with which the land-recovery,
system was being carried out in his native province. His eloquence and audacity rather interested
Charles XI. in his favour; but his representations
were disregarded and the violent and offensive language with which in another petition, addressed to
the King three years later, he renewed his complaints

involved him in a trial for high treason. To
save himself he fled to Switzerland and was
condemned, *in contumaciam*, to lose his right
hand and his head. For the next four years
he led a vagabond life; but, in 1698, after
vainly petitioning the new King, Charles XII., for
pardon, he entered the service of the Elector of
Saxony and it now became the main object of
his life to ruin his King and country. Patkul was
certainly no ordinary man. His gigantic stature,
enormous strength, handsome face and figure and
dogged courage would alone have made him remarkable, and he possessed, besides, great intellectual
gifts which had been fostered by a careful education.
He could be wondrously eloquent in four languages;
could write both Latin and Greek and was well
grounded in history, mathematics and theology.
But this rare combination of unusual gifts was spoilt
by an overweening insolence and a narrow, selfish
pride. Some modern historians have strangely
idealised Patkul into a hero and martyr of liberty;
in point of fact he was neither the one nor the other.
The exclusive privileges of his noble caste were the
only liberties he ever fought for; he was as intolerant
of any independence in those below him as he was
impatient of any authority in those above him, and
his idea of a free Livonia was a handful of irrespon-
sible landlords tyrannising over a race of serfs. Even
as a young man he had been notorious for the
savage brutality with which he treated his depend-
ants and subordinates. With still less reason can
Patkul be considered a martyr. Vindictive hatred

was the ruling principle of his treacherous conduct.
He deliberately lived the life and justly died the
death of a traitor, and it was not the fault of the
injured master who punished him but of the hard
times that sanctioned such punishments if his fate
was unnecessarily shocking.

With an energy and an ability worthy of a better
cause, Patkul now laboured, day and night, to bring
about a grand coalition for the purpose of partition-
ing the Swedish empire. An alliance to that end
(though purely defensive at first) was concluded
through him between Denmark and Saxony (March,
1698), and in August of the same year he brought
about a meeting at Rawa between King Augustus
and the Tsar, at which the project took a more definite shape. Peter the Great, that "barbarian with
great progressive ideas," was more interested than
anyone else in its speedy realisation. He saw clearly
enough that Russia must always remain semi-barbarous until she had recovered her natural seaboard,
and he was ready to sacrifice everything, honour in-
cluded, to obtain this national requisite. Sweden
stood immediately in his way, and it was only over
the ruins of Sweden's greatness that he could erect
his own empire. Thanks to the restless activity of
Patkul, the coalition against Sweden was rapidly
formed. In August, 1699, the ambitious Frederick
IV. of Denmark, only a fortnight after his accession,
concluded a definite offensive treaty with Saxony
against Sweden, and in November of the same year
an alliance with the same object was concluded between Russia and Saxony. Brandenburg was invited

to join the allies but, with characteristic reserve, preferred to bide her time. All these negotiations quite escaped the vigilance of Sweden's ministers abroad. Even Vellingk, her ablest diplomatist, who was supposed to enjoy the personal friendship of Augustus, was completely hoodwinked, and confidently assured his Court that peace was certain at the very moment when invading armies were actually on the march. Both the Tsar and the King of Poland were profuse in hypocritical expressions of friendship while taking prompt measures to despoil their good brother and ally of his dominions. We shall see that this duplicity rankled deeply in the heart of Charles XII. who was the soul of honour himself and he could never either forgive it or forget it.

All this time the Swedish King was occupied by the Holstein question and espoused the cause of his brother-in-law with a zeal which angered and alarmed the neutral Powers. In the summer of 1699, without so much as consulting his ministers, he sent 24,000 troopers from Wismar to Holstein to re-build the fortifications there. Denmark immediately began to arm, whereupon Charles reinforced his German troops with 5000 men from Sweden, quite regardless of the formal protests of England and Holland and the indignant remonstrances of Louis XIV. On October 24, 1699, Denmark addressed a circular to the Powers declaring and justifying her intention of attacking Sweden while Charles, who had, at last, received disquieting rumours of the hostile manœuvres of Russia and Saxony, strengthened his

PETER THE GREAT.
BASED ON THE PORTRAIT BY KNELLER.

position by a definite defensive alliance with the
Maritime Powers (Treaty of The Hague, January 23,
1700). He was determined not to be the aggressor;
but it is certain that, full of martial ardour, he impatiently awaited the outbreak of hostilities. He
had not long to wait. On February 12, 1700, the
Saxon troops invaded Livonia and laid siege to
Riga without any previous declaration of war and,
a fortnight later, the Danes occupied Holstein.
Charles was at a bear-hunt when the news was
brought him, and he received it with a nonchalance
which was absolutely unintelligible to his suite.
Turning with a smile to the French ambassador, he
said: "We will soon make King Augustus return
by the way he came." He at once hastened back to
Stockholm to make his final preparations and there
he learned, for the first time, that Russia also had
joined the league against him. The imperturbable
coolness of the young King filled everyone with
astonishment. The approach of danger seemed to
have made the boy a man. "I have resolved," he
said to the Senate, "never to begin an unrighteous
war; but I have also resolved never to finish a
righteous war till I have utterly crushed my enemies." At a later day the whole nation had good
cause to remember these ominous words. Finally,
on April 20, 1700, Charles XII. quitted his capital
which he was never to see again.

CHAPTER IV.

BEGINNINGS OF THE GREAT NORTHERN WAR— NARVA.

1699–1701.

Siege of Riga—Erik Dahlberg—The war in Holstein—Lethargy of Sweden's German allies—Charles in Scania—His financial embarrassments—Arrival of the Anglo-Dutch fleet in the Sound—The Swedish fleet puts to sea—Hans Wachtmeister—Difficulties of a junction with the English and Dutch—Sharp correspondence between Charles and his admiral—The junction effected—The Swedes land in Zealand—Danger of Charles's position—Peace of Travendal—Preparations for the Livonian expedition—Remonstrances of the Swedish Chancellor—Taciturnity of the King—Description of his chief officers, Rehnskjöld, Stenbock, Horn, Levenhaupt—Landing of Charles at Pernau—Advance upon Narva—Hardships of the march—Description of the Russian camp—Battle of Narva—Sensation caused thereby—Charles refuses all mediation—Winters at Lais Castle—Correspondence with his sister.

EANWHILE the war had already begun in two opposite quarters. In February, 1700, relying on the promises and representations of Patkul, who himself accompanied the army thither, Augustus had ordered the Saxon troops to invade Livonia. Patkul's plan was to surprise Riga by a *coup de main*. Success, he said, was certain and would be imme-

diately followed by the defection from Sweden of
the whole of the Livonian gentry.   The project was
defeated, however, by the providence of the aged *
commandant, Erik Dahlberg, indisputably the
greatest engineer and the bravest officer in the
Swedish service, who had won his first laurels fifty
years before under Charles X.   It was he who had
suggested to that monarch the hazardous passage
across the barely frozen Belt which resulted in the
glorious Peace of Roskilde, a feat for which his
superior officer, Marshal Wrangel, who had pronounced it a sheer impossibility, never forgave him.
The subsequent regency, of which Wrangel was a
member, accordingly took good care that Dahlberg
should get no further promotion, but one of the first
acts of the youthful Charles XI. was to re-employ
and recompense his father's faithful servant, making
him, in rapid succession, a Count, a Field-Marshal
and a Governor-General, and it was under Charles
XI.'s son that the veteran was now to perform his
last exploits.   Early in February, Dahlberg repulsed
the Saxons from before the walls of Riga, and won
the engagements of Wenden and Neumühle, but was
not strong enough to prevent them from capturing
the small fortress of Dünamünde, which, as its name
implies, commands the passage of the Dwina.   A
second Saxon invasion of Livonia in May was also
repulsed with the aid of troops from Finland and
Esthonia, and Patkul was publicly denounced as a
traitor at a Landtag held at Riga in June.   But
want of men and money hampered the Swedish

---

* Now in his seventy-fifth year.

generals at every step, and when the Saxons, largely reinforced, crossed the Dwina for the third time, in July, they met with no opposition, and King Augustus sat down before Riga and held it closely invested for the next six weeks.

In Holstein hostilities began in the middle of May, when the Lüneberg Princes, uniting with a small Swedish army under Gyllenstjerna, took the field against the Danes, who had by this time occupied the whole of Holstein, and were then actually besieging the Duke's last but strongest fortress, Tönning, which was stoutly defended by the Swedish General Johan Gabriel Banér. The allies were commanded by George of Hanover (afterwards George I. of England), but the anxiety with which the Hanoverians saved their powder and carefully avoided every chance of an engagement, gave to the whole campaign the character of a mere military demonstration. The approach of the allies indeed, slow as it was, did induce the Danes, at last, to raise the siege of Tönning; but, for the next two months, both armies did nothing but cautiously observe each other within speaking distance while the neutral Powers strenuously though fruitlessly endeavoured to mediate. Then it was that Charles XII., impatient of the circuitous methods of diplomacy, suddenly brought the war to an end by himself drawing the sword.

In April Charles had arrived at Carlscrona to superintend the mobilisation of his army and the equipment of his fleet, dashing backwards and forwards between Gothenburg, Malmö and Carlscrona

as occasion demanded. His energy and enthusiasm
were extraordinary, but even more so were the
obstacles that encountered him at every step, chief
among which was a paralysing poverty. Now, if ever,
Sweden was sorely in need of money and no money
was forthcoming. The whole country was still suffering from the effects of a terrible famine that had
lasted three years; the Treasury was empty; the
gentry, impoverished by the grinding requisitions of
the Reduction System, could give little or no help
to the distracted and embarrassed Government which
found itself absolutely at the end of its resources on
the eve of a costly war with a powerful coalition.
No wonder if many of the King's most experienced
counsellors shook their heads and murmured that
the enterprise on which he had just embarked was
too great for Sweden. Charles alone remained immovable. "Nothing is impossible!" was his constant motto, and he took an almost incredible
delight in wrestling with apparently insuperable
difficulties, while those about him looked on with
an admiration not unmingled with uneasiness. The
most arbitrary and unusual expedients were employed to raise a little ready money. The taxes
were anticipated a year in advance; the Senators
lent the Crown what cash they had; the Governors
of the Provinces, by the King's command, *persuaded*
the local magnates to make *free* gifts to the Crown,
and small loans were obtained from Holland and
the Lüneberg Princes. By these means and after
three months of the most strenuous exertions, the
fleet was ready to put to sea, an army was mobilised

in Scania, and Charles prepared to make his first
military venture. The united remonstrances of the
whole *Corps Diplomatique* in Sweden were powerless
to hold him back. For the first time in the course
of a century France and the maritime Powers spoke
the same language, for the understanding they had
come to by the partition treaty regulating the Spanish Succession made them anxious to prevent a war
which they might not be able to localise. But
Charles would not listen. He rid himself of the im-
portunities of these ubiquitous diplomatists by the
simple but irritating expedient of constantly referring them all to the Swedish Chancellery at Stockholm, five hundred miles off, and never answering
any of the despatches addressed to him from that
quarter. He himself was only awaiting the arrival
of the English and Dutch fleets which were daily
expected in the Sound. They were coming ostensibly as the friends of both Powers but with secret,
though somewhat indefinite, instructions to co-
operate with Sweden so far as to make Denmark
amenable to reason on the Holstein question. At
length, on June 12th, twelve English liners under Sir
George Rooke, and thirteen Dutch liners under
Alamonde, arrived at Gothenburg, and four days
later the Swedish fleet, consisting of thirty-eight
ships of the line and a number of smaller vessels,
carrying 2700 guns in all, also put to sea. This
magnificent fleet, the finest Sweden ever had till the
days of Gustavus III., was the life-work of her greatest admiral, Hans Wachtmeister, who had served
his apprenticeship in the science of naval warfare

CARL GUSTAF REHNSKJÖLD.

as a volunteer on board the English fleet during the
brief but bloody Dutch war of 1665–6. But his
great opportunity came in the Swedo-Danish war of
1675–79, which he entered as a post-captain and
quitted as admiral-general. He took a brilliant
part in the great sea battles of Öland and Möen
when the Swedish fleet was defeated by the combined Dutch and Danish navies, on the latter occasion fighting victoriously in his flagship against seven
Dutchmen ; while, at the second battle of Öland,
two years later, he defeated twelve Danish liners
with a little squadron of only six vessels. At the
close of the war, Wachtmeister devoted himself entirely to the reconstruction of the Swedish Navy,
and now, after twenty years of incessant labour, he
had the privilege of commanding the fleet that he
himself had created. Meanwhile the English and
Dutch fleets had passed through the Sound. The
Danish Admiral, Gyldenlöve, with his forty-five
liners, had fallen back upon Copenhagen and taken
up a position guarding the entrance of the strait
called the *Kungdjup*, the only safe channel from the
Baltic into the Sound, thus cutting off the allied
squadrons from the Swedish fleet which lay to the
south off Malmö. Gyldenlöve had strict orders to
prevent the junction of the fleets by attacking them
separately but not to risk a conflict against the three
combined. Charles, meanwhile, had gone ashore at
Malmö where he received a message from Admiral
Rooke urging him to bring up his fleet as soon as
possible and unite with the Anglo-Dutch squadron
in the Sound. Charles at once ordered Wachtmeis-

ter to comply with the request of the English Admiral, but the grave question now arose: How was
the junction to be effected? The superior Danish
fleet, in an almost impregnable position, guarded
the usual channel, the *Kungdjup*, and though there
was another strait, the so-called *Flintrännen* (Flint-
furrow), between the isle of Saltholm and the
Swedish coast, it was known to be very dangerous
and no ship of war had ever passed through it. A
fortnight of anxious suspense ensued. Brave as he
was, Wachtmeister hesitated to trust his fleet in the
narrow, rocky *Flintrännen*. He knew better than
anyone else what such a fleet was worth. It was the
only one Sweden had, it had cost twenty years to
build and the safety of the state depended on its
preservation. But the English and Dutch Admirals
becoming more and more urgent and Wachtmeister
still hesitating, Charles could control himself no
longer, and his angry impatience found expression
in a letter of remonstrance to the aged Admiral, in
which he even hinted at cowardice, concluding with
these words: " We cannot refrain from expressing
to you our *great displeasure* which will not be withdrawn unless you endeavour hereafter by valiant behaviour and riper *conduite* (conduct) to make up for
what you have been wanting in hitherto." Wachtmeister was cut to the heart and declared, in his
brief reply, that he had never felt anything so much
in all his life. His conduct would show, he added,
that he was second to none in valour. This note
was dated July 6th, the day after that on which the
Swedish fleet under his command had actually passed

through the dangerous strait. Five vessels indeed
had grounded and thirteen more had to be left behind on the south side of the *Flintrännen ;* but the
feat was accomplished none the less, and its decisive
result justified the venturesome insistance of the
young King, though he might well have dealt a little more tenderly with his father's old and faithful
servant. The Danish fleet, inferior as it was to the
three opposing fleets combined, was now compelled,
perforce, to look on while the Swedish troops were
rowed across the Sound in large, flat-bottomed boats
under cover of the escorting liners and frigates, and
effected a landing on the coast of Zealand which had
been carefully reconnoitred beforehand by Quartermaster-General Stuart. The plan was carried out
with such dexterity and despatch that the small
Danish force ashore mistook, at first, the real landing
point and only discovered its mistake when the vanguard of the invaders was already drawn up in position. Charles, who had impetuously thrown himself
out of his boat into water up to his waist and waded
ashore sword in hand, was one of the first to land,
and after a short but sharp skirmish the Danes were
driven back and the Swedes established themselves
in an entrenched camp.

So far all had gone well, but Charles's position
was, for the moment, most perilous. His little army
numbered but 4000 men ; it was only provisioned
for five days ; he had no cavalry to levy requisitions on the country round ; the Danish forces were
assembling, and the burgesses of Copenhagen, full
of martial ardour, clamoured to be led against the

foe *en masse*. If the Danish Admiral were to regain the command of the sea, or if any accident
were to interrupt Charles's communications with
Sweden, he was lost. Fortunately, the Danish Government, which had relied entirely on its fleet, was
so stupefied by the suddenness of this unexpected
descent that it did nothing at all for another week,
and, by that time, Charles's reinforcements had also
been ferried across the Sound and he found himself
at the head of 11,000 men. He was preparing to
fall upon Copenhagen forthwith when a courier
from the South arrived in the Swedish camp with
the news that peace had already been concluded at
Travendal between the Duke of Holstein and the
Danish Crown whereby the latter had acceded to all
the Duke's demands. There was, therefore, no
longer any occasion for the presence of a Swedish
army in Zealand. But Charles was ill-disposed to let
go this golden opportunity of crushing the Danish
Monarchy, and still persisted in his martial designs
even after Admiral Rooke had officially informed
Wachtmeister that since all the demands of the
Allies had now been complied with, no further assistance was to be expected from the English fleet
which was under orders to return home forthwith.
Then it was that Count Piper and his colleagues in
the Swedish camp energetically represented to the
King the criminal folly of running counter to the
wishes of all his allies. God's anger and the world's
hatred, they insisted, would overwhelm him if he
recklessly plunged his country into an unnecessary
war now that he could obtain a righteous peace,

especially when the hardly pressed Livonia offered him a fresh field for martial exploits if he was that way inclined. These cogent reasons, skilfully presented, at length prevailed.

Thus Charles XII.'s first campaign had ended gloriously and its success was mainly due to himself. The audaciously conceived plan of a descent upon Zealand in the teeth of a formidable Danish fleet and the still more audacious means by which he effected it, despite the objections of his most experienced officers, were entirely his own. He had given the first proofs of that astonishing resolution, of that gigantic force of will, which were, ere long, to achieve triumphs little short of miracles, and he had also shewn that he could listen to reason and moderate the fierceness of his martial ardour. On all who saw him at this time he seems to have made the most favourable impression. The Danish officers were amazed at the stern discipline enforced by a young general whose conquering army was content to starve in a fat land rather than pillage it, and Admiral Rooke, who had an audience with Charles on board the royal yacht, was strongly attracted by his frank and open manners and is reported to have said that if anyone wanted to see the ideal of a brave warrior he could not do better than go to the young King of Sweden for it. The Admiral, moreover, wanted to place his own sumptuously furnished yacht at the King's disposal but was privately dissuaded from doing so " because his Swedish Majesty had no great liking for such luxuries."

For the next two months Charles remained in

5

Scania preparing for his Livonian expedition. A
whole train of ambassadors followed him wherever
he went, but his dislike of diplomatists seemed to
increase every day and he persistently refused them
audiences, always referring them to the Chancellery
at Stockholm. Yet, if he had been wise, he
would have listened to the advantageous terms of
peace which Augustus of Saxony, alarmed at the
sudden and unexpected collapse of Denmark, was
now eager to offer the Swedish monarch through
the medium of France. But to every pacific over-
ture from that quarter Charles remained deaf. Disgust at Augustus's treachery, the desire to punish
him, above all the stimulating taste of victory, had
whetted his appetite for fresh adventures. Meanwhile he concealed his real sentiments beneath the
cloak of an impenetrable taciturnity. The despatches
of his ministers at Stockholm (and they reached him
every other day) remained unanswered for weeks
together; the proposal of the importunate French
ambassador who suggested that Sweden should
make peace with Poland and accede to the Spanish
Partition Treaty, was dexterously parried by impossible counter-proposals; and when Count Polus, the
King's ex-tutor, seized a rare opportunity of opening
his mind to his master in private and began eloquently setting forth the pacific views of himself
and his colleagues, Charles, after listening to him
for a few moments with an amused smile, rose and
politely bowed him right out of the room without
uttering a word. Charles XII.'s career, it has well
been said, was a combination of marvellous adven-

tures and neglected opportunities, and his obstinate refusal at this time to come to terms with a foe from whom he could not hope to obtain any solid advantage was the first grave mistake in his career. A haughty, self-centred reserve, which loved to stand alone and go its own way in spite of everything, was his chief fault as a ruler and the cause of all his future calamities. And all this time his financial embarrassments were becoming more and more pressing, to many it seemed doubtful whether he would even be able to mobilise his army. Ominous warnings too were heard from the most unexpected quarters. The Chancellor, Oxentsjerna, who had all his life long been the successful champion of a pacific policy and whose long experience had taught him the danger of neglecting opportunities, Oxenstjerna, the most cautious and circuitous of ministers, now fairly lost all patience and, in a letter to his colleague Polus, expressed his disgust and alarm at the turn things were taking in the most direct and emphatic manner. He bitterly complained of the ignorance in which he and his colleagues were kept as to the King's intentions; deplored the obstinacy which, instead of playing off one foe against another, would fain make head against them all and with truly prophetic foresight pointed to Russia as the one antagonist who could not safely be neglected. " If once the Tsar gets a place on the Baltic," wrote Oxenstjerna, " he 'll stick to it come what will." Whether this document ever reached the King's eyes is doubtful, but on September 25th, Charles at last broke his long silence by addressing a short note to his Chancellery declaring that he could not admit the possibility of any mediation but was determined to obtain due satisfaction for "an unjust and treacherous invasion" by means of his "lawful weapons," nor would he consent to listen to any negotiations till full and complete restitution had been made beforehand. The same week the news reached him that the Tsar had invaded Ingria whereupon the Senate was commanded to throw the Russian Resident into prison and confiscate all Russian ships and wares throughout the kingdom. Charles's preparations were now completed and he determined to embark at once with his troops. On October 1st he went on board the flagship *Westermanland* and on the following day the coast of Courland was sighted.

And now, before following Charles through his second campaign, we shall do well to learn something of his chief lieutenants, those men who for the next eighteen years were to follow their indomitable master through all his vicissitudes. Amongst the little band of heroes who surrounded the heroic young King, four stand forth conspicuously, Carl Gustaf Rehnskjöld, Magnus Stenbock, Arvid Bernhard Horn, and Adam Ludwig Levenhaupt.

Carl Gustaf Rehnskjöld was born at Griefswald, August 6, 1651, studied under Puffendorff at the University of Lund, and entered the army as an ensign in 1673. He gave the first proofs of his prowess during the Danish war of 1673-9, took a prominent part in Charles XI.'s three great victories at Halmstadt, Lund and Landscrona and won thereby the

CHARLES XII. AND MARSHAL STENBOCK.
BY EDELFELT.

rank of a lieutenant-colonel and the reputation of a " valiant stout-hearted soldier " (the King's own words). He subsequently reaped fresh laurels in the Low Countries in the often beaten but never routed army of William of Orange, so that on the accession of Charles XII. he was one of the ripest generals in the Swedish service. His neck-or-nothing tactics were after Charles's own heart, but he was bitterly hated· in consequence by those of his less-favoured fellow-generals who preferred the more deliberate procedure of the Dutch school, and some have even gone so far as to deny him generalship altogether. But even if his brilliant victory at Fraustadt were not proof positive to the contrary, it is absurd to maintain that an officer who satisfied two such exacting masters as Charles XI. and Charles XII. and was victorious in twelve pitched battles and thirty engagements owed everything to fortune. Rehnskjöld, however, was cursed with a provocative, almost brutal, surliness which made him many enemies and his memory has suffered accordingly.

Magnus Stenbock, the future victor of Helsingborg and Gadebusch, and the one blithe and brilliant figure of the sternly austere Caroline period, was born at Stockholm in 1664. After a six-years' tour abroad (1683–9), in the course of which he studied mathematics under Ozanam at Paris, and served as an ensign in William of Orange's life guards, he returned to Stockholm and had the good fortune to win the heart and hand of Eva Magdalena Oxenstjerna, the Swedish Chancellor's daughter. Another six-years' Odyssey followed, during which he fought under the Dutch flag with distinction, and on the accession of Charles XII. he was already a colonel. Stenbock's history is, as we shall see, inextricably bound up with that of Charles XII., whom he absolutely idolised. It is also noteworthy that he became Charles's solitary disciple in the art of war, most of the other Swedish generals belonging to another school or a former generation. Of all the great Caroline heroes, the radiant, versatile, kindly Stenbock was the most beloved. The memories of his heroic deeds and pathetic sufferings live to this day in the minds of the common people; in Scania, where for a time he was Governor-General, his sayings are still treasured as household words, and next to Charles XII. he approaches most nearly to the national idea of heroism.

Arvid Bernhard Horn, who, to use his own favourite quotation, was " taken out of the mire to be set among princes," came of a Finnish stock noble indeed, but so poor that the future Chancellor was forced to enter the army as a common soldier and keep away from church for want of decent clothes. Like Stenbock, whose acquaintance he made there, he had served in the Low Countries; Charles XII. on his accession made him a captain and a baron, and we shall see how under that young hero Horn won both fame and fortune. But we shall also see how, gradually, a breach opened between them, a breach so wide that even respect on the one side and gratitude on the other could not shake hands across it. Horn loved his king much, but he loved his country still more, and he had no wish, as it has finely been said, to see "Sweden shed her last drop of blood as a libation to Charles XII.'s caprices." So long as his master lived he could, indeed, only look on and see his country bleed, but it was reserved for him, after his master's death, to heal his country's wounds and nurse her into convalescence.*

Adam Ludwig Levenhaupt, born 1659, "our Latin Colonel," as Charles XII. called him because he was one of the few Swedish officers who could negotiate in that language, was, after Magnus Stenbock, perhaps Charles's best general ; but, belonging, as he did, to the cautious and circumspect Dutch school of tacticians (he had served for seven years in the Low Countries), he was somewhat undervalued and overlooked by his master, who is said to have even expressed his surprise on hearing of Levenhaupt's great victory at Gemaurthoff. He was also, as we shall see, the only one of Charles's generals who held an independent command for many years, and so long as he acted alone he did excellently well. But he was never a favourite, and the exploits of his more brilliant colleagues have thrown his own more sober if more solid services somewhat into the shade.

On October 6th, after a severe passage, Charles reached Pernau. He had intended at first to relieve Riga, but finding that the fortress of Narva, the key of Esthonia, was in still more pressing danger from the Russians, he finally decided to turn northwards against the Tsar. He fixed his headquarters at Wesenburg, a small town midway between Reval

---

* See R. Nisbet Bain's *Gustavus III.*, vol. i., ch. i.

and Narva; the next five weeks were spent in col-
lecting and mobilising his forces and on November
13th the King joined the army which set off to relieve Narva forthwith.   To all the Swedish officers,
however, the enterprise had seemed most hazardous.
The Russians, at the very lowest computation,* outnumbered the Swedes five to one and were protected besides by a strongly entrenched camp.   It
was a seven-days' march from Wesenburg to Narva
through a wasted land along dangerous boggy roads
defended by no less than three formidable passes
which a very little engineering science could easily
have made impregnable.   Even Rehnskjöld and
Stenbock, the bravest of Charles's captains, wavered,
and, supported by the new French ambassador,
Guiscard, whom Charles, to his intense disgust, had
found awaiting him at Reval, whence he had, so far,
followed the King everywhere like his shadow,
earnestly remonstrated against the expedition, but
in vain; Charles would not so much as await the
1000 cavalry that was daily expected from Reval.
He maintained that even a day's delay might be
dangerous and that the only way of neutralising
the superiority of the Russian forces was to take
them by surprise.   When his officers hinted at the
ruinous possibility of a defeat, he replied that he
was sure God would defend his righteous cause, and
that with his brave blue boys † behind him he feared
nothing.   So the army set out and the march to

---

* The Russians were not 80,000 in number, as commonly supposed,
but a little over 40,000.

† The Swedish uniform was blue, the flag blue and yellow.

ADAM LUDVIG LEVENHAUPT.
FROM AN OLD PRINT.

Narva proved even more terrible than was anticipated. During the last five days of it the way lay
through a land devastated with fire and sword and
the whole army had to bivouac in the open air.
They had no commissariat with them and the Russians had taken good care that they should find
nothing to pick up anywhere. As the march proceeded matters grew worse and worse. The mud
and mire reached up to the soldiers' knees, they were
drenched to the skin by driving storms of snow and
sleet, and during the last two days the men had
scarce a bit of bread to eat, the horses not a straw.
Fortunately the Russians had neglected to occupy
two of the dangerous passes in the Swedish line of
march, while the third, Pyhäjoggi, supposed to be
defended by Sheremetev with 6000 men, was carried by a dashing charge of 400 Swedish horse led
by the King in person. On the 19th the little army,
nearly starving and half frozen, reached Lagena, a
village about nine miles from Narva, and signalled
its approach to the beleaguered fortress.

In the Russian camp, meanwhile, all was alarm
and confusion. Sheremetev's wild flight from Pyhäjoggi had filled the Tsar with such panic terror as to
make him completely lose his head. He determined
not to await the arrival of the Swedes, but hastily
transferred the supreme command of his forces to
the Duke de Croy, who happened to be with the
Russian army as a spectator. That unhappy nobleman at first refused the dangerous distinction on the
plea that he was a perfect stranger to the ways, language and mode of warfare of the semi-barbarous

Russians ; but Peter, drunk with brandy and mad
with fear, came to the Duke's tent at midnight and
raved, coaxed and stormed till De Croy gave way.
Then Peter, fortifying himself with more brandy,
fled precipitately, giving out that he had a pressing
engagement with King Augustus, whom everybody
knew to be at least five hundred miles away. *

But abandoned though they were at the decisive
moment by their own leader, the Russians, well
clothed, well fed and well armed, in a commanding
position behind formidable entrenchments and out-
numbering the wearied and famished ragamuffins
opposed to them five to one, seemed certain of victory. The town of Narva is situated on a narrow
neck of land round which the river Narova makes a
wide bend. South of the town, commanding the
only road by which the enemy could approach, the
Russians had entrenched themselves between a
double line of circumvallation which cut off the town
from succour and at the same time protected them
from an outside attack.† The outer line of circumvallation had a rampart nine feet high and a trench
six feet wide, and was defended by one hundred and
forty cannons. Early in the morning of the 20th
November, when it was still quite dark, the Swedish
army broke up from Lagena. On debouching from

---

* The Swedes struck a medal ridiculing this shameful flight. On
the obverse the Tsar is represented holding his hands over his mor-
tars with the inscription : "Peter sat by the fire and warmed himself." On the reverse he is shown in full flight with his cap and
sceptre falling to the ground, with the accompanying device : "And
Peter went out and wept bitterly."

† See plan facing page 76.

the forest into the plain before Narva, the little
army was taken by De Croy for the mere vanguard
of a larger host and he would have sent out 15,000
men to drive them back but the Russian officers refused to quit their lines. The Swedes now formed
in battle array with the infantry in the centre and
the cavalry on the wings. Vellingk commanded the
right wing, Rehnskjöld, who had planned the attack,
the left. Charles was at the head of a small separate
division on the extreme left with Arvid Horn and
Magnus Stenbock. At two o'clock in the afternoon,
the signal for áttack was given by firing two rockets
and the whole Swedish line advanced under a vigorous fire from the hostile camp. At that moment
the sky was suddenly darkened by a violent snow-
storm. Some of the Swedish generals would thereupon have postponed the attack until the storm had
blown over. " Nay ! " cried the King, " don't you
see that it is at our backs but full in the enemy's
face, so that he cannot see how small our force is ?
Let us seize this favourable opportunity while we
can." No sooner said than done. The Russians,
who could not see thirty paces ahead because of the
snow, were not aware of the approach of the Swedes
until they were actually upon them, and the assault
was so impetuous that in a quarter of an hour the
Swedes were masters of the outer entrenchments,
scaling them in as perfect order as if they were on
parade. The Russian right wing was speedily thrown
into disorder, wavered and fled. A large number of
the fugitives were drowned in attempting to cross a
bridge which broke down beneath them ; the rest

hastily entrenched themselves behind a barricade of
wagons round which a bloody conflict waged till
it was dark. The King, who seemed to be wherever
the fight was hottest, was several times in great
danger, lost one of his jack-boots in a morass and a
bullet was found flattened against his cravat after
the fight was over. The Russian left was disposed
of equally expeditiously by the Swedish right under
Rehnskjöld, so that by nightfall the battle was practically over, and Charles, after promptly occupying
a height where the enemy had planted his principal
artillery, thus separating the remains of the Russian
right wing from the remains of the Russian left,
allowed his weary troops a brief repose in a safe
position between the inner line of circumvallation
and the fortress. At break of day General Wrede,
who commanded on the Russian left, capitulated,
the famished and utterly exhausted victors willingly
allowing him and his 6000 troops, a number pretty
nearly equal to the whole of the conquering host, to
lay down their arms and depart home. De Croy and
the other foreign officers in the Russian service had
already surrendered to escape being massacred by
their own ignorant, panic-stricken troops, who smelt
treachery in a disaster due entirely to their own cowardice. On the following day the remainder of the
Russian troops, who were scattered all over the vast
camp, surrendered unconditionally ; but the rank
and file were discharged at once lest they should
discover the weakness of their conquerors.* The

---

* It is said that 12,000 men alone laid down their arms at the feet
of Magnus Stenbock who had only 600.

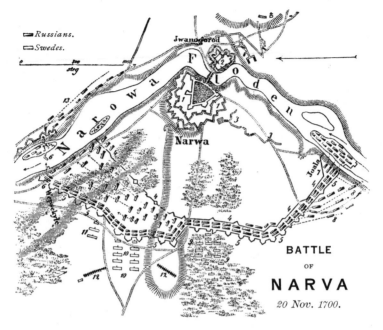

1. Narva. 2. Ivanogorod. 3. Russian trenches and batteries. 4. Russian line of contravallation over against Narva. 5. Russian line of circumvallation to repel attack from without. Between these two lines lies the Russian host. 6. Wepsekyle with bridge. 7. Joala. 8. Russian cavalry flight at beginning of battle. 9. Swedish right wing. 10. Swedish left. 11. Troops apart under Charles, Horn, and Stenbock. 12. Swedish artillery. 13. Russians' flight

enemy's camp, the whole of his artillery, and an immense amount of booty fell into the hands of the Swedes. The Russian loss has been estimated at between nine to ten thousand, the Swedish at not quite two thousand Well might Stenbock exclaim, in a letter to his father-in-law: " 'T is God's work alone; but if there be anything human in it at all, it is the firm, immovable resolution of his Majesty . . . and the ripe dispositions of General Rehnskjöld." Charles was justly proud of his soldiers, and their discipline was fully equal to their value. It is said that when the conquerors entered the enemy's tents and found the tables there covered with silver plate and all sorts of meat and drink they marched through them in pursuit of the foe without so much as touching a piece of bread although they had eaten nothing for two days.*

Thus Narva was delivered after a ten-weeks' siege. On the day after the battle the King held his entry into the town amidst the hurrahs of the inhabitants, and hastened first of all to the church where, on his knees, he thanked God for a victory any share in which he himself modestly disclaimed.

The battle of Narva caused a great sensation throughout Europe. Many had given Charles up for lost when he set out on his adventurous expedition. The French ambassador, Guiscard, who had

---

* It is true that there was a reaction *after* the battle, for Caspar Wrede wrote home to his father that all the common soldiers were so full of brandy, which they had found in the Russian tents, that it was impossible for the officers to arrange their prisoners, so they had to let them go. " If they had attacked us," he adds, " they would indisputably have got the better of us."

stopped behind, was so surprised at the news of the victory that he could not say a word for several days afterwards. Its consequences, too, were not inconsiderable. Ingria was rescued, the Russians were panic-stricken and it was only the absolute necessity of rest for the utterly fagged-out little army (more than half of which was already in the hospital) that prevented Charles from following up his advantage. But, on the other hand, this victory was mischievous also, for it gave the young King an altogether exaggerated idea of his own invincibility and filled him with an unjustifiable contempt for his rival Peter which he was one day to rue bitterly. In the middle of December the Swedish army went into winter quarters around Dorpat and Charles, for the next six months, took up his abode at Lais, a castle midway between Dorpat and Lake Peipus, so as to be on the spot when hostilities were resumed in spring.

Meanwhile an event had occurred which completely changed the face of European politics. In November, 1700, died Charles II. of Spain, bequeathing the whole of the possessions of the Spanish monarchy to Philip of Anjou, the second grandson of Louis XIV., who thereupon openly repudiated the Partition Compact which he had made with the Maritime Powers and declared his intention of putting his grandson into the full possession of his rights. A war between France and the Maritime Powers was now therefore only a question of days and both sides looked to Sweden for assistance. The competing French and Imperial ambassadors appeared in the Swedish camp, while the English

and Dutch ministers were equally busy at Stockholm. Chancellor Oxenstjerna saw in this universal
bidding for the favour of Sweden another opportunity of ending "this present lean war and of making
his Majesty the arbiter of Europe," and he instructed
his son-in-law, Magnus Stenbock, who was now in
high favour with his royal master, to represent the
advantages of concluding peace with Saxony and
Russia and taking up a neutral observant attitude
during the now imminent war of the Spanish Succession, which would give Sweden the same commanding position she had enjoyed under Charles XI.
during the war of the Palatinate. This was sound
and safe counsel and if Charles had only had the
wisdom to follow it the benefits to his country
would have been incalculable ; but, as usual, he condescended to give no reply one way or the other
and to all about him he remained an impenetrable
enigma. The ambassadors were referred to Oxenstjerna, and Oxenstjerna's numerous despatches, if
read at all, were never answered. "His Majesty,"
wrote Stenbock to his father-in-law, despairingly,
"his Majesty seems to receive his inspirations from
God alone and has got the idea of a war so firmly
fixed in his head that he can attend to nothing else."—
"God only knows what will be the end of it all,"
wrote Cederhjelm, another of Charles's officers, "both
politics and economics are treated cavalierly enough
and we jog on as best we can." The urgent representations of his Minister at The Hague, Lillieroth,
to the effect that both William III. and the Grand
Pensionary, Heinsius, were uneasy at the unnecessary

prolongation of the Northern war and desirous of
knowing the real sentiments of Sweden, drew at
length a reluctant reply from the saturnine young
hero. " It would put our glory to shame," he wrote,
" if we were to lend ourselves to the slightest treaty
·or accommodation with one who has so vilely pros-
tituted his honour." This reference to Augustus of
Saxony clearly showed that Charles was determined
to punish his treacherous antagonist at all hazards,
and that, till he had done so, nothing was to be
expected of him.

For the next six months Charles remained at Lais
among his officers, in the best of spirits, hunting,
dancing, sledging, storming snow bastions ingeniously
contrived by Stenbock, taking part in concerts (also
of that versatile officer's invention) and even playing
blind-man's-buff with the hearty gusto of a healthy
school-boy. His letters to his sister and ultimate
successor, the Princess Ulrica Leonora,* short and
scrappy as they are, give us an interesting glimpse of
the hero in *déshabillé* so to speak. In this correspondence he is always affectionate and sometimes
even jocose as, for instance, when he sends the
respects of his dog Pompey to his sister's pet poodle,
" Madame Menisse and any other dogs that may
happen to be at Court." Once he gives her a de-

---

* *Carl XIIs Bref-vexling . . . 1698-1709.*—They are all written
in great haste and with a magnificent disregard of orthography. The
word *cœur*, for instance (he always addresses his sister as *Mon
Cœur*) is spelled three or four different ways often on the same page.
Compare *Konung Karl XIIs Egenhändiga Bref*, quite recently (1893)
published and edited by G. Carlson, in- which the above smaller
collection is incorporated.

scription of a Livonian peasant-wedding which shews a considerable sense of humour. It is remarkable, however, how extremely reticent Charles always is about himself. He never says how he is or what he is doing or about to do. His longest letters relate to his sister's ailments or devotions, on both of which points he never fails to give her plenty of good advice. There are frequent enquiries also about his baby nephew, the future Duke of Holstein, whom he always alludes to as "little C. F." (*i. e.*, Charles Frederick). As a rule, however, this correspondence consists of very brief apologies for the writer's inability to write more at the time. Moreover, all his letters bear the marks of extreme haste, many of them not even being signed.

6

CHAPTER V.

THE KING-MAKER IN POLAND.

1701–1703.

Despondency of Augustus—Patkul revives his courage—Campaign of 1701—Charles at Riga—The passage of the Dwina—Charles occupies Courland—Condition of the Polish Republic at this time—Precarious position of Augustus—The Sapiéhas—Cardinal Radziejowski—Charles in winter quarters at Würgen—Refuses to negotiate with Augustus—William III. of England counsels moderation—Obstinacy and venturesomeness of Charles—The mission of Aurora von Königsmarck—Advance of Charles upon Warsaw — Warsaw occupied — Fruitless negotiations — Charles marches southwards—Battle of Klissov—Fall of Cracow.

EANWHILE, Sweden's enemies were arming to renew the contest with her. The Tsar was particularly alert. He had been inclined, indeed, immediately after the battle of Narva, to come to terms with his conqueror; but his dogged resolution had speedily got the better of his momentary panic, and during the winter he had been prudently engaged in strengthening his frontier fortresses and collecting fresh armies behind them. He had also sent an extraordinary embassy to Copenhagen, to persuade the

King of Denmark to a fresh rupture with Sweden, and at an interview, a few days later, with Augustus at the castle of Birse in Samogitia, he revived the drooping courage of the Polish monarch. Augustus had now almost as serious difficulties to contend against as Charles XII. himself. The finances of his Saxon electorate were in a wretched condition ; in Poland his position, never very strong, was every day becoming more and more precarious, and his best friends in that country counselled him to make peace with Sweden on almost any terms. On the other hand, there was constantly by his side the man who had first kindled the Great Northern War, and was now devoting all his energies to keep it alive. For Patkul was still the chief counsellor of Augustus, and his extraordinary abilities, inspired by his revengeful hatred of Sweden, made him her most formidable foe. He was in constant correspondence with all her actual and potential enemies ; is, with good reason, suspected of having brought about the interview between the Tsar and the King of Poland, and was never weary of urging the latter to snatch Livonia from the grasp of the exhausted and diminutive Swedish army there. Still Augustus wavered. He attempted, first of all, to secure a peace with Charles through the mediation of the Elector of Brandenburg, but Charles persisting in his determination never to negotiate with one who had once played him false, Augustus was driven to the ultimate arbitrament of battle, and on March 27, 1701, Field-Marshal Steinau set out from Warsaw, to take the command of the Saxon army in Livonia.

His instructions were not to cross the Dwina (the boundary, at that time, between Swedish Livonia and Poland) until he had been joined by the Russians, but at all hazards to prevent the Swedes from crossing it.

The Swedish army had already taken the field, and indeed it was high time, for it had no longer anything to eat. Luckless Livonia, after being ravaged thrice in one year by the enemy, had been sucked absolutely dry by her own defenders, for the pressing exigencies of the Swedish King had compelled him to treat it like a conquered province. An offensive war had therefore become an absolute necessity, and the impatiently awaited reinforcements from Sweden, amounting to nearly 10,000 men, which reached Livonia in the late spring of 1701,* enabled Charles to shew himself on the battlefield once more. On June 17th, his birthday, he set out to seek the foe, marching southward at the head of 15,000 men; on July 7th the army stood under the walls of Riga. On hearing of the Swedish advance, the Saxon army had concentrated itself on the opposite side of the river Dwina, facing the city. It consisted of 10,000 Saxons and 19,000 Russians. Misled by a rumour that Charles intended to cross the Dwina at Kockenhausen, some miles lower down

---

* Under constant pressure from the King, Sweden had now put forth all her resources. Seldom had she had such a large and w ll equipped host. Her total forces at the beginning of 1701 have b estimated at 80,000 men. Of these 17,000 remained at home to fend her frontiers, 18,000 were in Pomerania to hold Denmark Saxony in check and nearly 45,000 were distributed through Livon.a, Esthonia and Ingria.

AUGUSTUS OF POLAND.
FROM AN OLD PRINT.

where the stream was narrower, Steinau had hastened thither with the pick of his troops, leaving Patkul and the Duke of Courland in command of the main army. They relied upon their superior numbers, their commanding position behind well fortified trenches, and above all upon the tried valour of the Saxon veterans. " If the Swedes even numbered 100,000," the Duke of Courland is reported to have said, "it would be impossible for them to cross successfully." Both generals agreed therefore not to lead their troops down to the river's bank to arrest the passage of the foe, but to take up a strong position on rising land a little distance away, wait till a few thousand of the Swedes had crossed and then fall upon and crush them in detail. They also counted upon making Charles a prisoner, well aware that his habitual audacity would make him court rather than avoid danger.

On July 8th the Swedish troops began to embark. Old Dahlberg, who had been instructed long before as to the King's design, had got together a number of boats and vessels of all sorts. He had also invented a peculiar kind of flat-bottomed prahm, big enough to hold both cannons and cavalry, and protected in front by huge stiff hides which could be hoisted like sails during the passage and let down to serve as landing-boards on reaching the other side. A few minutes after four o'clock in the morning, the whole river was covered with rafts, prahms and boats full of Swedish troops. In front of them all went sailing boats filled with damp straw which had been ignited and gave forth volumes of smoke which the

wind blew right into the faces of the Saxons, so that
the enemy could not exactly make out what the
Swedes were about till they were already half way
across the Dwina.   Then, however, the Saxon artillery began to play upon the advancing flotilla, but
most of the balls and bullets were stopped by the
protecting hides.   After a passage of about three
quarters of an hour, the first convoy of troops
reached the shore.   The grenadiers of the guard
were the first to land, and among them was the King.
" My lads," he cried, as he leaped ashore, " we 've
got so far with God's help, and He will help us on
still farther."   All his generals had implored him
beforehand not to venture his life in so risky an
enterprise.   He had given no answer at the time, but,
seizing his opportunity, had slipped away and crossed
with the very first boat-load.   It now seemed to
Patkul that the time had come for falling upon the
still disordered little band, and the whole Saxon
host advanced accordingly, but they found that the
King had already drawn up his forces in battle array
and put down *chevaux de frise* where their position
was least secure.   The fight was hot, especially on
the left wing where Charles suffered severely for
want of cavalry.   Fortunately, however, he had with
him two of his best regiments, the horse guards and
the life guards, which offered a stubborn resistance,
especially the former, led by Arvid Horn, who, despite a bullet through the leg received at the beginning of the engagement, kept his saddle till the fight
was over.   The Saxons were finally compelled to
fall back, whereupon the whole of the Russian con-

tingent fled wildly without striking a blow. Just at this moment, however, Marshal Steinau returned from Kockenhausen, rallied his Saxons, and again led them on, while the Duke of Courland made a deter- mined onslaught on the Swedish right at the head of a large body of horse. But despite the valour of the Duke, who had two horses shot under him, and the stubbornness of the Saxons, this attack was also repulsed, and so it fared with a third and still more desperate assault led by Patkul and Steinau in per- son, both of whom were wounded. Then the Saxons also took to flight. The battle had lasted from five o'clock till seven and the fugitives were pursued till ten. The Swedes had lost 500 killed and wounded, the Saxons 2000 (not including 400 Russians who had entrenched themselves on an island and were cut down to a man) and about 1000 prisoners.

The fruits of this second great victory were much more considerable than those of Narva. The Saxon troops never stopped in their flight till they had reached Prussian territory, thus exposing Courland,* which Charles instantly invaded, traversing it from east to west without the slightest opposition, and capturing its capital Mittau which was found to be full of stores and ammunition. For the next few years the whole Duchy was treated like an incor- porated province, administered by a Swedish Gov- ernor-General, and the inhabitants of Livonia were permitted and even encouraged to cut timber freely in its forests. All the Swedish fortresses on the

---

*Courland at this time was a semi-independent fief of the Polish Republic.

Dwina were now recaptured one after another; the
land was cleared of Saxons and Russians in every
direction, and in the beginning of September Charles
went into winter quarters in western Courland around
Würgen, a place not far from Libau, on the confines
of Poland.

And now, before following Charles through his
wonderful adventures in Poland which read more
like an episode from some mediæval chronicle of
chivalry than like a chapter of modern humdrum
history, it will be well to take a brief glance at the
theatre of his crowning exploits—seventeenth-cen-
tury Poland.

The Polish Republic, although its former gigantic
proportions * had, by this time, shrunk considerably,
was still one of the largest states in Europe. Its
territory touched the Baltic on the north, and Moldavia on the south, and embraced the whole of that
vast plain which lies between the Oder and the
Dnieper. Yet this huge state was already mori-
bund, and only lived on because its neighbours were
not yet big enough and strong enough to give it the
coup-de-grâce. Its decline had begun in the middle
of the sixteenth century when the government was
abruptly changed from an hereditary into an elective
monarchy, and the introduction of the *liberum veto*
gave every member of the sovereign *Sejm*, or Diet
(which, by the way, was composed exclusively of gentry, the towns having no share whatever in the repre-

---

* It had already lost territory equal to the total area of the United
Kingdom, plus Holland and Belgium, but was still half as large
again as modern France.

sentation of the country), the right of suspending its proceedings, a right so freely exercised that no less than forty-eight of the fifty-seven Diets held between 1652 and 1764 had been entirely inoperative. The difficulty of government was also very considerably increased by the fact that Poland was really a dual state consisting of the Kingdom of Poland, and the Grand Duchy of Lithuania, acknowledging indeed a common King and Diet, but each possessing its own army, judicature and great officers of state. Moreover each of the provinces, or palatinates, into which both Poland and Lithuania were subdivided, had its own local independent Diet or *Sejmik*** which could refuse to sanction the decrees of the great national Diet or *Sejm.* The only corrective which the constitution could devise for this chaotic state of things was the privilege conceded to every member of the Diet of forming an armed confederation to support the views of the majority or minority, as the case might be, whenever an injudicious use of the *liberum veto* had brought legislation to a deadlock. If the King and the Senate (which was composed of the great officers of state, and administered the country between the sessions of the Diet) joined such confederation, any question that the Diet had decided or refused to decide might be re-opened ; but, inasmuch as a counter confederation could be formed by anyone else at any moment on any pretext, such an expedient generally resulted in civil war. Thus the government of Poland was a legalised anarchy tempered by rebellion. That such a

---

* *I. e.*, little Diet.

metaphysical sort of government, as it has well been
called, could have actually lasted a century and a
half was due, not so much to the valour of the
Polish chivalry, though that, no doubt, must count
for something, as to the apathy or weakness of
Poland's neighbours, as already stated.* Besides,
there were seasons of partial recovery, especially under such able warrior kings as Stephen
Bathory and John Sobieski. The latter had
even attempted to secure the succession to the
throne in his own family ; but his intentions, which
might, perhaps, have saved his country, were frustrated by French intrigues, and on his death, in 1696,
after a stormy interregnum, Austrian influence and
Austrian gold had given the throne to Augustus of
Saxony who abjured his religion for the sake of a
crown. But Augustus's position in Poland was insecure at best. Both the Sobieskis and the adherents
of the French candidate, the Prince of Conti, were
secretly intriguing against him in Poland proper,
while his personal interference in Lithuanian quar-
rels had made the family of the Sapiéhas, the mightiest magnates in the Grand Duchy, his irreconcilable
enemies. The Sapiéhas at this time had much the
same sort of extraordinary influence in Lithuania as
the Radziwills had had fifty years before, and the
Czartoryskis were to have fifty years later. The
family, of Galician origin, was first heard of in the

---

* The Jesuits are sometimes held responsible for the fall of Poland,
unjustly I think. Their influence, so far as it extended, made for
stability and cohesion. On the other hand, the spread of Protestantism, whose inherent property it is to split up into sects, could only
have added a fresh element of disintegration.

middle of the fifteenth century, though it was not till the middle of the seventeenth that it obtained senatorial rank. Its chief representative at this time was Casimir Paul John, Grand-Hetman, or, as we should say, Commander-in-chief of Lithuania, an ambitious, turbulent nobleman, open-handed and amiable enough to his friends, but a veritable tyrant to all who in any way opposed him. His despotic endeavours to degrade Lithuania into something very like a family fief had raised against him the majority of the gentry of the Grand Duchy under the Oginskis who had succeeded, after bringing about a state of things which in any other civilised country would have been considered civil war, in breaking the power of the great magnate and depriving him of most of his private property besides. In him therefore Charles XII. was to find a partisan ready-made. In Poland proper the most considerable personage was Cardinal Radziejowski, Archbishop of Gnesen and Prince Primate of Poland, who had been trained for the profession of arms in his youth, but having had the misfortune to kill one of his fellow-students at the Harcourt College in Paris, was expelled from that institution, and, returning to his own country, took holy orders. His superior abilities were first discovered by Sobieski who protected and rapidly promoted him, and as Bishop of Warmia he was noted for his truly apostolic energy and fervour. The bestowal of the red hat upon him by Innocent XI. seems, however, to have completely turned his head, at any rate from henceforth his less fortunate brother prelates remarked a steady

deterioration of character in their metropolitan.
Amongst other vices he now exhibited a pride
which had not been suspected before ; and he was
soon found to possess an itching palm likewise. On
the death of Sobieski, when, as interrex, he for some
months ruled the land, Radziejowski took money
from France to secure the election of the Prince of
Conti, and then sold his influence to Augustus of
Saxony who bid still higher. But neither did this
Prince quite fulfil the exorbitant Prelate's expecta-
tions, and at the time of the arrival of Charles XII.
on the Polish frontier at the head of a conquering
army, Radziejowski was, on the whole, more inclined
to welcome the hero as an ally than to fear him as a
foe, though his measures were marked throughout
by a commendable caution which aimed at getting
as much as he could out of both parties without in
any way binding himself to either.

Charles XII. remained at Würgen from the middle
of September to the end of December, 1701, exercising his troops, disposing of arrears of business,
and, as we shall see presently, negotiating with the
Polish magnates. He was in excellent spirits, and
chiefly amused himself by bombarding his officers in
their quarters with snow-balls, and card-paper gre-
nades, and repeatedly breaking their windows by way
of comical protest against their unsoldierly love of
comfort in lodging in well built houses, while the
rank and file had to put up with huts of clay, and
he himself was roughing it in a thin tent only very
occasionally warmed by a pile of hot cannon balls.
Charles's proximity to the Polish border had seri-

ously alarmed Augustus, and Cardinal Radziejowski, at his request, had written to the Swedish monarch reminding him that Poland was at peace with Sweden, forbidding him in the name of the Republic to cross the frontier, and offering to mediate between the two monarchs. Charles's reply cut off all chance of negotiation. He bluntly demanded the deposition of Augustus, and in a subsequent despatch to the Polish Senate repeated and justified his demand on the ground of Augustus's treachery both to him and them, threatening, in case of non-compliance, to punish his foe himself. Such an outrageous ultimatum from a foreign Prince to an independent and friendly Power naturally stung the pride of the Polish chivalry to the quick. A reaction in favour of Augustus began ; many of the local Diets or *Sejmiks* declared themselves ready to defend him to the last drop of their blood, while the Cardinal sent a letter of courteous but earnest remonstrance to the King of Sweden, refusing indeed to entertain the deposition project but almost imploring Charles to evacuate Polish territory forthwith. Most of the foreign Powers to whom Charles had already communicated his fresh triumphs from his camp at Würgen, spoke the same language. William III. of England, who had an extraordinary admiration for the young hero, even went the length of writing to him personally in a paternal spirit, counselling moderation and urging him, both for his own advantage, and for the good of Europe, to make peace at once, especially as he was now in a position to fix his own terms. William had just succeeded in bringing about the grand alliance of The Hague (September, 1701) which bound the neutral Powers to resist to the uttermost the extravagant pretensions of Louis XIV.; but he felt that he should never live to head the coalition himself, and there is good reason to believe that he had fixed upon the conqueror of Narva and Dünamünde as his successor as generalissimo.* On the other hand the Swedish statesmen who followed the triumphal progress of their King with ever increasing anxiety and alarm, while also desiring peace with Poland and Saxony, were ill disposed to allow Sweden to fight the battles of the Maritime Powers in the West, so long as the Tsar remained a standing menace to her in the East, and again and again they insisted that Russia was the foe against whom the King should direct all his efforts. There can be no doubt that this was Sweden's best policy, and the matter was ably submitted to the King, but in vain; he persisted in his dethronisation project against a consensus of opinion which was virtually European. Such strength of will in a youth of twenty confounded his would-be counsellors. Yet perverse as Charles's obstinacy undoubtedly was, it is not to be confounded with the brutal obstinacy of a dull, violent man who makes up his mind beforehand *not* to listen to reason. Charles always listened politely and patiently to the arguments presented to him ; carefully weighed them one against another, before he came to the de-

---

* Louis XIV. too had spared no pains to win Charles over to his side. Piper had been secretly offered enormous bribes if he would only bring his master over to the French interest.

cision which seemed to him to be the best, and on the very rare occasions on which he condescended to explain the reasons for his actions, surprised everyone by the almost mathematical clearness and precision of his ratiocination. In the present case, moreover, he had ready to his hand an excellent opportunity of directly interfering with a good grace in the internal affairs of Poland. In September, 1701, Casimir Sapiéha placed himself under Swedish protection, and 600 of Charles's best cavalry, under his bravest subaltern, Alexander Hummerhjelm, were sent forthwith into Samogitia to assist the Grand Hetman against the Oginskis, thus Polish territory was actually violated. Charles himself about this time gave his army a scare by suddenly disappearing from camp with 400 horse, and for the next few weeks there was not a trace of him to be seen. Arvid Horn was promptly sent after him with 500 of the horse guards, and it was resolved at a council of war hastily convened by Piper, that the ragged, half-starving and leaderless army should remain where it was till January 2, 1702, but, after that, move elsewhere in search of food. Three days before that time, however, the King returned. It appears that, impatient of his long idleness, he had taken it into his head to have a dash at the Oginskis himself, and had accordingly chased the Polish light cavalry 180 miles through the fens and forests of Lithuania, swarming though they were with foes, and after inflicting no inconsiderable damage on the enemies of Sapiéha, and narrowly escaping death half-a-dozen times at least, returned to the

camp unhurt. It was with an immense relief that
his warriors again beheld him, and many a merry
glass we are told was drained at Stockholm also, when
the news of the King's safe return to camp reached
that city.

Three weeks later Charles quitted Courland, which
was also drained dry, and boldly established himself
at Bielowice in Lithuania. Thither in the middle
of January, Augustus, who had all this time been
knocking in vain at every court of Europe for assistance, sent, close upon each other's heels, two extraordinary ambassadors in whose powers of persua-
sion he now placed his last hopes. The first of
these special envoys was the beautiful Marie Aurora, Countess of Königsmarck, for three years
his mistress, and the mother of two of his 365
children. This lady, whom Voltaire has enthu-
siastically described as the most famous woman
of two centuries, was now in her prime, and
for wit, grace and *savoir-faire* she had not her
equal in Europe. The siren, who was instructed to
offer Charles whatever he liked to ask, had already
prepared her way by secretly negotiating with
Rehnskjöld and Piper and she now addressed a flat-
tering letter to the young King, explaining the
nature of her pacific errand, hinting at the advantages he might derive from it, and desiring the
honour of kissing his royal hand. Receiving no
answer, she travelled all the way to the Swedish
camp in the depth of winter, but Charles sedulously
avoided her and absolutely refused to grant her an
audience. Nothing daunted, the lady waylaid him

AURORA KÖNIGSMARCK ON HER WAY TO CHARLES XII.
BY EDELFELT.

one day when he was out riding, and, descending
from her carriage, knelt down before him in the
muddy road. Charles, somewhat taken aback, courteously raised his hat and bowed low, but immediately afterwards put spurs to his horse and galloped away at full speed, so that the baffled beauty
had to return whence she came, with her mission
unaccomplished.* Immediately after her departure,
Charles drummed together all the loose women who
had crept into his camp, and, after compelling them
to listen on their knees to an ingeniously prolonged commination service, had them driven with
scorn and contumely from his camp. This was
generally taken to be a pretty broad hint to the
fair Aurora not to shew her face there again. Still
worse fared it with Augustus's second envoy, Count
Viszthum, who came with his pockets full of bills on
good Dutch houses wherewith to bribe the Swedish
generals, and a draft treaty in his pocket which it
was thought would satisfy the most exorbitant
demands of the Swedish monarch. Charles, however, not only refused to see him, but ordered him
to be arrested and sent a prisoner to Riga. His
bills were confiscated. In fact, Charles had already
made up his mind to treat with neither friend nor
foe. A deputation from the Polish Senate and Diet,
which waited upon him at this time, was put off with
but scant courtesy; and after issuing a proclamation
to the effect that he came as a friend of the Republic to punish and depose their traitorous King, the

---

* The story that Charles looked at her and exclaimed : " Ah, ha !
you rogue, then you are still beautiful ! " is a fable.

7

young Swede in the beginning of March, 1702, set out for Warsaw. He met with no opposition worth speaking about, though he had frequent skirmishes with the Lithuanian guerillas and laid heavy contributions on Grodno and Wilna as he passed. At Jürgenberg he was joined by Casimir Sapiéha who became, for the time, one of his chief counsellors, and eight miles beyond Grodno he was overtaken by a magnificent deputation of 500 mounted noblemen from the Polish *Sejm*, which he received in his tent with military pomp, surrounded by his generals. Mutual compliments were exchanged but no business was done, and the deputation departed at last full of consternation at the stubborn sternness of this "modern Attila," as the Cardinal called him. Charles then continued his advance along the villainous Polish roads. His army is described, at this time, by an eye-witness as " 16,000 wretched, half-naked, ill-fed ragamuffins with broken-down horses and no artillery, but absolutely unmatched for endurance and martial prowess." It took them a week to cross the broad and swiftly flowing Memel, where only two little rafts were available for the transport of the troops, but this was the only serious impediment in the way and on the 14th May Charles arrived safely at Warsaw. On entering Poland proper he had issued another proclamation declaring that "the Elector of Saxony," as he now persisted in calling Augustus, had forfeited the Polish crown for his breaches of the Polish constitution, and that the Swedes were simply there to assist the Republic in getting rid of him. The first thing Charles did on reaching the capital was to march into the great square before the palace, and there sing a *Te Deum* in the midst of his soldiers, whereupon the troops were quartered upon the city, and, leaving the splendid mansions of the magnates to his generals, the King chose for his lodging a little uncarpeted room in the suburb of Praga, where he lived in his usual simple style. A contribution of 30,000 riksdaler was levied upon the city, because, as Charles expressed it, " the Swedes cannot live on wind and weather, and the Poles ought to sustain them because they sent for them," * but the strictest discipline was maintained, the lives and property of the inhabitants were rigorously respected, and the Swedish officers fraternised with the Polish gentry and found some consolation for their past hardships in balls and banquets. The King, however, held aloof from these festivities, and his austerity, modesty, sobriety and earnest piety, so uncommon at that time in one of his age and rank, filled all who beheld him with astonishment and admiration.

At Warsaw, however, there was nobody to negotiate with, Augustus having fled from thence to Cracow, the coronation city, with all his valuables, a week before Charles arrived. The Cardinal, indeed, was lingering at Lowitz, a small place about twelve miles from the capital, in fear and doubt as to what would happen next; but it was only after being thrice summoned by Charles that he ventured to appear before the conqueror at Warsaw, and

---

* Since Sapiéha joined him, Charles could fairly pose as the conederate of the Poles.

there, in one of its palaces, had a long interview
with the young King, who peremptorily demanded
that a *Sejm* should be convened forthwith to depose
Augustus, and elect someone else king in his stead.
The Cardinal objected that, according to the Polish
constitution, a new king could not be elected while
the old one was still alive ; that it was highly improbable, in any case, that a free Polish Diet would
elect a king under compulsion ; and, finally, that it
would be much more reasonable and advantageous
for Charles to use his exceptional advantages to extort guaranties from Augustus which would reduce
that monarch's power in Poland to a mere shadow,
assuring him that, in the latter case, the Poles would
be willing to go all lengths with him.   These representations seemed so just and reasonable to the
Swedish generals and statesmen that they earnestly
urged the King to listen to them, recapitulating all
the safe old arguments about the exhaustion of
Sweden, her present isolation and her insecurity in
the future amidst so many watchful foes.   But
Charles remained immovable.   He calmly declared
that he would not depart one hairbreadth from his
deposition project, and meant to carry it through
though the whole Republic rose in arms against
him.   Piper hotly remonstrated, but in vain, and the
Cardinal, with tears of vexation running down his
cheeks, quitted the presence in despair.

A fortnight later Charles broke up from Warsaw,
with his little army, to seek Augustus.   His generals
urged him to wait at least till he had been joined by
the Pomeranian contingent (some 16,000 strong)

under Gyllenstjerna, or by Mörner's division of 5000, which (a grave strategic blunder) he had detached and left behind in Lithuania to assist the Sapiéhas against their personal enemies. All that Charles would consent to do, however, was to send an *estafette* to Mörner, commanding that officer to join him without delay, whereupon he himself set out for Little Poland.* In this act of foolhardiness, for, under the circumstances, it was nothing else, Fleming, Augustus's best general, saw his master's opportunity and advised him to instantly fall with his Saxon troops, and the *banderia* of the southern Polish palatinates, úpon Charles's little host and crush it before it was reinforced. Augustus at once acted on the suggestion. On July 2d the whole of the Saxon army, 19,000 strong, quitted Cracow, and four days later Augustus pitched his camp at Klissov where he was joined shortly afterwards by a Polish army of about 6000, under the Grand-Hetman Lubomirski. On the 7th Charles arrived within a mile of the enemy's camp, and would have attacked it there and then without even awaiting the arrival of Mörner, although that general was now only a day's march off, had not Piper happily suggested that as the morrow happened to be the anniversary of the battle of Dünamünde, it would be more glorious to postpone fighting till then so as to be able to win a second victory on the anniversary of the first. The idea caught Charles's fancy, and he therefore con-

---

* Little Poland was the southernmost division of the Kingdom of Poland, and comprised the palatinates of Lublin, Sandomir and Cracow.

sented to give his weary soldiers a few hours' rest. At eight o'clock the same evening, Mörner's division arrived, thoroughly fatigued by its long forced marches, but Charles, who would not hear of postponing the battle any longer, set off at six o'clock the following morning to seek the foe; his army now numbered about 10,000 men. After a six-miles' march, the Swedes came within sight of the enemy's position which had been well chosen. The Saxon right wing, resting on a wooded height, had its front protected by a long reach of morass which extended to the extreme end of the left wing also. Behind the camp stretched, in a semicircle, a deep bog, which in case of retreat * might prove disastrous. On a hill in front of the camp stood the artillery commanding the whole plain and the woods beyond it. By midday the Swedes had passed through these woods, and marched straight toward the Saxon camp. Augustus at once ordered his left wing to move forward, follow the Swedes if they attempted to retreat, and *compel* them to fight. The whole Saxon host was accordingly marshalled in front of the camp; its line extended for nearly a quarter of a Swedish mile,† and was double as long as the Swedish line. Charles, however, who saw at a glance the impossibility of attacking breast to breast, with any chance of success,

---

* Such an eventuality, however, was considered impossible. The Saxons, confident in their superior numbers, were so sure of victory, that their officers, when the battle began, told the cooks to keep their dinner warm, as they should be back to eat it within an hour.

† A Swedish mile is equal to six English miles.

BATTLE

OF

KLISSOV

9 July 1702.

☐ *Swedes.*
▥ *Saxons.*
■ *Poles.*

1. Stream and marsh between the two armies. 2. Swedish army's first position. 3. Its second position when battle began. 4. Saxon army's first position. 5. Saxon artillery. 6. Polish army. 7. Saxon army's second position when battle began. 8. Swedish left wing. 9. Road by which Steinau went to take the Swedish right in the rear. 10. Saxons' attack on Swedish right wing. 11. Swedish right driving Saxons back. 12. Flight of Poles. 13. Flight of Saxons.

an army so strongly posted, suddenly commanded his own army to turn sharply to the left, and make for the height on which the enemy's right wing rested near to which the ground was free from morass, a manœuvre that was instantly executed and deprived the enemy of most of the advantages of his position. His right wing had now to face about, so as to meet the Swedish attack, while his left was prevented by a morass in front of it from engaging without making a considerable detour. The Polish army now came marching up to unite with the Saxons. Its commander, Lubomirski, had claimed the post of honour in the battle, on the extreme right wing, thereby considerably cramping the Saxon right wing, and hindering it from freely deploying. At two o'clock in the afternoon the battle began. Charles, who commanded his left wing in person, gave the signal to advance, and the same instant his brother-in-law, the Duke of Holstein, who commanded the Swedish right, was mortally wounded,* and his place was taken by General Otto Vellingk. The magnificently attired and excellently mounted Polish cavalry charged the Swedes in gallant style, but were met not only by the Swedish horse, but by their infantry also, for the King had providently placed foot soldiers, armed with long pikes, in the gaps between the

---

* " I hope," wrote Charles to his younger sister some days after the battle, " I hope that our Lord may comfort you all in this exceeding great sorrow of ours, and especially sister Hedwig [the widow], that she may not fret herself too sorely over this calamity, but bear it as best she can, and I hope that [you] my dear sister and the Queen [his grandmother] will do your best to comfort her."—Hedwig, by the way, was his favourite sister.—*Carl XIIs Bref*, pp. 34, 35.

horsemen.   When then the Poles charged with their
short lances they were unexpectedly brought to a
stand by the front ranks of the Swedes, while the
rear ranks sent in a murderous fire at close quarters
into the midst of the Polish lancers.   The Poles
stood only one salvo, and then turning tail, galloped
from the field pell-mell,* thereby exposing the Saxon
right wing to the onslaught of the victorious Swedes,
who charged up the wooded height and scattered
the whole of the Saxon extreme right, though not
till after a sharp tussle, in the course of which the
Saxon general, Fleming, was twice wounded, and had
a horse killed under him.   But the severest struggle
was on the Swedish right, where the enemy's left,
having succeeded in crossing the morass in front of
them by a path unknown to the Swedes, suddenly
fell upon them in front, rear and flank simultaneously.   The onslaught was so furious that for a
moment the Swedish dragoons wavered, but General
Rehnskjöld quickly brought up the horse guards
and the life guards to their assistance and made
them   form   into   squares   like   infantry.   Never
since the days of Charles X. had the Swedes displayed such splendid valour.   The enemy said of
them afterwards that they stood as solidly as though
they had been *welded together*.   Twice the onslaught
of the Saxons was hurled back, and then the Swed-

---

* Lubomirski, whose precipitate departure from the scene of action
when he was most wanted certainly stood very much in need of explanation, characteristically explained afterwards that his flight was
purely patriotic, as he had heard a rumour at the last moment that
Charles and Augustus were conspiring together to ruin Poland.

ish cavalry charged *en masse*, sabring everything in its
way and driving most of the hostile cavalry into the
morass behind where most of them perished. In
the centre, meanwhile, the two infantries were hotly
engaged. The Swedish foot had been considerably
weakened by the loss of the large detachments of
pikemen taken from it to support the cavalry on the
wings, and most of the Saxon foot regiments were
veterans; but while the fight was still at its hottest,
the King recalled his cavalry from pursuing the foe,
and sent them squadron by squadron, as they came
up, to the relief of the hardly pressed infantry, besides turning against the Saxon centre their own
captured artillery with deadly effect. By half-past
four the battle was over, and those of the Saxons
who had not already fled, laid down their arms. The
enemy had lost 3300 killed and wounded, the Swedes
about 2000.

The honour of the victory of Klissov belongs entirely to Charles XII. Stuart had devised the invasion of Zealand, Rehnskjöld had planned the attack
at Narva, and possibly at Dünamünde likewise, but
the tactics adopted at Klissov were the King's own
and the result was a conclusive testimony to his
genius as a commander. He had also not wantonly
exposed himself during this battle, though he was
always to be found where he was most wanted.

Three weeks after the battle of Klissov, Charles
XII., after driving Augustus before him from place
to place, stood before Cracow. The story of his
capture of that strong fortress sounds almost fabulous. The King and Stenbock with only three hun-

dred men marched boldly up to the gate, and Stenbock invited the commandant to come out. He
came accordingly and began parleying with Stenbock till Charles, who kept in the background,
growing impatient of the delay, cried impatiently:
"*Ouvrez la porte!*"—one of the very rare occasions
on which he was known to speak French. The commandant poked his head out to see who the imperious young gentleman was, whereupon Charles and
Stenbock rushed at the gate which had been left
ajar, forced it open, and the three hundred Swedes,
with nothing in their hands but canes and unloaded
muskets, penetrated into the inner citadel before
the cannons there could be turned against them,
and compelled the garrison to surrender unconditionally.   Charles himself, meanwhile, had disappeared and was, in fact, riding all alone through
the streets of the hostile city just as if it were his
own capital, and on returning to his army, which
was in no little trepidation about him, gave his
soldiers a humorously circumstantial account of the
curiosities of the place.   One of his first acts was to
appoint Stenbock governor and commandant of
Cracow, with a garrison of three Swedish regiments.
Thus, for a time, both the capitals of Poland were
in his hands.

CHAPTER VI.

STANISLAUS LESZCZYNSKI.

1703–1704.

Charles still refuses to negotiate—Remonstrances of Piper and Hermelin—Augustus at Warsaw—Charles breaks his thigh—Stenbock ravages Volhynia—Mediatory efforts of the neutral Powers
—The War of the Spanish Succession—The political situation—
Lillieroth, the Swedish Minister at The Hague—His efforts to
bring about peace—Interview of Mr. Robinson with Charles at
Lublin—Campaign of 1704—Engagement of Pultusk—Siege
and capture of Thorn—Magnanimity of Charles—Diet of Lublin—Confederation of Great Poland—Fresh Alliance between
Augustus and Peter—Diet of Warsaw—Arvid Horn as a diplomatist—Deposition of Augustus—The Sobieskis—Other candidates for the vacant throne—Stanislaus Leszczynski—Obstinacy
of the Cardinal—Horn forces the Polish gentry to elect Stanislaus.

OR the next two months Charles re-
mained inactive at Cracow, resting his
army (which, after the timely arrival
of the splendid Pomeranian reinforcements, was now more than 25,000
strong) and gazing impassively at the
chaotic state of things around him.
And indeed the unhappy Polish State seemed to be
on the verge of dissolution. All Lithuania was

wrapped in the flames of civil war. Jacqueries ravaged Red Russia and the Ukraine where the most appalling atrocities were of every-day occurrence. The Saxons here and the Swedes there levied contributions and extorted money in the heart of an independent country that was nominally at peace with them both. " Everywhere," says a contemporary letter from Warsaw, "there is wailing and gnashing of teeth." It is due to Augustus, to say that he made every effort to put an end to the war. Immediately after the battle of Klissov, he had released what Swedish officers he had in his hands, and sent them back to their master, loaded with gifts. Charles, not to be outdone in generosity, at once released still more Polish prisoners with still more precious gifts, but would not listen to any pacific overtures, refusing even to read Augustus's letters and referring all the mediating ministers of foreign Powers to Count Piper. But that faithful servant also now made a most determined effort to bring his obstinate young master to reason by addressing to him (29th August) a carefully drawn up memorial criticising with equal courage and ability Charles's perverse Polish policy and pleading energetically for peace. After arguing with telling force against the dethronisation project in the abstract, Piper proceeds to put a whole series of point-blank questions to the King, which would have made anyone else feel somewhat uncomfortable. Even if he *could* dethrone Augustus, how would he be able, enquired Piper, to keep his own candidate on the slippery Polish throne without the constant presence of

an army corps which he could ill-afford to spare?
Would not all Europe consider the Swedes a strange
sort of people to go on pursuing a profitless war in
a foreign land, while their own lands were being
ravaged by the Russians? Why should Sweden's
splendid army, the national safeguard and defence,
perish without rendering her the slightest service?
Finally, Piper presses home an irrefutable *argu-
mentum ad hominem.* Whenever Charles had been
fairly cornered hitherto by the arguments of his
counsellors, he had always taken refuge in his favourite contention of the justice of his cause and the
favour of Providence. Piper now deprives him of
even this loophole of escape. Is it the conduct of
a true Christian, he asks, to nourish an inexorable
hatred against an enemy who acknowledges his fault
and is not only ready to make reparation for the
past, but to give security against the future? If,
contends Piper, you still refuse to listen to your
penitent foe, your cause can no longer be just in the
eyes of a righteous and merciful God, and it is therefore sheer presumption to flatter yourself that God is
any longer on your side. Finally Piper points out
the immediate advantages of a peace with Augustus.
A Polish province (possibly Courland) might easily
be obtained from the Republic as a guaranty of
peace, and then, by turning all his attention to Muscovy, Charles could not only recover his lost provinces, but extort from the Tsar fresh accessions of
territory which would enable Sweden to cement and
consolidate her empire. The King took this memorial,
read it through carefully, and pondered over it for

many days; but he said never a word about it to any-
body, and it seems to have had no effect whatever
upon his resolutions. Yet, so far from being offended
by Piper's freedom of speech, Charles shewed his ap-
preciation of his servant's zeal by appointing him,
the same day, Chancellor of Upsala University.*
His field-secretary, Hermelin, who also frequently
ventured to remonstrate with him, Charles generally silenced by a repartee. For instance, Charles
had once, in Hermelin's presence, chanced to remark: "We have ten years yet to fight with the
Poles, and then we shall have twenty years more of
fighting with the Russians." "In that case," replied
Hermelin, "those of your Majesty's soldiers who happen to survive at all will certainly be well disciplined."
"Well," replied Charles, with a smile, "and soldiers
ought to be well disciplined, ought they not?"

Meanwhile both Charles and Augustus did what
they could to bring the Polish Republic over to their
side, for, by an absurd fiction, Poland at the very
time when it was being ravaged by the Swedes and
Saxons, was assumed to be at peace with them both.
After holding an abortive meeting of magnates at
Sandomir, Augustus, taking advantage of Charles's
absence from Warsaw, returned to that city and summoned thither a Diet. But the Province of Great Poland † refusing, at the instigation of the Cardinal, to
send deputies thither, the assembly was considered

---

* Piper, utterly baffled, wrote home to a friend that he had done
all he could, but God had hardened the King's heart.

† Great Poland was the extreme western portion of Poland proper,
and consisted of the palatinates of Posen, Kalisch and Sieradz.

KARL PIPER.

FROM AN OLD ENGRAVING.

informal and came to nothing. The conduct of Augustus's Saxon troops at Warsaw, moreover, was so bad that even the Swedes were tearfully regretted there. Charles, meanwhile, growing impatient at the procrastination of the Poles, was devastating the southern palatinates with fire and sword. He himself had been disabled, for a time, by an accident that might have proved fatal. During one of his headlong gallops, his horse had stumbled and fallen on him, breaking his left thigh bone. He himself, with his usual sangfroid, had laughed at the misadventure as a mere trifle, and had himself carried round the camp in a litter the same evening, to show his soldiers that he was alive; but the affair seriously alarmed his officers, and caused some sensation throughout Europe.* Charles, however, would not allow his accident to interfere with his strategy. In October he broke up from Cracow to seek fresh quarters, while Stenbock, with 2000 men, was despatched on a marauding raid into Volhynia, which he traversed, to use his own expression, "torch in hand." Stenbock, who was as kind-hearted as he was valiant, would have proceeded with " moderation and *douceur*," but the King would not hear of it. "The Polish gentry," he wrote, " must either be constrained to follow us *nolentes volentes*, or be ruined so thoroughly that they may not be able to help our enemies." Charles, indeed, was always merciless to

---

* His death was universally credited at first, and this verse of Martial was applied to him : " *Dum numerat palmas credidit esse senem.*"—" Judged by the number of his laurels, he was already a veteran."

the obstinate and rebellious, and his natural severity seems to have been hardened into a cruel sternness by the horrors and necessities of war.* So Stenbock continued his devastations,† securing a rich booty, the proceeds of which went to clothe and pay the Swedish army, but making little impression upon the stubbornness of the Poles.

In January, 1703, Charles went into winter quarters round Lublin, after despatching Rehnskjöld and Sapiéha with ten regiments into Great Poland to protect his partisans there whom Augustus sought to punish for refusing to obey his summons to assemble at Sandomir and Warsaw. The presence of Rehnskjöld inspired the Philo-Swedes with confidence, the Cardinal even going the length of calling together the Senate at Warsaw when measures, hostile on the whole to Augustus, were adopted. Augustus, on the other hand, held a counter-meeting at Marienburg, declaring the Cardinal's meeting invalid, and condemning all the Philo-Swedes as traitors. But hostile as he was to Augustus, the Cardinal could not incur the responsibility of dethroning him, although Charles, in a long four hours' interview

---

* Thus, shortly afterwards, he advised Rehnskjöld to devastate all the country around him, so that the superior forces of the enemy might not be able to get at him, advice which Rehnskjöld, though by no means a particularly soft-hearted soldier, disregarded, just as Catinat disregarded Louvois's savage counsel to "*bien bruler*" the Palatinate.

† It should be said for Charles, however, that he was led a good deal at this time by the advice of the Sapiéhas and the Sobieskis, who counselled him to bring Augustus's partisans to reason by burning their houses over their heads.

with him at Praga, exhausted all his threats and
cajoleries to persuade him to it. Charles himself,
however, was equally inaccessible to argument from
other quarters. During the winter of 1703–4, England and her allies made strenuous efforts (purely in
their own interests it is true) to put an end to the
Polish quarrel. Ever since the summer of 1701,
the war of the Spanish Succession had been raging,
but hitherto with no definite result. Whatever we
may think of the morality of France in provoking
such a war, splendid was the energy with which she
sustained it. Six French army corps under six of
her greatest captains confronted the allies on the
Meuse, the upper and lower Rhine, in Savoy, the
Tyrol and the Pyrenees, and, on the whole, gave a
good account of themselves. It is true that Prince
Eugene defeated Catinat at Carpi and Villeroi at
Chiari, while Marlborough captured the fortresses
on the Maas, one after the other ; but, on the other
hand, Vendôme had checked Eugene's further progress, the French had taken Breisach and Landau,
and Villars had defeated the Austrian general, Sty-
rum, at Höchstadt, so that at the beginning of 1704
the antagonists were, after all, pretty much where
they had started. Under these circumstances both
France and the Maritime Powers had begun to look
out for fresh allies. But for the Great Northern
War, England might have counted on the assistance
of Denmark, Brandenburg and the smaller German
Protestant Powers, who were now wholly occupied
in anxiously watching the progress of Sweden. It
was her object therefore to release·these contingent

8

auxiliaries by persuading Charles XII. to sheath his sword. France, on the other hand, had no desire to see some 40,000 fresh Protestants let loose upon her, and consequently did her best to foment the Polish discord. The Swedish Ministers, so far as they could, seconded England. Indisputably their ablest representative was Nils Lillieroth, Charles's ambassador at The Hague, then the centre of European diplomacy, one of the many self-made men who had achieved distinction under Charles XI., and who from the Peace of Ryswik, 1697, to his death in 1705, was one of the most influential diplomatists in Europe. Lillieroth was on intimate terms with all the English and Dutch Ministers, and had been able to render his country important services. It was to him that Charles always applied for money, and Charles's Ministers for advice, and both Marlborough and the Grand Pensionary, Heinsius, now approached him as the person most capable of persuading his royal master to listen to pacific counsels. Lillieroth had a difficult part to play, but he played it with consummate ability. Like the Chancellor, Bengt Oxenstjerna, he insisted all along that the Tsar was the foe whom Sweden had most reason to fear, and prophesied that if Russia once got a firm footing on the Baltic she would speedily become one of the greatest powers in Europe. Though uncertain of the support of, and for months together without any instructions from, his master, Lillieroth contrived to hold his own against the persistent diplomatic intrigues of Russia and Denmark, while he mollified Prussia by persuading

Charles to acknowledge at last the newly founded
Prussian Monarchy.* He also continued to keep
England in a good humour by holding out promises
of the assistance of a Swedish army corps so soon
as the Polish war was over, and it was through his
influence that the English Minister at Stockholm,
Mr. Robinson, a *persona gratissima* with Charles
XII., received permission to set out from Stockholm,
in the depths of an arctic winter, and seek Charles
in his camp, which during the whole reign of that
warlike young monarch was the real though constantly shifting capital of Sweden. Robinson, on
his arrival at Lublin, took the whole Swedish camp
entirely by surprise, and the Swedish officers were
sorely exercised how to procure him an audience,
knowing as they well did what an aversion Charles
had to the very sight of a diplomatist. Fortune,
however, proved a friend to Robinson on this occasion, and gave him an opportunity which he did not
neglect. He was returning to camp one day after
dining with Piper, when he happened to meet the
King on horseback. Charles drew near to the carriage, curious to see who was inside, while Robinson,
recognising him, at once alighted, and began con-
versing with him in Swedish by expressing his
pleasure at this fortunate meeting, which he said he
regarded as equal to a formal audience. The suddenness of the encounter, the sight of the ambas-

---

* Nothing, I think, shows so clearly the commanding position of
Sweden in those days as her long hesitation to recognise the new
Hanoverian electorate and the new Prussian Kingdom, and the
eagerness with which both these Powers sought such recognition.

sador standing among the snow-drifts cap in hand, clad in furs up to the eyes, and with a wretched old wig on his head, tickled Charles's sense of humour, and made him unusually condescending. He also uncovered, jumped off his horse, and talked to Robinson bare-headed for more than an hour, finally giving him the rarely conceded permission to follow the camp as long as he liked. Nothing came of this visit. After following Charles about for a fortnight, the English diplomatist clearly saw that his presence in Poland was quite superfluous. He wrote to his friends in Sweden that the King was civility itself, but that his taciturnity surpassed even his civility— so he took his departure.

Hostilities were recommenced in the spring of 1704, when Charles, suddenly assuming the offensive, made one of his wonderful forced marches, and pounced upon the Saxon forces at Pultusk (21st April), scattering them in every direction, and filling them with such panic terror that the mere tidings of his approach was sufficient henceforth to put them to flight. Then he abruptly desisted from pursuing, and turning off in the opposite direction, sat down before the strong fortress of Thorn which Augustus had garrisoned with 6000 of his best infantry. For the next eight months, despite the tearful remonstrances of his ablest counsellors,* Charles re-

---

* Piper reminded him that Peter had already obtained his Baltic haven, and was building thereon a fortress which was worth more than the whole of Poland. Charles remained deaf to all remonstrances. " Well ! " cried Piper, " I 've spoken my mind, and saved my soul, but may I die before I see my country plunged into wretchedness."

mained immovable beneath the walls of Thorn, while
the Tsar was laboriously conquering Sweden's distant and deserted Baltic provinces,* one by one.
Charles's headquarters were within cannon-shot of
the fortress, and he recklessly and repeatedly exposed himself to danger in a spirit of imperturbable
fatalism which stupefied the bravest of his officers.
It was, by the way, the only siege he ever conducted,
except the siege of Pultawa where he was to lose his
glory and the siege of Fredrikshald where he was to
lose his life, and the slowness of the operations sorely
tried his patience. Once he actually proposed to
storm the walls at the head of a forlorn hope of only
600 men; but his officers positively would not allow
him to do so. It was, they said, rushing into certain
death, and to say nothing of the folly of needlessly
sacrificing his brave followers—what would become
of his country after such an irreparable loss as his?
Then it was that Charles uttered these memorable
words : " Where my soldiers are, there also will I be.
As for Sweden, I should be no great loss to her, for
she has had little profit out of me hitherto." Nevertheless he allowed himself to be persuaded, but the
siege was prosecuted with renewed vigour. The
bombardment began on September 13th, and the
grand old town-hall and other buildings were speedily in flames, though, by the King's special command, all the churches were spared, and finally on
October 4th, after the garrison had been reduced by
two thirds, the fortress capitulated unconditionally,
when 84 cannons, 1000 stands of arms and an

* See Chapter VIII.

immense booty fell into the hands of the victors.
The town had to pay 60,000 rix-dollars,* and surrender its church bells, because, contrary to the
usages of war in those days, they had been rung
during the siege, but the garrison and the population
were treated with that singular magnanimity and
gentleness which Charles XII. always showed to
open foes vanquished in fair fight.   Thirty oxen
and forty sheep were driven into the town to
serve as a banquet for the half-starving population ; the prisoners were released and sent home
to their wives and families with as much fresh
meat as they could carry ; the Saxon officers were
entertained at a grand banquet, and every Saxon
soldier's wife who had been at Klissov, and could
recognise the King, received from him a couple of
ducats.   In one thing only he was absolutely inexorable.   The walls of the fortress, despite the tears
of the inhabitants, were levelled with the ground.

The fall of Thorn, which cost Charles much
precious time indeed but only fifty men, made a
great impression upon the Poles, and considerably strengthened Charles's friends amongst them.
During the siege, the progress of events in Poland
had been rapidly leading up to a crisis.   Taking
advantage of Charles's absence, Augustus had held
at Lublin a *Sejm* or Diet mainly composed of his
own partisans, at which the Cardinal was humiliated
as never a prince of the Church had been humiliated
before, and compelled, on his knees, to take an oath
of eternal hostility against all Polish Philo-Swedes,

*About £15,000.

including the Sapiéhas, who were given six weeks
to submit to Augustus under penalty of outlawry.
The result of the Diet of Lublin was certainly a
triumph for Augustus, though a very short-lived one.
The tyrannous majority had needlessly irritated the
Province of Great Poland by excluding the deputies
from the palatinates of Posen and Kalish, and no
sooner had it dissolved, than Great Poland practically rebelled against Augustus by forming an armed
confederation which was presently joined by the
Cardinal, now become Augustus's mortal foe. After
vainly attempting to negotiate with the confederation, Augustus attempted to dissipate it by force of
àrms and actually crossed the Vistula, with that purpose, at the head of 10,000 men ; but Rehnskjöld's
little army, skilfully, handled, compelled the King
of Poland to retreat, and the confederates were
still further strengthened by the surrender of the
important city of Posen to Rhenskjöld, and a proclamation issued by Charles in which he declared
that he took the confederates under his protection.
But now Augustus's desperate fortunes also seemed
to take a turn for the better. On September 2,
1703, he was again joined by Patkul, who came to
him this time as the special envoy of the Tsar, with
a new treaty of alliance in his pocket. Peter had
now got hold of the long coveted Baltic provinces,
but he needed some time yet to firmly establish
himself therein, and it was therefore of the last importance to him that Charles should be detained
still longer in Poland. By this new treaty, which
was signed in October, 1703, Russia promised to aid

Augustus with 300,000 roubles per annum, and a
contingent of 12,000 men ; neither ally was to make
peace without the other, and Augustus undertook to
follow hard upon Charles's heels should he turn
against the Tsar.

This alliance, to which Augustus now clung as to
a last straw, alienated many of his Polish subjects
who had hitherto supported him. The intense
national hatred of Russia revived, and when the
Prussian palatinates * also joined the confederation
of Great Poland, the Cardinal, who ever since the in-
dignities practised upon him at the Diet of Lublin
had burned for vengeance, felt strong enough to summon, on his own responsibility, a General Confederation at Warsaw, which assembled there in January,
1704. Although numerously attended it could by
no means be regarded as a national assembly as all
the southern palatinates of Poland and the whole of
Lithuania were unrepresented ; but, such as it was, it
suited the purpose of Charles XII., who had now
gone into winter quarters round Heilberg in the
Bishopric of Ermeland, and he determined, with the
assistance of the Cardinal, to use it as an instrument
for deposing Augustus. As his special envoy to the
Warsaw Confederation he despatched Arvid Horn. It
was the first diplomatic mission with which Horn
had ever been entrusted, and many marvelled that
the King should have selected a mere cavalry officer
for such a difficult and delicate task; but Charles
knew his man, and Horn quickly developed those

* Polish Prussia consisted of the palatinates of Pomerelia, Marienburg and Culm.

rare diplomatic and political talents which ere long
were to stamp him as one of Sweden's greatest
statesmen. He found everything at Warsaw at a
standstill. The deputies were unruly and uncertain,
and the Cardinal was in favour of leading rather than
driving them. But Horn, to use his own energetic
language, " gave his Eminence the spur," and worked
upon the patriotic pride of the Poles by showing
them the letters which had been captured from
Aurora Königsmarck and Count Vizthum, in which
Polish territory had been secretly promised to
Sweden and Polish senators had been spoken of in
the most disparaging terms. So at last the confederation was persuaded to depose Augustus, and Horn
could write to his master that the Gordian knot was
cut. But it was only when the question of finding
Augustus's successor arose, that Horn's difficulties
may be said to have really begun. Weeks and
months of procrastination followed, and Augustus
himself did all in his power to throw obstacles in the
way of the confederation. He held a rival assembly at Cracow which solemnly declared the decree of
deposition illegal. He kidnapped the most likely
candidates, the Princes James and Constantine
Sobieski, as they were travelling on the highway
near Breslau in Imperial territory, and imprisoned
them in the fortress of Pleissenburg (an unheard of
violation of the law of nations which caused considerable sensation at the time), and made frequent
attempts to advance upon Warsaw with his Saxons,
which were all frustrated by the promptness and
vigilance of Rehnskjöld and his little army in Great

Poland. The capture of the Sobieskis, however, was
a serious embarrassment to Charles. Prince James
had been his candidate for the vacant throne, and
though James's youngest brother Alexander was
now solemnly escorted from Breslau to Warsaw, as
the King designate, by a Swedish army, nothing in
the world could persuade the young man to accept
the dangerous dignity. * Then the Cardinal suggested that some foreign prince should be selected
who would have power enough to hold his own
against Saxony, but here again there were insurmountable difficulties in the way. Charles could not
support the French candidate, the Prince of Conti,
without offending the Allies, and he could not support the Allies' candidate, the Prince of Neuburg,
without offending France. Francis Rakoczy, Prince
of Transylvania, was next proposed, but Charles
regarded him as a mere rebel against the authority
of the Emperor, and as such would have nothing
to say to him. Finally he determined to give the
crown to a native Pole, and selected the Palatine of
Posen, Stanislaus Leszczynski, a young man of
blameless antecedents, respectable talents and ancient family, connected, moreover, by his marriage
with the wealthy and beautiful Catherine Opalinska,
with many of the leading magnates. Stanislaus,
from the first a warm Philo-Swede, had won
Charles's goodwill by the ability and eloquence
with which, at the head of a Polish deputation, he
had pleaded for the remisison of the heavy war con-

---

* It is thought that Augustus secretly threatened to murder his two
elder brothers if he should accept the Polish crown.

tributions levied by the Swedes. He now resigned himself entirely into Charles's hands, though the prospect of such a crown as the crown of Poland had very little attraction for him. But now both the Cardinal and Horn united their opposition against any such choice. They had no fault to find with the candidate personally, indeed they were both of them his warmest friends ; but they were quite convinced that any native Pole, except a Sobieski, was an impossible candidate. The Cardinal declared that the reign of such a king could not last six weeks, and absolutely refused to nominate him, while Horn predicted what actually came to pass, that the departure of the Swedes would be followed by the immediate downfall of such a paper potentate, and that it would require the perpetual presence of a Swedish army to keep him on his tottering throne. But Charles had made up his mind once for all, and nothing could move him from his purpose. He declared that he meant not only to put his candidate on the throne, but to keep him there also, and he sent Horn a bribing-fund and an army corps to carry through the election of Stanislaus. Still the Cardinal held out, and he was encouraged by the growing indignation of the Polish deputies who were greatly averse to electing one of their own members as king. Leszczynski himself was beginning to tremble for his safety, so Horn sent him to the Swedish camp, that "your Majesty may preach a little heart into him." He returned resigned to his fate, but Horn had to keep a constant watch upon him, lest he should run away at the last moment.

With the Cardinal, however, nothing could be done. His political experience convinced him that it would be an unpardonable blunder on his part to nominate Leszczynski, and not even Charles XII., who had a long private interview with him at Warsaw, could convince him to the contrary. " I would rather be buried alive," said he to Horn, " than consent to proclaim such a candidate." " Your Eminence may spare yourself that inconvenience," replied Horn, " as I have already found another prelate who will do us that kind office." This substitute was Nicholas Swiecicki, Bishop of Posen, who had behaved all along " like a good Swedish Bishop," as Horn expressed it, and was now ready to nominate and proclaim Leszczynski if no other ecclesiastic could be found to do it. When, however, it came to the point, only the utmost pressure could prevail upon the Poles to accept Stanislaus Leszczynski as their king. At mid-day on July 2, 1704, the day appointed for the nomination of the new King, crowds of people assembled on the field of election which was situated a little to the west of Warsaw ; but the elective assembly itself only consisted of a few castellans and some scores of the lesser nobility. Not a single palatine was to be seen ; the only bishop present was the Bishop of Posen, the only high official Benedict Sapiéha, and he was a Lithuanian. On the other hand 300 Swedish dragoons and 500 Swedish infantry were marshalled close to the field of election, and Arvid Horn was conspicuous on horseback surrounded by his staff. The Marshal of the Diet hesitated under the circum-

STANISLAUS LESZCYNSKI.

FROM AN OLD PRINT.

stances to proceed to an election, and sent deputies
first of all to Warsaw to summon from thence the
Cardinal, and the other high officers of State who
were known to be there, but they refused to come.
Then Horn who had been frowning all the time, and
biting his nails for vexation, would hear of no
further delay, and roughly disregarding the protestations of the Podlachian * deputies who stoutly maintained that the election could not be called free so
long as the Swedish troops were present, rode
through the crowd right up to the Bishop of Posen,
and ordered him to proceed with the election at
once, whereupon the Bishop, turning to the assembly,
asked them if they would have the Palatine of Posen
for their King. The Podlachian deputies still protested, but the majority of the gentlemen from
Great Poland threw their caps into the air, and cried
" We will ! we will ! " " Then," cried the trembling
Bishop, " I proclaim Stanislaus Leszczynski King of
Poland and Grand Duke of Lithuania." The
newly-elected King was then hoisted by his partisans
on to a richly caparisoned steed, escorted back to
the capital by torch-light, and proceeded in state to
the cathedral where the Bishop preached an in-
augural sermon in an almost empty church, while
the Swedish troops fired salvos of rejoicing outside.
On the following day Charles rode forth to meet
and congratulate the newly elected King. He had
succeeded at last in placing his puppet on the Polish
throne, the question now was how to keep him
there.

---

* Podlachia was the central province of Poland.

CHAPTER VII.

CHARLES THE ARBITER OF EUROPE.

1704–1707.

EVER, surely, was there such a king of
shreds and patches as poor King
Stanislaus immediately after his election. Unrecognised by any foreign
Power but the one that had placed
him on his throne; with no ministers
of his own to serve him, no army of his own to support him, no money to reward his friends or convert

his enemies; elected without the consent of one half
of the nation, by the other half acting under extreme
compulsion, while the great dignitaries of the kingdom stood sullenly aloof, he may almost be said to
have depended upon his patron for the food he ate
and the clothes he wore. It was hard to see how he
could stand alone unless Charles stood constantly
beside him, and yet just at this very time, when
Charles's presence at Warsaw was most indispensable, that Hotspur among monarchs suddenly left his
defenceless puppet to take care of himself, and made
a mad dash southwards to capture a fortress which
could not be of the slightest service to him. This
was the remote city of Lemberg, which had an irresistible attraction for Charles for the simple reason
that it had never yet been captured by a foe. So
southward he marched, or rather raced, with such
rapidity as to soon leave his infantry and artillery
far behind him, and succeeded, at the head of his
dragoons, in capturing the virgin fortress by a *coup
de main* in a quarter of an hour, with the loss of only
forty men. On August 27, 1704, Lemberg fell,
but the day before that Augustus had recaptured
Warsaw. Knowing the weakness of the place, and
taking advantage of Charles's absence, he had advanced with an irresistible Russo-Saxon army.
Stanislaus, finding that his Poles absolutely refused
to fight, made the best of his way by circuitous
routes to Rehnskjöld's camp in Great Poland, where
he arrived a beggared fugitive; the Cardinal fled to
Danzig; Horn shut himself up with 480 Swedes in
the citadel, where Augustus bombarded him with

red-hot cannon-balls till he was forced to surrender ;
the Bishop of Posen, who had been guilty of the
unpardonable crime of proclaiming Stanislaus, was
sent to Rome to be dealt with by the Pope himself.
Meanwhile Charles was engaged in levying contributions upon the southern palatinates, and compelling
them, one by one, to recognise Stanislaus when the
news of the loss of the capital reached him.   At first
he would not believe the report ; but when Horn,
who had been released on parole, confirmed it, he
took speedy measures to repair his error, though the
autumn rains had now begun, and the roads in Poland, always bad, were by this time impassable for
ordinary travellers, to say nothing of an army.   But
nothing could stay Charles's impetuosity, and he set
off at once to seek Augustus.   That monarch, after
sacking the palaces of the Cardinal and his other
personal enemies, and reducing the environs of
Warsaw to a desert, thought it prudent to retreat
as rapidly as possible ; but Charles, after re-occu-
pying Warsaw, followed hard upon his heels, traversing 360 miles in nine days, never unsaddling
his horses, and allowing his soldiers and himself only a few hours' rest each day in the open
air.*   He thus contrived to overtake the Saxon
main army under Schulenburg at Punitz (October), forced them to fight at a disadvantage, and
utterly routed them after a sharp engagement, although the odds against him were nearly three to

---

* After hastily swallowing a piece of black bread, he would fling
himself down upon a little straw in front of a smouldering fire, and
sleep there till morning.

one. Nightfall alone saved the Saxons and Russians from utter destruction. Under cover of the darkness, Schulenburg retreated into Silesia, and Charles, after pursuing him into Imperial territory as far as Glogau, returned to Poland, pitching his camp at Ravitz on the Saxon frontier, thus completely cutting Augustus off from Poland, and at the same time menacing Saxony. Here, for the next eight months, he remained motionless but vigilant, transacting arrears of business, settling his domestic affairs, and receiving in his camp the overtures and congratulations of a multitude of ambassadors.

The star of Sweden was now indeed in the ascendant in the political firmament, and her friendship was eagerly sought from every quarter. Charles had only to choose between half-a-dozen advantageous offers of alliance, but he listened to them all with a haughty tranquillity bordering upon indifference, and only condescended to reply after long intervals and in a high tone. To the enquiry of Louis XIV. whether he would mediate between France and the Allies, he replied that he would only consent to do so at the request of *both* belligerents. He was evidently more and more possessed by the idea of leaning on his good sword alone, and did not seem to care whom he offended. Thus, about this time, he had a quarrel with the friendly English Government, which threatened to become serious. A Swedish naval hero, Captain Psilander, who was convoying a merchant fleet, had refused to salute the English flag in English waters, and consequently

9

had drawn upon himself a battle with eight English men-of-war, which he valiantly sustained till his own vessel was placed *hors-de-combat*. Queen Anne's Ministers remonstrated against Psilander's insolence, but Charles, through his Chancellery at Stockholm, gave a sharp reply, which was scarcely distinguishable from a declaration of war. Fortunately Mr. Robinson, the English Minister at Stockholm, found a decent excuse for not delivering this note to his Government, so the dispute died a natural death. Charles's dictatorial conduct, too, towards the free city of· Danzig, which had harboured some of Augustus's refugees, very nearly led to a rupture with both the Maritime Powers who had extensive commercial connections there. Fortunately the sudden appearance of two regiments of Swedish dragoons at Danzigwerder induced the civic magistrates, at the last moment, to submit to the King of Sweden's terms. Another attempt of the Emperor through his ambassador, Zinzendorf, to bring about an accommodation between Charles and Augustus, on the most humiliating terms for the latter, so long as he might be permitted to retain his kingdom, also came to nothing. Nor would Charles, in his overweening self-confidence, even agree to an alliance with Prussia, though it was an alliance which all the Swedish diplomatists, and Stanislaus himself, eagerly desired. And indeed there can be no doubt that in thus standing aloof from the Court of Berlin, Charles committed another of his many political blunders. With an insecure Poland on his hands, and a war *à l'outrance* impending with Russia, Prussia with her

central position and her excellent army of 47,000
men would have been an invaluable ally for both
Charles and Stanislaus to have fallen back upon in
case of need. And just now too she could have been
bought cheaply. Polish Prussia and the reversion of
Courland was all she required, in return for which
she offered to place 20,000 men at Sweden's disposal.
The Swedish diplomatists thought the bargain
should be clinched at once, and suggested that
Poland should be compensated by a still larger slice
of Russian territory ; but Charles thought that Prussia asked too much, and that any cession of Polish
territory beyond the little bishopric of Ermeland
(which he was willing to let go) would be highly im-
politic under the circumstances. Thus the negotiations with Prussia, at one time so promising, entirely
fell through.

Meanwhile Charles used all his efforts to firmly
establish Stanislaus, and the first and most essential
step was of course to get him crowned—the reign of
a Polish king always being reckoned from the date
of his coronation. The Cardinal was at last persuaded, though only after six months of the most
irritating negotiation, to summon a coronation *Sejm*
or Diet, which met at Warsaw in July, 1705.
Augustus attempted to nullify it by obtaining a
papal bull forbidding the Polish bishops, under pain
of excommunication, to take any part in the coronation of Stanislaus. Nobody in Poland and Saxony,
however, could be found daring enough to force his
way through the Swedish lines and serve this bull
upon the Cardinal personally, but it was found one

morning posted up against his stable door. And
bayonets as well as bulls were called into requisition.
A Russo-Saxon army under Paikull, 10,000 strong,
advanced upon Warsaw to dissipate the Diet ; but
the Swedish general Nieroth with his little army
corps of 2000 men gallantly threw himself in its way,
and after an obstinate six hours' fight, completely
routed it, with the loss of 2000 men and nearly all its
officers, including Paikull himself, who was sent to
Stockholm and there beheaded as a traitor.* A
second and still larger Russian army under Sheremetev, had, by the advice of the ubiquitous and indefatigable Patkul, at the same time invaded Lithuania, so as to catch the Swedes between two fires
and overwhelm them, but Charles himself frustrated
this plan by making one of his astounding marches
(he covered the whole distance between the Silesian
frontier and the Polish capital in ten days), and in the
beginning of August suddenly appeared at Blonie, a
small place close to Warsaw. Levenhaupt, whose
recent victories (of which more anon) † had swept
Livonia clear of the Russians, though they came too
late to save Courland, strongly advised his master to
pursue Sheremetev forthwith, and give him the *coup
de grâce ;* but Charles would do nothing till the new
King of Poland had been crowned, and remained
idle, though not useless, at Blonie for the next four
months to overawe the Polish Diet. And indeed his
Polish friends gave him far more trouble than his

---

* As a Livonian he was, of course, a Swedish subject, and Charles
XII. never showed the slightest mercy to deserters.

† See Chapter VIII.

Russian and Saxon foes. The difficulties which be-
set the coronation of Stanislaus were innumerable,
and apparently insurmountable. First of all the
Polish magnates insisted that the ceremony should
be celebrated at Cracow, which time out of mind had
been the coronation city of Poland. Charles over-
ruled the objection by declaring that Warsaw would
do just as well as any other place. Then there was
a difficulty about the regalia which had been carried
off to Saxony by the prompt and provident Augustus, so that Charles, after already providing Stanislaus
with a kingdom, had to find him crowns * as well.
This difficulty had no sooner been settled than the
question arose : who was to crown the King ? The
Cardinal-Primate was the only legally authorised person, but as his Eminence laid down conditions which Charles would not accept, a more
compliant ecclesiastic had to be found, and so the
prelate next in rank, Dzielinski, Archbishop of Lemberg, was pitched upon. He, however, had disappeared so completely as to leave no trace behind
him ; but he was ultimately found hiding in the
midst of a remote sylvan swamp, whence he was
conveyed to Warsaw in triumph, and committed to
the care of " a guard of honour," which was held responsible for his due appearance when he was wanted.
Nothing now prevented the coronation of Stanislaus,
and that ceremony took place accordingly on September 24, 1705, with great splendour.† Charles, who

---

* One for himself and one for his Queen.

† The fullest description of the pageant is to be found in the Prince
of Würtemberg's *Reisen*, pp. 224-35.

disliked all pomp, looked on incognito from a small chamber over the choir, with Piper and the Prince of Würtemberg, leaving to Arvid Horn the honour of escorting the Queen into and out of the cathedral. Swedish troops occupied the chief place in the procession, and at the banquet which followed Ambassador Horn and his two colleagues were the only persons allowed to sit on the royal dais, the highest dignitaries of Poland being obliged to dine at another and lower table.* An alliance between Charles and the Polish Republic followed, on the basis of the Peace of Oliva, whereby each power contracted never to make peace without the other, Poland undertaking besides to aid Sweden against the Tsar until she had obtained from him the amplest satisfaction. There was one clause in this treaty which the more far-seeing of the Swedes regarded with grief and consternation. By this clause Charles engaged not to withdraw his forces from Poland, till Stanislaus had been thoroughly established there, thus disappointing the hopes of his subjects that he would now give his undivided attention to Russia, whose progress in the Baltic provinces had by this time become a menace not merely to the safety, but to the very existence of Sweden as a great power.

Charles took advantage of this rare interval of leisure to put his own house in order, and dispense rewards and punishments among his servants. Great changes had taken place in Sweden during the last few years. Bengt Oxenstjerna, Nils Lillieroth, Erik

---

* When the Tsar heard of it, he held a mock ceremonial at his Court, at which his jester was solemnly crowned King of Sweden.

Dahlberg, the leading politicians of the last generation, were dead, and the Senate had been reduced
to seven persons. Under the late King that august
college had consisted almost entirely of civilians,
Charles XII. now filled it with warriors. Three generals and six lieutenant-generals received the purple
on the same day,* and amongst them we find the
well known names of Rehnskjöld, Arvid Horn and
Nieroth. The Chancellorship, however, the highest
dignity in the realm, Charles conferred upon a diplomatist who had been one of his father's most useful
servants, and one of his own guardians, Count Nils
Gyldenstolpe. But the most remarkable event in
Sweden at this time was the judgment passed
upon Senator Count Nils Thuresen Bjelke, which
proves, if proof were wanting, that if Charles's
bounty was magnificent, his justice was inexorable.
Nils Bjelke was perhaps the mightiest magnate of
Sweden. His brilliant services under Charles XI.,
both as a statesman and a soldier, had been rewarded
by the highest offices in the State, and he had increased his renown in the Kaiser's service which he
quitted as a general and Count of the Empire. He
then obtained the lucrative office of Governor-General of Pomerania, and it was while he was still holding that dignity that the heavy displeasure of Charles
XII. fell suddenly upon him. He was accused of
enriching himself by debasing the coinage, of making

---

* The insignia of a Swedish Senator were a purple mantle embroidered with ermine, and a heavy gold chain. By an article of
the Peace of Westphalia they were to rank with English Dukes and
Spanish Grandees of the first class.

an unwarrantable use of the King's name and was
arraigned before the Supreme Court of Sweden for
these and other high misdemeanours, and, after a
trial lasting for eight years, was condemned to lose
his life and forfeit all his possessions. The same day
that the judgment was pronounced, the Queen Dowager and the two Princesses petitioned the King in
Bjelke's favour, and ultimately Charles remitted the
capital sentence on condition that Bjelke henceforth
resided on his estate in the utmost seclusion, and
there accordingly the fallen Minister, who listened
imperturbably to his sentence, and scorned alike to
petition or to plot against his King, spent the rest of
his days in prayer and penance.

And now in the late autumn of 1705 Charles prepared again for war. His officers represented that a
campaign in such a country, at that time of the
year, was a sheer impossibility, but he only laughed
at them. " My soldiers," he said, " have enjoyed
their winter quarters in summer ; it is only right
that they should take the field in winter." With
that he set off to encounter General Ogilvie, who
had occupied the fortress of Grodno with 20,000
Russians, plunging headlong into the interminable
forests and morasses of Lithuania, and disappearing
for whole months at a time, to the great perplexity
of the Swedish Senate, who expressed their amazement that a King at the head of 10,000 men could
succeed in hiding himself away so effectually. During this campaign the Swedish soldiers cheerfully
endured hardships which seem absolutely incredible.
After traversing 180 miles in mid-winter in seven-

teen days, Charles, at the beginning of January,
1706, appeared before Grodno.	The fortress was
too strong to be stormed, so Charles contented himself for the next two months with blockading Ogilvie, whose troops suffered severely from privations,
"dying off like flies." Meanwhile the anxiety of the
Tsar was terrible.	It was not a mere garrison, but a
whole army corps, that was shut up in Grodno, and
if that were captured, and a Swedish invasion of
Russia followed, Peter absolutely trembled for his
safety, as his recent reforms had revolted the con-.
servative instincts of the Moscovites, and it needed
but a convenient opportunity to convert secret dis-
content into open rebellion.	He pathetically im-
plored his good brother and ally Augustus to make
a diversion in the West, and that potentate, who
fancied it would be an easy task to crush the little
army under Rehnskjöld that had been left behind
to secure Poland and watch Saxony, crossed the
Oder accordingly with 15,000 men, while Schulenburg with 20,000 more, most of whom were Russians, set out to attack Rehnskjöld from the West
simultaneously.	So certain was Augustus of victory,
that he sent his Minister, Fleming, to Berlin to persuade the Prussian Government not to harbour the
Swedish fugitives.	But Rehnskjöld was not idle,
and his strategy, as usual, was swift, sure and deci-
sive.	He saw that he would have no chance against
both armies combined, so, assuming the offensive
forthwith, he fell suddenly upon Schulenburg at
Fraustadt, and completely routed him, the Saxons
losing two thousand more than the whole effective

strength of the Swedish army, whereupon Augustus disbanded his own forces, and shut himself up in Cracow. This glorious victory well deserved the Marshal's bâton which Rehnskjöld at once received from his delighted master. Charles meanwhile was pursuing Ogilvie, who had contrived to escape from Grodno, and was making the best of his way to Kiev. The break-up of the ice on the Niemen prevented the Swedes from crossing, so that Ogilvie got a start of some days, but Charles attempted to make up for this by taking a short cut through the morasses of Podlesia,* a trackless, uninhabitable wilderness where never the foot of a soldier had yet trod. After truly appalling hardships, the King himself frequently being obliged to go in front with the water up to his armpits in order to find a way for his hesitating and exhausted host, the Swedes reached the city of Pinsk, the centre of this marshy desolation, and here Charles ascended the tower of the Jesuit monastery to survey the country, when even he at last became convinced that any further progress was impossible. As far as his eye could reach stretched an endless waste of waters. "Non plus ultra!" he exclaimed as he descended the tower again. At Pinsk he stayed a month to recruit his soldiers, and convert the surrounding palatinates to the cause of Stanislaus by the irrefutable arguments of fire and sword.† His own exertions all this time

---

* Podlesia was that part of Poland that formed the watershed of the Pripietz and its numerous confluents. It was midway between Black Russia and the Ukraine.

† Pinsk and the regions round about were the property of the Radziwills and the Wiesnowieckis, who, as the personal enemies of the Sapiéhas, were the friends of Augustus.

border upon the fabulous. Once, for instance, after riding 180 miles in twenty-two hours, accompanied only by young Prince Maximilian of Würtemberg, whom he was much attached to and frequently took with him on his eccentric excursions,* their way was suddenly barred by a large lake. After searching about for some time, they found at last the hollowed out trunk of a tree which served the rude fishermen of these parts as a boat: Charles at once jumped into it, seized the paddles, and bade the Prince sit behind, and hold the horses by the bridles as they swam after them. When they got into the middle of the lake, and were out of sight of land, the horses grew so restive that they nearly upset the boat, and for some hours the King and the Prince were in extreme peril ; and this was only one of many similar escapades.

All this time the Tsar lay at Kiev intensely anxious, but his anxiety was at last relieved. Ogilvie joined him with the remains of his army (stress of weather and manifold privations had reduced it from 20,000 to 10,000 men), and shortly afterwards the news reached him that the King of Sweden had stopped short at Pinsk. Then Peter thought that he himself might safely return to Petersburg.

Thus Charles had failed to overtake and destroy Ogilvie's army, but on the other hand he had brought over Volhynia and Podlesia to the cause of Stanislaus. The Lithuanian nobility now hast-

---

* The Prince's memoirs, *Reisen und Campagnen durch Teutschland Polen, Lithauen,* etc., Stuttgart, 1730, is one of our best authorities on Charles XII., and full of personal anecdotes. This episode is recorded on pages 288, 289.

ened to make their peace with the new King of
Poland ; the Radziwills and the Wiesnowieckis, Augustus's most obstinate supporters, rubbed shoulders
with their mortal foes the Sapiéhas in the royal antechamber ; and, for the first time in his life, Stanislaus found himself the centre of a brilliant Court.
Yet he did not feel himself secure so long as Augustus remained his rival, and, he therefore pressed his
protector to crown his work by making the Elector
of Saxony perfectly harmless.   Charles desired
nothing better.   Orders were given for the whole
Swedish host to proceed westwards, and though its
destination was kept a profound secret even from
such confidants as Piper and Hermelin, it was soon
pretty obvious to the Swedish officers that their
master meant to invade Saxony.   On August 5,
1706, Charles effected a junction with Marshal
Rehnskjöld at Strykow in Great Poland, and three
weeks later he crossed the Vistula and entered Saxony, reassuring the defenceless inhabitants by a
manifesto declaring that he took them under his
protection (and we shall see that he kept his word)
and filling the rest of Europe with the most profound consternation.

For the war of the Spanish Succession was now
approaching a crisis, and the belligerents so evenly
counterpoised each other that the slightest deflection
of the political balance must have infallibly brought
one of them to the ground.   It is true that Marlborough had crushed Villeroi at Ramilies shortly
before Charles's irruption into Saxony, while Eugene shortly after it had rescued Italy from the

French by the equally brilliant and bloody victory
of Turin ; but the subsequent successes of Villars
and Vendôme in Germany and of Berwick in Spain
showed that the resources of France were still far
from being exhausted, and that even after the retire-
ment of Catinat and the disappearance of Tallard
she still possessed generals who were invincible. The
sudden apparition of Charles XII. and his army in
the very heart of the *Reich*, at such a time, very
naturally fluttered all the statesmen of Europe, more
particularly the Allies, who saw in it, at first, a deep-
laid plot of Louis XIV.* the real state of the case,
Charles's personal hatred of Augustus, being much
too simple a solution of the enigma to recommend
itself to the tortuous minds of that age's political
intriguers. Marlborough, whose diplomatic finesse
was fully equal to his military genius, determined to
travel all the way from The Hague to the castle of
Alt-Ranstadt near Leipsic where Charles was staying, in order to pay his respects to the King of
Sweden in person, and " endeavour to penetrate his
designs." † He was fully alive to the danger of irritating Charles in any way ; counselled both his own
Government and the Court of Vienna to temporise
at any price ‡ with a Prince of such a particular humour,§ and frankly declared it to be his opinion that

---

* See *Letters and Despatches of the Duke of Marlborough.* Ed.
Sir G. Murray. London, 1845, vol. iii., 281.

† *Correspondance Diplomatique et Militaire du Duc de Marlborough,*
Ed. Vreede, Amsterdam, 1850.

‡ *Marlborough Despatches.* Ed. Murray, vol. iii., 390.

§ *Correspondance Diplomatique,* pp. 117, 118. " Care must be
taken," writes Marlborough on this occasion, " that there be no
threats in the letter for the King of Sweden."

any other policy would mean the total ruin of the
Allies. On the evening of April 26, 1707, Marlborough arrived at Alt-Ranstadt, and at ten o'clock
next morning had an audience of the young King.
Crowds of people had assembled round the castle to
see something of the meeting between the two world-
renowned generals, and a couple of regiments had to
be in the courtyard to keep order. The interview
lasted till dinner-time, and was afterwards renewed
for a considerable time.* Marlborough opened the
conversation by presenting Charles with a letter from
Queen Anne. "I present your Majesty," he observed,
" a letter not from the Chancery, but from the heart
of the Queen, my mistress, and written with her
own hand. Had not her sex prevented it, she would
have crossed the sea to see a prince admired by the
whole universe. I am, in this particular, more happy
than the Queen, and I wish I could serve some campaigns under so great a general as Your Majesty,
that I might learn what I yet want to know in the
art of war.† Charles was visibly pleased by this adroit
compliment from the only man in Europe who could
pay it to him without impertinence. He expressed
through Count Piper " great tenderness and respect "
for the Queen, and even seemed " very well inclined "
to the interest of the Allies. ‡ Personally, however,
neither of the great captains was very favourably

---

* *Marlborough Despatches*, p. 247.

† *Memoirs of the Duke of Marlborough*, by Coxe, vol. ii., 45, 46.

‡ *Marlborough Despatches* p. 347. Marlborough spoke in French,
Mr. Robinson being his interpreter to the King, though Charles, as
Marlborough said, understood most of it. Piper, on the other hand,
interpreted Charles's Swedish to Marlborough.

impressed by the other. Charles thought Marlborough more of a dandy than a true soldier ought to be, while Marlborough put down Charles's rugged simplicity to vain-gloriousness and a love of singularity. He soon convinced himself that western Europe had nothing to fear from Charles XII. It is true that the young monarch's reserve and taciturnity proved absolutely impenetrable even to the keen-sighted Duke, but it did not escape Marlborough that Charles's eye flashed and his cheeks kindled whenever the name of the Tsar was mentioned, and he also observed that the table was covered with maps of Russia, whence he shrewdly concluded that no bribes were necessary to turn the Swedish arms from Germany to Moscovy,* and departed much relieved.

Five months after his interview with Marlborough, Charles XII. compelled Augustus to sign the Peace of Alt-Ranstadt. By this treaty Augustus not only resigned the Polish crown (he was allowed to retain the empty title of King) but solemnly declared that all his acts of government as King of Poland from the time that the Swedes first invaded that land, were invalid. He engaged besides to renounce every anti-Swedish alliance; to deliver over to Charles all deserters, especially Patkul,† as prisoners of war,

---

* Marlborough had brought a large sum of money with him to bribe Charles's ministers, especially Piper, and it was long supposed, on the sole authority of Marlborough himself, that most of it found its way into their pockets. Later investigations tend to prove that Marlborough appropriated most of it himself.

† The Swedes took him with them when they left Saxony, and he was ultimately (10 Oct., 1707) tried by court-martial at Kasimir and

as well as all the Russian troops actually in Saxony,
to release the Sobieskis, restore the Polish regalia
and obtain the guarantee of the Emperor and the
Maritime Powers to this treaty within six weeks.
But although the treaty of Alt-Ranstadt was thus a
bitter humiliation to Charles's enemies, it cannot be
said to have been of the slightest benefit to his country, and that, of course, from a statesman's point of
view, is its worst condemnation.   Sweden got absolutely no consideration or satisfaction whatever for
all the damage that Augustus had done her during
the last six years.   Her interests were altogether
lost sight of in her sovereign's desire to satisfy his
personal vengeance to the uttermost.

Still, now, at any rate, peace was concluded with
Saxony, and so far the Swedish statesmen considered they had great cause to be thankful.   But suddenly fresh and still more alarming complications
arose, this time with the principal continental potentate, the Emperor.   And it cannot be denied that
Charles had many just grounds of complaint against
the Court of Vienna.   Austria had not been backward in aiding King Augustus in his extremity.
She had supplied him with able officers; she had
allowed his forces a free passage through Silesia;
she had assisted fifteen hundred of his Russian mer-
cenaries, who had escaped the carnage of Fraustadt,
to regain their own country through Bohemia and
Hungary.   Moreover, she had supported the Danish

---

condemned to be broken on the wheel, and then beheaded and quartered.   The sentence was literally enforced and the traitor died
heroically.

candidate for the Bishopric of Eutin against the Swedish candidate, Christian Augustus of Holstein-Gottorp * and, finally, she had, treated the Protestants of Silesia with a tyrannical severity in direct contravention of the terms of the Peace of Westphalia, of which Sweden was one of the guarantors. Charles demanded instant and complete satisfaction on all these points in such a dictatorial tone that the Emperor in his first irritation got ready for war with " the Lion of the North." France and Russia were alike jubilant, though from very different reasons, while Marlborough moved heaven and earth to prevent a rupture between the two Powers. It was the religious question which presented the most difficulty. The Emperor was quite willing to give the amplest satisfaction on every other point, but he resented Charles's championship of the Silesian Protestants as an interference with his sovereign rights. But it was just on this one point that Charles was most obstinate. As the successor of Gustavus Adolphus, whose memory he venerated, he regarded himself as the divinely appointed guardian of German Protestanism, and zeal for the faith, as he had been taught it, was the ruling principle of his life. He was determined not to quit Saxony, till the Silesian Lutherans had been confirmed in all their ancient rights and privileges, and this was the chief cause of his twelve months' sojourn in that country after the signing of the Peace of Alt-Ranstadt, to the infinite alarm and vexation of England and her allies, who could never be sure from one week's end to

---

* Chiefly remarkable in history as the grandfather of Gustavus III.

10

another what would happen while such a storm-cloud was brooding over their heads. Nay, more, Charles's presence in the centre of Europe had the effect of seriously hampering the movements of the allied armies and thus indirectly giving relief to France. It was this consideration which finally induced the Emperor to gulp down the bitter draught which the King of Sweden insisted upon his swallowing. Within the time fixed by Charles, Joseph I. conceded to the Silesian Protestants all that their protector demanded for them and, immediately afterwards, the ambassadors of England and Holland declared that their respective Governments had agreed to guarantee the provisions of the Peace of Alt-Ranstadt. Thus Charles had succeeded in forcing his demands upon both Saxony and Austria without coming into direct collision with either of them. Nothing therefore now prevented him from at last turning his victorious arms against the Tsar. On August 23, 1707, Charles gave the order for his army to evacuate Saxony. He was now at the head of the largest and finest host he had ever commanded. It consisted of over 24,000 cavalry and 20,000 infantry, all in excellent condition. Every man had received his arrears of pay in full and, to prevent waste, the King had started military savings-banks in which the soldiers were obliged to deposit half their money, which could only be withdrawn at the discretion of their officers. And all this had not cost Sweden a penny. It was Saxony that had paid the invader to go. Yet the departure of Charles was viewed with unaffected regret by the population of the Electorate. The contributions he had levied had fallen for the most part on the privileged classes who pleaded their exemption from taxation in vain before a King whose cardinal economical maxim it was that the rich and noble should pay not less but more than their poorer brethren of the commonalty. On the other hand the peasantry were protected and it was as much as the life of a Swedish soldier was worth to steal so much as a hen or a goose from the country folks. The piety and simplicity of the Swedish King had also produced a very favourable impression upon the people. Thousands came from all parts of the country to see and speak to him, and they drew comparisons between their own ruler, the magnificently attired Augustus who sat down to his splendid banquets in gold brocade encrusted with pearls and gems, and his youthful conqueror who went about in plain blue cloth and mud-stained elk-skin boots and dined contentedly off a steak and a piece of bread, comparisons which were not very favourable to the former. It is not often that a conqueror takes away with him the good wishes of the conquered population.

CHAPTER VIII.

THE RUSSIAN WAR FROM NARVA TO HOLOWCZYN.

1700–1708.

Awakening of Russia under Peter I.—Necessity of a seaboard for her—A struggle for the possession of the Baltic inevitable—Activity of Peter after Narva—Weakness of the Baltic provinces—Russian invasion—Fall of Nöteberg—Of Nyen—Of Dorpat—Siege and capture of Narva—Levenhaupt's victories over the Russians—Charles marches against the Tsar—Refuses peace—Gyllenkrook's plan of campaign—Charles decides to advance on Moscow—Passage of the Berezina—And of the Drucz—Battle of Holowczyn—Its results—Charles rests at Mohilev—Sufferings of the army—Engagements of Czerikow and Malatitze—The way barred at Tatarsk—Embarrassment of Charles—" I have no plan ! "—Gyllenkrook advises a retreat—Charles marches towards the Ukraine.

ND now, before following Charles through his Russian campaigns, we must go back seven years and briefly review the course of events in the Baltic provinces since the young conqueror turned his back upon them after the battle of Narva.

That dazzling victory proved, ultimately, more mischievous to Charles XII. than half-a-dozen

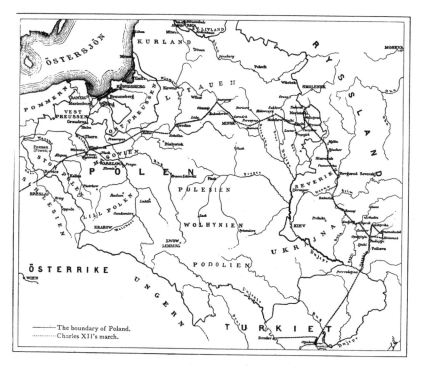

MAP TO ILLUSTRATE THE CAMPAIGNS OF CHARLES XII., 1707-1709.

defeats, for it blinded him to an ominous fact
which the leading Swedish statesmen had begun
to recognise—the sudden and alarming awakening
of that sluggish colossus, Russia, from a slumber of
centuries. For it did not escape the attention of
such observant politicians as Bengt Oxenstjerna and
Nils Lillieroth that Russia under Peter I. had at
last become conscious of her power, and that the first
use she meant to make of it was to obtain a seaboard * (without which she could not hope to
properly develop her immense resources) as the first
step towards gaining her natural frontiers, in her
case no mere diplomatic phrase. Her nearest road
to the sea lay in a north-westerly direction where the
Swedish provinces of Ingria, Esthonia and Livonia
barred the way. These transmarine possessions
formed no integral part of Sweden ; but she could
not let them go without abandoning her dream of
empire, descending at once to the level of a second-
rate Power and resigning the hegemony of the North
which she had now held for more than a century.
Whether Sweden could have permanently excluded
Russia from the sea is more than doubtful. Taking
into consideration her superior civilisation, her
splendid armaments, the concentration of all her
resources in the hands of an absolute monarch of
extraordinary force of character and, to all appearance, with a long life before him, she might perhaps
have kept the Muscovite back for a generation or, at
the most, for half a century ; but, in order to accom-

---

* The White-Sea, ice-bound as it was ten months out of the twelve,
could scarcely be dignified with the name of a seaboard.

plish even so much as this, she would have had to devote all her energies to the herculean task. Unfortunately, Charles XII., who never seems to have realised what a flimsy thing the Swedish Empire at its best really was, took an unwarrantably sanguine view of the situation. His contempt for the Russians after Narva was unbounded, nor did their panic flights before him during his Polish campaigns tend to raise them any more in his estimation. Henceforth they were to him a nation of poltroons whom anyone could be trusted to thrash. Peter he seems to have left out of sight altogether. If he thought of him at all, it was, doubtless, only as the man who had run away from his first battle and from such a one, he would naturally argue, there was little to fear. Peter was, of course, a treacherous foe whom he would one day have to chastise; but that chastisement might safely be postponed to more urgent business. So he quitted provinces that, properly defended, had ever been the bulwark of Sweden in times of war and her granary in times of peace, and plunged recklessly into the quagmires of Lithuania in pursuit of political will-o'-the-wisps that were to lure him to destruction. His great rival was not slow to perceive his mistake. Peter's proceedings immediately after Narva show how clearly he understood the state of things, indeed, he knew what Charles ought to have done better than Charles knew himself. Anticipating, as every one else did, that the Swedish King would follow up his first advantage by advancing against the fortresses of Pleskov and Novgorod before the Russians had recovered from their panic, he made superhuman efforts to strengthen those places and collect fresh forces behind them. And yet, all the time, his own position was most critical. The Russian nation was secretly chafing against the newly introduced reforms; the Boyars detested a war which, to their limited vision, seemed aimless and hopeless; the appearance of a Swedish army on Russian territory would pretty certainly have been followed by a general defection if not an open rebellion. But no Swedish army appeared, and Peter, always well informed, no sooner discovered that Charles had left his Baltic provinces to take care of themselves than he resolved to attack them forthwith in his own methodical way.

Even under the most favourable circumstances the Baltic provinces had a very poor chance of withstanding the whole force of the Russian Empire, and the circumstances were anything but favourable. They had been impoverished by a series of bad harvests; they had suffered from the ravages of their enemies before Narva and from the exactions of their friends after it, for the heavy burden of supporting the victorious army of Charles XII. had rested almost entirely on their shoulders and, finally, when Charles quitted them at last, he not only took away with him the pick of their troops, but strictly enjoined the Government at home to send all reinforcements to himself in Poland via Pomerania; not a regiment, not a frigate was to be wasted on his Bothnian possessions. Nor was this all. Discord and jealousy, personal and official, were presently superadded to

the other troubles of the wretched Baltic provinces.
The four Governor-Generals of Ingria, Esthonia,
Livonia and Finland could do nothing but lay the
blame of each successive and inevitable disaster at
each other's door, and address piteous appeals for
help to the King in Poland and the Senate at Stockholm, which the former would not, and the latter
dare not, listen to.   The generals and admirals,
moreover, too independent to act together, too feeble
to act alone, clearly foresaw the ruin that was coming
upon them, for the three little handfuls of half-
starving ragamuffins, dignified by the name of army-
corps, could not seriously attempt to defend against
a tenfold odds the twentieth part of a frontier
extending from Lake Ladoga to Lake Peipus, from
Lake Peipus to the Dwina, and from the Dwina to
the Gulf of Riga.   Only beneath the walls of the
fortresses did the invader meet with any prolonged
resistance, and the fortresses themselves, ill-pro-
visioned, undermanned, in many cases half in ruins,
would have surrendered at the first summons, had
they not been defended by veteran soldiers of heroic
antecedents.   Slowly and deliberately, Peter advanced with irresistible forces behind him, feeling
his way cautiously along, step by step, risking as
little as possible, retreating without hesitation whenever it was necessary; but never idle for a moment,
neutralising his losses in one direction by fresh gains
in another and clearly acting all along on a systematic
plan.   Repulsed from Livonia by the gallant Schlippenbach, in the summer of 1701, he was back again
in the early spring of 1702, ravaging Ingria and

Livonia simultaneously, driving the tiny Swedish
armies before him, and in the autumn his perseverance was rewarded by the capture of the fortress of
Nöteberg, the key of Ladoga*, after a splendid
resistance. In 1703 he followed up this success by
taking the fortress of Nyen at the head of the Gulf
of Finland, and, a fortnight later, a little lower down
the Neva, on the island of Jenisaari, were laid the
foundations of a Russian fortress which the Tsar called
Petersburg after himself : by the end of the same year
the whole province of Ingria was in his hands. Em-
boldened by his successes, Peter in 1704 laid siege
simultaneously to Dorpat, the central fortress of
Livonia, commanding Lake Peipus, and Narva, then
the strongest bulwark of Sweden's eastern frontier
and the key of the Baltic. Dorpat fell † after a
determined resistance of six weeks which cost Peter
5000 men, whereupon he concentrated all his forces
round Narva, which only four years before had been
the scene of his humiliating overthrow. The Swedish
Government made a supreme effort to save the place.‡
The Finnish and Esthonian forces were ordered to
co-operate for the purpose, and a small fleet under De
Prou was sent to the mouth of the Neva to make a
diversion against Petersburg ; but the generals missed
the right moment and the admiral found that Petersburg and the newly-built galleys and brigantines
around it were too strong to be attacked by his

---

* Called now, for that very reason, Schlüsselburg.

† In this, as in every other instance, except Narva, the garrison was
allowed to march out with all the honours of war.

‡ After the fall of Nyen, Charles XII. gave the Senate leave to
reinforce the Baltic provinces.

puny squadron, so the commandant of Narva, Rudolf Horn, was left to do as best he could. From April to August the fortress was closely invested. On August 7th the ancient bastion called *Honor* suddenly collapsed, leaving a breach in the walls large enough for twelve men to storm in through it abreast. Then Peter, anxious to avoid unnecessary bloodshed, offered the commandant an honourable capitulation; but Horn replying with an insulting allusion to the battle of Narva, the infuriated Tsar bombarded the town and then ordered a general assault. The garrison defended itself heroically; 3000 Russians fell in the breach; but might prevailed at last and by vespers the Tsar was lord of Narva. *

The fall of Narva produced a most painful impression in Sweden. When the news first reached Stockholm there was a general panic there, many persons even sent their money and jewelry to Hamburg for better security. The Senate at once addressed a most solemn remonstrance to the King painting in the darkest colours the condition of the realm and representing that peace with Poland was now the only means of saving it from destruction, as thereby the army would be released and his Majesty enabled to come to the succour of his afflicted people. The Senate insinuated at the same time that the King would greatly strengthen his position by making an alliance with Prussia who was only waiting to be

---

* The town, despite the personal efforts of the Tsar who is said to have cut down fifty of the marauders with his own hand, was savagely plundered by the Russians. Yet Peter was much more merciful than Cromwell at Drogheda.

asked. Charles's reply was evasive but not un-
gracious. Peace, he said, was in God's hands. He
also was labouring towards the same end, but his
people must patiently abide God's will and not lose
heart. The more vigorously the war was prosecuted
the more certainly and speedily it would lead to a
general peace. And with these and similar pious
commonplaces, the Senate had to be content.

During 1705 the Swedes were too feeble to do
anything but prevent the Russian fleet which the
Tsar, after incredible efforts, had already built upon
Ladoga * and the Neva, from running out into the
Baltic. On the other hand, three expeditions under-
taken against St. Petersburg failed utterly. Peter
meanwhile had repaired to Lithuania to aid his friend
Augustus whose prospects were then at their
gloomiest; but he had an eye at the same time upon
Riga, and would certainly have captured that great
fortress also but for the presence in those parts of
one of Charles's most reliable lieutenants who, like
his master, could work wonders with that excellent
war material, the Swedish soldier. This was Colonel
Adam Ludwig Levenhaupt who had now begun
that wonderful career which was to end, all too
briefly, in unmerited disaster. His first exploit was
in April, 1703, when with only 1300 men he utterly
routed 5200 Poles and Russians, for which he was at
once made a Major-General and Governor of Courland. For the next five years Levenhaupt continued
to be a sort of connecting link between the King's
forces in Poland and the Baltic provinces and was

* He had helped to build some of these ships with his own hands.

supposed to keep open the communications between the two and assist whichever needed it most. Thus, in 1704, he acted in Lithuania with the Sapiéhas (though they were always more of an impediment than a reinforcement) and with 6000 men defeated 12,000 Russians and Poles under Prince Wiesnowiecki at Jakobstadt, besides capturing the important Polish fortress of Birse. But his crowning achievement was in the following year against Peter's best general, Sheremetev. The Tsar, as I have said, had, in the beginning of 1705, invaded Lithuania with the double object of assisting Augustus and capturing Riga, and Sheremetev was sent with 20,000 Russians to, drive off Levenhaupt who had planted himself in the way with his 7000 men. But the Swedes stood firm at Gemauerhof, an old castle not far from Mittau, and there, on June 16th, was fought one of the bloodiest engagements of the Great Northern war, in which the Russians were finally routed with the loss of 6000 men. But Levenhaupt was too weak to hold Courland and protect Riga (of which he was now made Governor) at the same time, so he wisely resolved to sacrifice a useless province for an indispensable fortress and fell back upon Riga to the infinite chagrin of Peter who had now to be content with occupying Courland. During 1706 and 1707 the Baltic provinces were spared any further invasion, for the mere rumour that Charles was moving eastwards sufficed to send the Tsar back in hot haste to guard his own frontiers.

But the rumour of Charles's advance proved a false alarm. The King of Sweden quitted Saxony

indeed in the autumn of 1707, but he was delayed
for months in Poland by the non-arrival of the expected reinforcements from Pomerania so that not
till November was he able to take the field. Then,
everything pointed to a *combat à l'outrance* between
the two great rivals. Charles had told the Imperial
Ambassador at Alt-Ranstadt that he intended to depose Peter as he had already deposed Augustus
and there is reason to believe that he had made
up his mind to give the crown of Russia to James
Sobieski as some compensation for the loss of the
crown of Poland. Peter who was at Warsaw, where
he had summoned a Diet under Russian protection
to elect a new King, now made a last attempt to
negotiate through the French Minister, offering to
surrender all his conquests except the river Neva
and a strip of land on both sides of it as he euphemis-
tically called St. Petersburg and its cordon of depend-
ant fortresses. But Charles, well aware that the possession of the Neva was vital, declared at once that he
would rather sacrifice his last soldier than leave St.
Petersburg in the hands of the Russians and, without more ado, set off against the Tsar. By Christ-
mas Day he had already reached the Vistula, and by
New Year's Day he had crossed it, although the ice
was only three inches thick and he very nearly lost
one of his finest regiments in consequence. Peter,
gloomy and depressed, rapidly retreated from Warsaw and would have intrenched himself behind the
Memel at Grodno to dispute the passage of the river ;
but Charles, advancing with unsurpassable swiftness,
anticipated him, snatched Grodno from his very

grasp (28th January, 1708) and, continuing the pur-
·suit, actually came up with Peter at Wilna, but the
Swedish cavalry was too exhausted to attack the foe
the same day and by next morning Peter had de-
camped. Then Charles gave his weary army a
brief rest at Smorganie, a small place not far from
Wilna.

It was the opinion of Charles's ablest officers that
he should now turn towards the Baltic provinces,
recover Ingria, destroy St. Petersburg, capture the
strong Russian fortress of Pleskov and use it as a base
for further operations. Much the same plan had been
suggested immediately after the battle of Narva and
then it would have been easily practicable. Even
now, with such a leader as Charles XII. at the head
of an army of veterans, it was not impossible, and
Quartermaster Anders Gyllenkrook * very carefully
worked out the whole project and submitted it to
the King who approved of it but told its author to
put it by and keep it secret. Gyllenkrook naturally
supposed that his plan was now being followed out
as the Swedish army continued advancing steadily in
the direction of the Baltic provinces and Pleskov ;
but he was soon undeceived, for on breaking up
from Smorganie, the King ordered the army to turn
to the southeast and pitched his camp at Radoskowice, a few miles from Minsk. The route now followed led straight to Moscow and it became pretty
evident to Charles's officers that thither he had re-

---

* This able officer was born in 1665, and, as we shall see, was captured by the Russians. He died in 1730 a lieutenant-general and a
baron.

solved to go.* Now there can be no doubt that
there was something grand and fascinating in the
idea of striking at the very heart of the Russian
Empire and so ending the war at one blow, and had
Charles only well weighed all the chances and carefully provided against every adverse contingency
the idea might even have been realised. But this he
had not done and his officers knew it and told him
so. Every one of his lieutenants, except Marshal
Rehnskjöld who seems to have had a blind confidence in his master's luck, objected energetically to
this change of front and pointed out the danger of
exposing the one army that Sweden now had to depend upon to the risk of destruction in a vast wilderness where it might easily be cut off from its
communications and would always be uncertain of
its supplies. But Charles whose contempt for the
Russians was only equalled by his sublime confidence
in his own soldiers only smiled at the timely counsels of Piper, Levenhaupt † and Gyllenkrook and in
the beginning of June the army broke up from
Radoskowice and turned off to the south-east. Peter,
who had been watching his foe all this time at the
head of 70,000 men, was doubtful, at first, which
direction Charles would take ; but perceiving that he
was bent upon reaching Moscow by way of Smolensk,
the Tsar at once took vigorous preventive measures,

---

* There can now be very little doubt that he meant to go thither
from the first.

† Levenhaupt had been summoned to Radoskowice to receive in-
structions as to the part he was to take in the ensuing campaign.
He returned shortly afterwards to Riga to make his final preparations.
Arvid Horn, Magnus Stenbock and Nieroth were now in Sweden.

fortifying the whole line of the Dnieper from Mohilev to Orsza so as to entirely cover that part of central Russia which lay in the Swedish line of march and sending forward 8000 men under General Goltz to dispute the passage of the first considerable river, the Berezina. But Charles, skilfully out-manœuvring Goltz, succeeded in crossing the Berezina without loss and pursued his way towards the Dnieper over, marshy ground that grew more and more difficult every mile he advanced,* the enemy meanwhile steadily retreating but burning all the bridges on his way and sending forth crowds of Tartar horsemen to hang upon the invader's flank and harass him at every step. Still Charles imperturbably led the way onwards at the head of his Guard and the army hungry and weary but still victorious followed him without a murmur. The next stream, the Drucz, was also crossed without difficulty, but when Charles came to the river Wabis, he found the enemy strongly posted on the opposite side, near the little town of Holowczyn, evidently bent upon barring his passage. The position of the Russians seemed, at first sight, almost impregnable. Between themselves and the river there was a morass and behind them stood a thick forest. The line extended for six miles † along the river, they far outnumbered the

---

* Charles admits as much himself in his letter to his sister Ulrica : " All this summer the marching has been pretty difficult owing to the weather and bad roads. The enemy seldom shewed himself the whole way except in small parties and at the rivers."—*Egenhändiga Bref*, No. 70.

† This was to escape being outflanked as at the Berezina and the Drucz. They never thought that the Swedes would dare to cross.

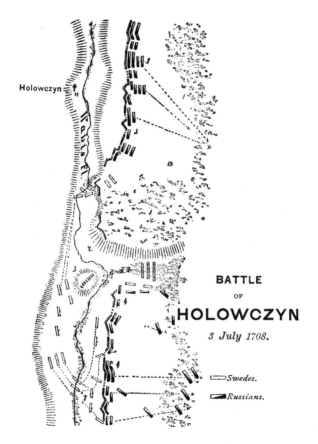

Holowczyn

BATTLE

OF

HOLOWCZYN

3 July 1708.

☐Swedes.

☐Russians.

1. Forest.   2. Morass.   3. Russian right wing.   4. Russian
left.   5. Hill on which Charles placed battery.   6. The point where
Charles crossed the Wabis with the infantry.   7. The point where
Rehnksjöld crossed the Wabis with the cavalry.

Swedes already and fresh masses of infantry and
cavalry reinforced them continually. Sheremetev
was in command of the right wing, Repnin of the
left, the cavalry was led by General Goltz. Charles
waited three days, till about two thirds of his forces
had come up and then, impatient to fight and fearing lest the Russians, might decamp, he determined
to attack them forthwith. His measures were well
chosen. With the eye of a true general, he had de-
tected the vulnerable point in the enemy's long line,
an unguarded gap between their left and right wings
where there was a morass in front of them which they
deemed impassable, and against this point he hurled
all his forces. At daybreak on July 4th, the battle began with a general cannonade and then Charles, on
horseback, at the head of his foot-guards plunged
first into the river and then into the morass, 1500
yards long, covering the Russian front, in the face of
a vigorous enfilade which visibly thinned the Swedish
ranks. But nothing could stop the impetuous advance of the Swedes. With their weapons raised
aloft, for the water came up to their shoulders,
they advanced as calmly as if they were on parade
and Charles, after giving up his horse to a wounded
officer, charged with his little band as soon as they
reached dry ground. Repnin, fearing to be cut off
from Sheremetev, now fell back on the wood behind
him and there at half-past five in the morning the
Swedes closed with them and a murderous struggle
began. Repnin's cavalry thereupon advanced to assist his infantry by taking the Swedes in flank, but
Marshal Rehnskjöld, perceiving the King's danger,

dashed across the stream in his turn with a few
squadrons of dragoons who repulsed nine times in
succession the two-fold odds hurled against them, but
were themselves in extreme peril for a time till gradually reinforced by the remainder of the Swedish horse
who engaged immediately they had crossed the river,
and after a life-and-death struggle the enemy's horse
was at last driven back. The prodigies performed
by the Swedish cavalry on this occasion have led an
eminent German military, critic * to declare that the
battle of Holowczyn must always be the standing instance in tactics of the utmost capability of cavalry.
Meanwhile the rest of the Swedish infantry had also
crossed the Wabis and now Charles ordered a general
advance. Again there was some very severe fighting (or " a merry scrimmage," † as his Swedish Majesty chooses to call it), but at last the whole of the
Russian left wing was forced to abandon its artillery
and camp and fall back upon the woods behind,
where it rallied for the last time but was finally
routed and dispersed, Charles at the head of his cavalry chasing the enemy for no less than six miles.
By eight o'clock all was over. The Swedish attack
had been so swift and sudden that the Russian right
wing had not had time to assist their left which bore
the whole brunt of the fight and by the time Charles
returned from pursuing, he found the battle-field en-

---

* Sarauw, *Die Feldzüge Karls XII.*, Leipzig, 1881.

† The best account of the battle is to be found in Charles's letter to
his sister Ulrica, of Aug. 4, 1708. His narrrative is remarkable for
its lucid marshalling of the facts and his modest self-effacement. He
never mentions his own name once.—*Egenh. Bref*, No. 70. Compare Carlson, *Carl den Tolftes tåg mot Ryssland*, pp. 368–71.

tirely deserted, for Sheremetev also thought it prudent to retire. The Swedes had lost about 1300, the
Russians more than 3000 men.

The victory of Holowczyn was not without effect.
Not only did it open up the way to the Dnieper and
relieve, for a time, the more pressing difficulties of
the Swedes, but it was also not without its influence
on public opinion in Europe generally. At Stockholm people began to think that the Russian expedition might succeed after all, while the ardour with
which Augustus of Saxony had been endeavouring,
at the instigation of Peter, to form a fresh coalition
against Sweden cooled considerably. Nevertheless
this battle had no decisive results and, moreover, it
opened the eyes of the Swedes to the very significant
fact that the Russian soldiers they now had to fight
against were very different to the men who had run
away at Narva. Then the Swedes had triumphed
easily over a five-fold odds, now a two-fold odds was
almost too much for them. The struggle had been
severe and the victory by no means an easy one.
Still, a victory it was and had the Swedes been able
to follow it up instantly, they might have gained incalculable advantages. But this in their exhausted
condition was impossible, in fact Charles would not
even risk an attack upon the next obstacle in his way,
the village of Horki, which the Tsar had hastily
transformed into a fortress, but left it behind him
and turned aside to Mohilev on the Dnieper which
he reached on July 8th. Here he rested for a month
while Peter employed the respite thus gained by
prudently but pitilessly devastating the whole region

for miles around. On August 6th Charles resumed
his onward march. The Swedish army now began
to suffer severely. Bread was running short and
there was scarcely any fodder for the horses, but the
soldiers still had meat for they had captured and
brought away with them whole herds of bullocks.
Both officers and soldiers now began to show the first
symptoms of weariness of war ; dysentery and other
diseases caused by bad water made their appearance,
and both high and low fervently desired that rest
which peace with the Tsar alone could bring. But
Charles had come there to fight, and not to treat, and
he did all in his power to bring on an engagement
with the two large Russian armies that carefully and
constantly kept him in sight but as carefully and constantly avoided a pitched battle. There was, indeed,
a sharp skirmish at Czerikow on the river Sosz which
the Russians vainly attempted to prevent the Swedes
from crossing, and a much more serious combat at
Malatitze where they had the unheard-of audacity to
attempt to cut off an outlying Swedish division, and
very nearly succeeded ; but still Peter would not yet
risk a general engagement but slowly retired before
the invaders, burning and destroying everything in
his path till, at last, the Swedes had nothing but a
charred wilderness beneath their feet and a horizon
of blazing villages before their eyes, while sometimes
the air was so full of smoke that they could not see
the sun. Nevertheless the indomitable young King
continued the pursuit, occupying every evening the
camp the Russians had quitted the same morning
and striving in vain to overtake his elusive foe. He

was now only three miles from the Russian border,* but that border he was never to cross. His army was still intact, it is true ; but its sufferings were terrible and it was becoming plain to everyone but Charles himself that the limits of human endurance had very nearly been reached. For weeks together the soldiers had had next to no rest, and loiter behind they dare not for every straggler was instantly cut off by the watchful Tartar and Bashkir horsemen who hovered around the advancing host and harassed it night and day. Their bread and provender, moreover, were now nearly all gone and there seemed no prospect of getting any more. Two things had become quite plain to them : the Tsar meant to gradually starve them out and then fall upon them,† and the King's project of reaching Moscow was utterly impracticable. Even Charles felt, at last, that a crisis was at hand, and, for the first time in his life, he was doubtful what to do. In his embarrassment he took counsel with the very officer whose plan of campaign he had previously rejected—Anders Gyllenkrook. One morning while the army was stopping at Tatarsk, on a tributary of the Sosz, Gyllenkrook was surprised to see the King enter his tent and still more surprised was he when Charles said to him : " In what direction think you the army should march now ? " Gyllenkrook naturally replied that it was impossible for him to counsel anything so long as he remained

---

* That is to say the border of early eighteenth-century Russia. He was already in the very heart of the Russian Empire of to-day.

† Letters intercepted from the Russians said as much.

ignorant of the King's plans. "*I have no plan !*"
replied Charles. Astonished by such a reply at such
a moment, Gyllenkrook did not know what to say,
but, after consulting with his brother officers and
finding them unanimous as to the impossibility of a
farther advance upon Moscow, he proposed that the
army should fall back upon the Dnieper, there await
the arrival of Levenhaupt who was advancing from
Riga with reinforcements and a whole caravan of
stores and ammunition and then return to Lithuania. It was calculated that Levenhaupt could now
be only a few days' march off and until he arrived
Gyllenkrook undertook to find provisions for the
army. This was, under the circumstances, the wisest
plan that could have been adopted, as it would not
only have recruited the army but enabled the King
to recommence the war, if he chose to do so, under
very much more favourable conditions. Unfortunately, Charles XII. had an invincible repugnance to
any strategical movement which had the remotest
resemblance to a retreat. He enquired therefore
whether there was any alternative. Then Gyllenkrook, very reluctantly, admitted that it was also
open to the army to march southwards through
Severia to the land of the Cossacks who were supposed to be friendly. There, too, provisions might
be found, for Severia and the Ukraine had hitherto
escaped the ravages of war. But, on the other hand,
Gyllenkrook pointed out that in those remote regions
the Swedes would be entirely cut off from their communications, and he strongly insisted that, in any
case, they should wait till they had been joined by

Levenhaupt and his 14,000 veterans. But to this the King would not consent. He considered it as unnecessary to await Levenhaupt now as it had been to await Gyllenstjerna before Klissov * and he gave orders that the army should break up at once, sending General Lagercrona on in advance to hunt up provisions. So the army first retraced its steps to the river Sosz by the way it had come and then turned off in a south-easterly direction towards Severia and the Ukraine. It has well been said that this march northwards from Tatarsk was an inexcusable strategical blunder which led inevitably to the final catastrophe. †

---

*See Chapter IV.

† E. Carlson, *Karl XIIs ryska fälttågsplan*, 1707–1709 (*Nordisk Tids.*, 1889). This valuable monograph is the latest contribution to the history of this disastrous campaign.

CHAPTER IX.

THE RUSSIAN WAR FROM HOLOWCZYN TO PULTAWA.

1708-1709.

Ivan Stefanovich Mazeppa—His negotiations with the Swedes—
Advance of Levenhaupt with a relief army from Riga—His
extraordinary difficulties—Battle of Lesna—The march through
Severia—Mazeppa joins the Swedes at Horki—Passage of the
Desna—The Ukraine—Winter quarters at Romny and Had-
yach—The black frost of 1708-9—Horrible sufferings of the
Swedes—Instances of Charles's rough sympathy—Engagements
of Oposznaya and Krasnokutsk—Charles advances towards
Pultawa—Is joined by the Zaporogean Cossacks—Charles's plans
—Siege of Pultawa—Charles wounded and disabled—Battle of
Pultawa—Useless heroism of the Swedes—Escape of Charles—
Surrender of the Swedish army at Perewoloczna.

HEN Charles XII. turned southwards
in the direction of Severia and the
Ukraine he hoped to find a serviceable
ally in Mazeppa, the Hetman of the
Ukrainian Cossacks. As the connec-
tion of this man with the Swedish
King has been much misunderstood,
and his influence on the events of 1708-9 greatly
exaggerated, it is necessary to briefly explain who he
was and what he really did.

Ivan Stefanovich Mazeppa, whom art and poetry
have conspired to make one of the most picturesque
figures in Slavonic history, was the illegitimate son
of a Polish nobleman, and took his name from the
castle of Mazeppa near Bialozerkiew the place of his
birth. In his youth he served as a page at the Court
of King John Casimir, but, being caught in adultery
with the wife of a Polish magnate, was tarred and
feathered, bound naked on the back of his own horse
with his face to its tail and his legs tied beneath its
belly and let loose upon the steppes of the Ukraine.
Here he was rescued from the carrion crows by the
Cossacks who adopted the lad. He grew up among
them, and in 1687 they unanimously elected him
their Hetman. In this position he greatly distin-
guished himself by his valour and capacity, clearing
the land of the Tartar hordes, and rendering signal
services to Peter the Great during his earlier Turkish
wars. But it was the secret ambition of Mazeppa to
become independent of both Russia and Poland, and
the successes of Charles XII. seemed to present him
with his long sought for opportunity. During
Charles's march through Poland in 1708, Mazeppa,
who had long been vacillating between loyalty and
rebellion, began secretly negotiating with the Swedes
through King Stanislaus. For the Cossack Hetman,
although bound by all the ties of honour and gratitude to the Tsar, had been much disturbed by Peter's
far-reaching military reforms which seemed to him
to be undermining the independence of the Cossacks,
and he was quite prepared to shake off the Muscovite yoke, if only he had a powerful friend behind

him. Such a friend he now hoped to find in Charles XII., and the reward he claimed for his defection was the erection of a principality for himself consisting of the Ukraine and a couple of adjacent Polish palatinates, yet all the time he adroitly hoodwinked Peter by pretending to reveal to him the secret plans of Charles and Stanislaus. It was while Charles was resting at Mohilev, after the battle of Holowczyn, that Mazeppa took the decisive step by sending a special envoy to the Swedish monarch, offering to place 30,000 horsemen at his disposal, if he would take the Cossacks of the Ukraine under his protection. Charles consented. Hitherto indeed the possibility of Mazeppa's active assistance seems scarcely to have entered into his calculations,* and he received all the Cossack Hetman's earlier overtures with the most frigid indifference. It was not in Charles's nature to willingly seek help from anyone, and the monarch who had rejected the offer of 40,000 picked troops from Prussia, on practically his own terms, was not likely to attach too much importance to the promises of a discontented freebooter in the Russian steppes. It was only when necessity compelled him to abandon for a time the advance on Moscow, that he gave a thought to Mazeppa, though the knowledge that he actually possessed an ally in the Ukraine was an additional argument for turning in that direction

* See F. F. Carlson, *Carl den Tolftes tåg mot Ryssland.* The supposition of Voltaire, and of Fryxell after him, that Charles, in quitting Saxony, was tempted from the first to the Ukraine by Mazeppa's offers, has absolutely no foundation in fact. Compare also Würtemberg, *Reisen und Campagnen*, pp. 399 *et seq.*

now that there was nothing better to do, or hope for. The wish moreover to join Mazeppa as soon as possible was his chief reason for not awaiting, and so sacrificing, Levenhaupt and the valuable caravan of stores and provisions which that unfortunate general was now painfully endeavouring to bring with him all the way from the Gulf of Riga to the banks of the Dnieper, a distance of more than four hundred miles.

In fact Charles had laid upon the shoulders of his lieutenant a burden too heavy for him to bear. On May 26th the King had sent Levenhaupt a command to set out from Riga at the beginning of June, march straight to the Dnieper, and there await further orders. This letter did not reach Levenhaupt till June 8th and he at once replied that with the best will in the world it was impossible for him to get all his baggage wagons together till the end of the month. By that time he was ready, and set out with 11,000 men, and sufficient provisions to feed the main army for twelve weeks. It is said that each company took with it ten four-horse wagons. Hampered as he was by these impediments, Levenhaupt's progress was necessarily slow, and it was made slower still by the bad roads and the heavy rains, so that it was not till the middle of September that he reached the Dnieper at Sklow where fresh orders bade him follow southwards after the main army as best he could, along and across the rivers Dnieper and Sosz, to Starodub in Severia, some hundred and fifty miles farther on. Levenhaupt, who had expected to find the King waiting for him

on the Dnieper, was thunderstruck at thus being
abandoned by the main army from which he was
now separated by no less than five large rivers, and
his dismay was not diminished when he learned that
the Tsar was marching rapidly towards him, with a
threefold odds, to surround and cut him off. He
felt that he was indeed in evil case, but he prepared,
like the brave man he was, to loyally carry out the
King's orders and his strategy at this crisis was not
unworthy of his great reputation. Within a week he
had crossed the Dnieper, and, fighting incessantly
with the Russian vanguard, forced his way towards
the Sosz, but, when only a day's march from that
river at Lesna, Peter threw himself in the way with
30,000 men, and Levenhaupt and his 8000 had
nothing for it but to conquer or die. Early on
September 29th, the battle began, and lasted till
dusk, the Swedes gallantly repulsing four determined
attacks. The same night the Russians received
large reinforcements,* so that Levenhaupt thought
it prudent to quit his camp, and make for the Sosz
which he hoped to cross at Propoisk before he was
overtaken. But the Russians followed hard upon
him ; part of his army missed its way, and was lost ;
the passage of the Sosz at Propoisk proved impracticable ; so Levenhaupt, after sinking his cannon in
the morasses and burning the whole of his stores and
ammunition, to prevent them from falling into the
enemy's hands, retreated with barely 6000 men,
and succeeded, after incredible hardships, in reaching
Severia.

* Some say as many as 15,000.

Well might Peter the Great exult over the victory of Lesna, and consider it cheaply bought even at the cost of 6000 men. To say nothing of the very serious material damage inflicted on the Swedes by the total loss of indispensable stores and ammunition, it was the first time they had been defeated in a pitched battle by the Russians, and the moral effect of such a reversal of the usual course of things was incalculable. Not without reason did. the Tsar call the battle of Lesna "the mother of Pultawa."

Charles received the tidings of this disaster with his usual sangfroid, nay more, having regard to the fact that the larger portion of Levenhaupt's army had got off, he chose to regard it as "a lucky action."* He himself, meanwhile, was continuing his march through Severia. Severia was the name then given to the plain lying between the rivers Desna and Sosz, corresponding almost exactly with the modern government of Chernigov. It consists, for the most part, of forest and morass, which made progress, especially for the baggage, very slow and difficult. The country here was not wasted like the Dnieper district, and in some places a little forage could be scraped together, but the Swedes found all the villages they came to deserted, while in the towns (which were few and far between) the inhabitants suspiciously watched the invaders from behind their walls, armed to the teeth. Food became scarcer and scarcer as the march proceeded, even the more squeamish of the officers being now glad enough to live upon

* *Egenh. Bref*, No. 252.

black bread and tisane. *   In the beginning of October Levenhaupt effected his junction with his master,
but both armies had now shrunk so much from their
former proportions, that the King ordered the new-
comers to be incorporated with his own regiments,
and thus many officers, including Levenhaupt himself, had no longer any command. Shortly after this
junction, when Charles reached the little Severian
town of Horki, he was joined (6th November)
by Mazeppa who came with all the ceremony of a
Hetman of Cossacks, having the silver staff borne
before and the horse-tail standard behind him, but
bringing with him only 1500 horsemen instead of
the 30,000 he had promised. Mazeppa, in fact, had
lost nearly everything, and was now himself a fugitive. He had for long succeeded in hoodwinking
the Tsar, but his double dealing had at last come
to light, and Peter took prompt measures to make
his rebellious vassal a useless ally to anyone else.
Menshikov, with a large Russian army, suddenly appeared in the Ukraine, reduced Baturin, Mazeppa's
capital, to ashes (previously confiscating the treasure
accumulated there estimated at 2,000,000 gulden);
placed Russian garrisons in the fortresses of Starodub and Novgorod Seversk † ; caused Mazeppa to be
publicly excommunicated by the Archbishop of
Kiev, and made his former lieutenant, Skoropadzki,
Hetman in his stead. Mazeppa, therefore, to save
his head, was obliged to flee to the Swedes, and

---

* *Des Printzens Max. Emanuels Hertzogs in Würtemberg Reisen
und Campagnen*, pp. 410-12.

† The Swedes arrived too late to occupy these places.

though he was no longer a potent ally, his sagacity, courage and intimate knowledge of the country made him a valuable counsellor and guide.* Charles seems to have been very favourably impressed by the wit and vivacity of the wiry little man who, despite his sixty years, was still full of fire and energy, and spoke Latin as fluently as the King himself. Ten days after meeting Mazeppa, Charles reached (November 15th) the broad and rapid Desna which separates Severia from the Ukraine. The Russians had assembled in large numbers on the opposite bank, and the banks on the Swedish side were so steep that the soldiers had to be hoisted down on to the rafts prepared for them ; but the passage was nevertheless safely effected, and, after a severe skirmish, the enemy was put to flight. And now, at last, Charles found himself in the Ukraine.

The Ukraine, the " border-land " † in those days between Europe and Tartary, nominally belonging to Russia and Poland, but actually in the possession of the Cossacks, was the name given to that district which extended on both sides of the lower Dnieper, south of the city of Kiev. It was a fat and fruitful land abounding in cereals and rich grasses, and covered with flocks and herds, and here the Swedes were much better off than they had been for some time, although they had come to it at the wrong season, and were now as good as cut off altogether from the rest of the world. After marching past the

---

* He also lent Charles a large sum of ready money.

† Hence the name. Beyond it lay the land of the **Tartars, stretch-**ing north-eastwards as far as the Crimea.

smoking ruins of Mazeppa's former stronghold, Baturin, Charles fixed his head-quarters at Romny, a little place to the south-east of it, situated on the River Sula. Throughout his march he was harassed incessantly by the light horse of the Russians, whose main army now lay towards the north, with its fore-posts extending as far as Lebedin and Veprik.* It was from Romny that Charles issued a manifesto (written in excellent Latin by his field secretary Hermelin) to the Cossacks, warning them against Peter's treachery, and offering to take them under his protection ; but it produced far less effect than a previous proclamation by the Tsar, appealing to the cupidity of the freebooters by offering rewards on a graduated scale,† for every Swedish captive brought into the Russian camp, alive or dead. All this time the Swedes had little or no rest. The Russian armies, reinforced by thousands of Cossacks, were closing in upon them on every side, rendering it more and more difficult every day to collect supplies. At length Romny became too narrow for them, and in December they shifted their quarters to Hadyach, still farther to the south-east. It was while the ragged, half-starved army was making its way tow-ards this place that a terrible frost, the like of which had not been known for a century, devastated all Europe. In Sweden and Norway elks and harts

---

* See Map.

† Two thousand rubels were to be paid for every general, 1000 for every colonel, down to 5 rubels for every live, and 3 rubels for every dead, common soldier. In many places, moreover, circulars were left behind, promising the Swedish soldiers plenty of good food and hand-some pay if they would desert.

were found frozen to death in the forests. The Baltic became a mass of ice, the Belt and the Sound solid roads. In Central Europe the fruit trees were killed by thousands, the canals of Venice, the estuary of the Tagus, even the swift-flowing Rhone, were covered with ice. But it was in the vast open steppes of the Ukraine that the cold was most severe. There birds dropped down dead from the trees and wine and spirits froze into solid masses of ice. It was while the unhappy Swedes were painfully toiling on their way between Romny and Hadyach that this new and terrible enemy fell upon them. They hastened as rapidly as they could to Hadyach for warmth and shelter, but on reaching the place it was found that there was only a single gate through which they could enter, and that was speedily blocked by wagons and cannon, horses and men. Only a fraction of the army could get inside the town that same evening, the rest had to pass three or four nights among the snow-drifts under the open sky, and the consequence was a loss of life greater than the carnage of a pitched battle. Three to four thousand men were frozen to death, and of the remainder there was scarcely one who was not seriously injured by frost-bite. Even those who lay well covered with sheepskins in beds of straw were afraid of falling asleep lest they should freeze to death and many had not even skins to protect them. It was no unusual thing to find a sentinel frozen to death on horseback, and sledges full of corpses were driven every day into the little town, every house of which now became a veritable hospital, the patients being

12

crowded together on benches and under benches, so that there was no room to move about. The sufferings of the unhappy wretches were aggravated by ignorance or recklessness. Many thought it absurd to rub their frozen limbs with snow, the only sure remedy ; others tried to drown their woes in bad brandy and crude Tartar wine, while others again were too weak and helpless to attempt to do anything for themselves. " Nevertheless," grimly exclaims the young Duke of Würtemberg, a participator in these horrors, " nevertheless, although Earth, Sky and Air were now against us, the King's designs had to be accomplished, and the daily march to be made."* Charles himself in his letter to his sister Ulrica, some months later, passes lightly enough over the intense sufferings of his soldiers,† and evidently thinks it a suffi-

---

* *Des Printzens Max. Emanuels Hertzogs in Würtemberg Reisen und Campagnen*, pp. 428–30. Compare what is perhaps the most circumstantial account of this awful campaign, viz.: Daniel Krmann's *Historia ablegationis . . . ad Regem Sveciæ Carolum XII.*, a document published only last year (1894) by the Hungarian Academy of Sciences, and, so far as I am aware, quite unknown to Swedish historians. Krmann, a Hungarian Protestant, came all the way to Lithuania to place himself under Charles's protection, and accompanied him to the Ukraine and to Turkey.

† " Things are well enough with the army here, although there has been a little fatigue as is usual when the enemy is near. Moreover this winter has been very cold and the frost has *almost seemed to be unusual* (sic) inasmuch as several of the enemy as well as of our own people have been frozen to death sometimes, or have lost parts of their hands, and feet and noses. Nevertheless, for all that, this winter has been a *merry* (sic) winter too. For although some have been unlucky, inasmuch as the sharp cold has damaged them, nevertheless we have always managed to find a little *pastime.*" The pastime alluded to is the skirmishing with the enemy.—*Egenh. Bref*, No. 71.

cient compensation that they were able now and then to have some lively skirmishes by way of diversion; but, though a long experience of war had had the natural effect of making him somewhat callous, there is no reason to exclaim against him as altogether heartless. A thorough soldier himself, he naturally regarded warfare entirely from a warrior's point of view. He knew that the profession of arms was as grim as it was glorious; but he argued, not unreasonably, that a man enters it with his eyes open, and that a true soldier is in duty bound to cheerfully take the rough with the smooth in the trade of his own choosing. He himself in this respect always set the example. Throughout the awful winter of 1708–9 he took more than his fair share of fatigue and hardship with perfect equanimity, exacting nothing from his soldiers that he did not cheerfully undergo himself, and it is a fact that his soldiers regarded him more as a comrade than as a master. Then, too, as a prudent general ought to do, he minimised difficulties as much as possible, making light of what could not be altered or denied. On one occasion he was accosted by a soldier who held out to him a piece of black bread almost as hard as a stone, exclaiming: "That, your Majesty, is what we have to eat!" Charles at once took the bread, broke off a bit, chewed and swallowed it, and then said: "It is not very good to eat, my lad, but it *can* be eaten." On another occasion he was riding by an ambulance wagon in which lay a young ensign, a relative of Count Piper, who had lost both feet at Hadjach from frost-bite. Charles stopped and asked him how he was. The youth replied that he would never be able to walk again as the greater part of his heels and toes was gone. "Stuff! Stuff!" replied the King, then baring his own leg up to the ankle, he added: "I have seen fellows who have lost their legs up to there, yet when they stuffed them into their jack-boots, they have managed to walk all right." On riding away, however, he said in an undertone to his adjutant: "I'm sorry for him though, poor fellow! he is so very young." Such anecdotes have some-times been given as instances of the young King's * hard-heartedness. I prefer to see in them a rough perhaps, but certainly kind intention to make the best of things, and it is a fact that so long as he was able to mingle with his men, and lead them personally, they endured their torments without a murmur.

All this time Charles was consumed by a restless energy which was rewarded by several successes. Early in January, 1709, the little fortress of Veprik surrendered to the Swedes though not till after they had lost 1000 men beneath its walls. At the end of February Charles suddenly assumed the offensive, and defeated the enemy in two very sharp engage-ments at Oposznaya and Krasnokutsk, on the latter occasion driving ten thousand Russians headlong be-fore him. Then the spring floods put an end to all active operations for a time; the Tsar set off for Voronets on the Don, to inspect his Black Sea fleet, while Charles encamped at Budiszcze, between the Prol and the Worskla, two tributaries of the Don.

---

* He was only 26 at the time.

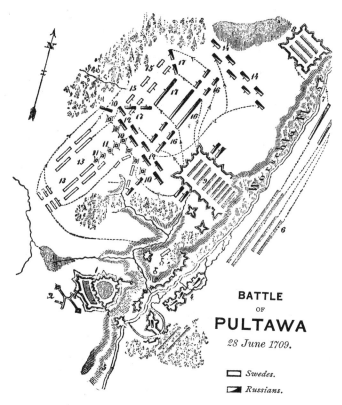

BATTLE

OF

PULTAWA

28 June 1709.

▭ *Swedes.*
◣ *Russians.*

1 Pultawa.   2. Swedish trenches.   3. Swedish strand-batteries.   4. Russian strand-batteries.   5. The spot where Charles was wounded.   6. The Russian army before crossing the river.   7. Place where the Russians crossed on the 17th, entrenching themselves at 8.   9. Entrenched camp which Russians made on June 24th and to which they retired.   10. The trenches the Russians made on the 25th and 26th June.   13. Swedes advance to the first conflict.   14. Russian cavalry driven back in first conflict.   15. Swedes drawn up for the second conflict. 16. Russian army likewise.   17. Russians surround Swedes who subsequently fly past Pultawa southwards.

By this time the situation of the Swedes was not
merely serious but alarming. The army had dwin-
dled down from 41,000 to 20,000, of whom about
18,000 were able-bodied, the loss of superior officers
being particularly ominous.* Supplies were running
so short that it was as much as the men could
do to keep body and soul together. Saltpetre
had now to be used instead of salt, and there
was not sufficient wine left to give the sacrament
to the dying soldiers. All communication with
Central Europe had been cut off by the Russians.
The nearest Swedish army, Krassau's, † was nine
hundred miles away. Once more his officers tried
to persuade Charles to return to Poland, so as
to co-operate with Stanislaus and Krassau, but the
King would not hear of such a thing because "a
march back to the Dnieper would look like a flight
and make the enemy all the bolder." He resolved
instead to march still farther north, lay siege to the
fortress of Pultawa, and there await the reinforcements he had ordered from Poland and Sweden, and
solicited from Turkey and the Tartar Khan. What
his ulterior plans were, it is impossible to say. Some
think he had none at all, others suppose that, after
giving his soldiers a long rest, he intended to make
a second attempt upon Moscow. It was while on
his way to Pultawa that Charles concluded an alliance

---

* To take only one instance, the six adjutant-generals, whom
Charles had appointed on his departure from Saxony, had all perished.

† When Charles quitted Saxony, he left Major-General Ernest
Detlev Krassau with all the Swedish troops remaining in Poland.
Krassau had orders to join the King in the Ukraine if possible, but
was obliged to give up the idea as totally impracticable.

with the Zaporogean Cossacks, who, as their name
implies,* dwelt behind the rapids of the Dneiper,
southwards of the Ukrainian Cossacks, and had been
persuaded by Mazeppa to throw off the Russian
yoke. They now occupied most of the places to the
south of Pultawa, while Charles took up a position to
the north of that fortress. To attack it the Swedes
were much too weak. It was not so much that his
army had notably diminished (his Polish exploits had
been performed with half as many men) as that he
had next to no artillery left, and his powder was not
only running short, but had so deteriorated with repeated wetting as to be almost useless. It is said
that when a shot was fired off it sounded no louder
than the clapping together of a pair of gloves, while
the bullets fell down in the sand scarcely thirty paces
from the mouth of the gun that fired them. There
was such a dearth of bullets too, that the Swedes
were glad to collect, and make use of, the spent balls
of the enemy. And on the other side of the river
Worskla, on which Pultawa is situated, lay the Tsar
with an army four times as numerous as Charles's, so
that he was always able to throw provisions and reinforcements into the town. In May, 1709, the siege
began. Charles did all in his power to encourage
his men. He took up his quarters so close to the
fortress that the walls of his house were literally rid-
dled with bullets. When his engineer officers were
shot down one after the other, he himself gave the
sappers and miners the necessary instructions. Day
by day the situation of the Swedes grew more dis-

---

* *Za*—behind, *porog*—a rapid or waterfall.

tressing. The summer heat was oppressive, and caused most of the wounded to die of gangrene. The narrow district occupied by the Swedes was soon drained dry of food. At last the soldiers had nothing to eat but horseflesh and black bread, and a tin of brandy in the canteens cost from 15/- to £1.5 in silver. And now a fresh misfortune befell the besieging host, a misfortune but for which the culminating catastrophe might never have happened. Hitherto, although Charles had exposed himself to danger with such utter recklessness that many believed he was courting death, he had escaped unhurt, but on the 17th June, his birthday, he received a wound which placed him *hors de combat.* He was riding with Levenhaupt backwards and forwards along the banks of the Worskla, at break of day, within range of the fortress, when a bullet pierced his heel, passing through his foot, and finally lodging inside it, close to the great toe. The wound must have been a painful one, yet Charles did not so much as flinch, but continued riding about as if nothing had happened, though the blood dripped so fast from his boot that his attendants fancied at first that it was his horse that had been struck till the ghastly pallor of the King revealed the truth. Even then he would not return to his quarters till he had given some directions which took him over to the opposite end of the camp ; when he did at last get back his foot was so swollen that the boot had to be cut off. On the foot being examined, it was found that several of the smaller bones had been crushed, and the surgeon hesitated to make the deep and painful incisions

necessary for removing the splinters. "Come,
come," cried Charles impatiently, "slash away, slash
away!—it won't damage me!" and, firmly grasping
his leg, he watched the operation through, without
giving the slightest sign that he felt any pain. Nay,
more, when, subsequently the lips of the wound
swelled up, and the surgeons shrunk from cutting
away the inflamed and exquisitely sensitive parts,
advising instead the application of blue-stone, Charles
asked for a pair of scissors, and coolly removed the
affected parts himself. At first it was feared that
gangrene would set in, and the King might lose his
leg, especially as he obstinately refused for a long
time to take drugs, but fortunately he was prevailed
upon at last to swallow a sudorific, and the leg was
saved. For all fighting purposes, however, Charles
was now completely useless.

And it was just at this very time that his guidance
was most wanted. Hitherto Peter, though he could
oppose 80,000 to Charles's 18,000, had been careful
to avoid every manœuvre which might lead to a general engagement; but on hearing that Charles was
hors de combat, he immediately changed his tactics,
and threw the greater part of his forces across the
Worskla (June 19th–23d), though even now he was so
diffident of himself and his troops in the presence of
his great adversary, that he took the precaution to
strongly entrench his camp. On the 24th June he
moved into a still stronger intrenched camp, closer
to Pultawa, and on the 26th and 27th constructed a
line of small field batteries, extending between the
Swedish camp and his own. He evidently regarded

mere numbers as an insufficient safeguard against
the ragged veterans who had defeated him at
Holowczyn and Krasnokutsk. Meanwhile Marshal
Rehnskjöld, who had taken over the supreme command of the Swedish army, held a council of war at
which it was resolved to attack the Russians in their
batteries and intrenched camp. Levenhaupt proposed that the useless siege of Pultawa should be
raised, so that every available soldier might be sent
to the front, but this Charles would not hear of, so
2000 of his best troops were absolutely wasted upon
observing the fortress. Add to this that 2400 more
had to be told off to guard the baggage, while 1200
more were posted on the southern bank of the Worskla to prevent those of the Russians who had not
yet crossed, from taking the Swedes in flank, and it
will be seen that, not including the Zaporogean
guerillas, who numbered about 6000, Rehnskjöld had
barely 13,000 men at his disposal, and with these
13,000 he proposed to attack 80,000 men in a
strongly intrenched camp! The council of war
was held on the 26th June, and on the following
day, Sunday, after evening prayers, all the generals
were summoned to the King's bedside, and here the
plan for the morrow's attack was definitely arranged.
Then Charles had his wounded foot freshly band-
aged, and drawing his spurred boot on the other, and
taking his sword in his hand, he had himself borne
in a litter through the ranks to the front, and finally
took up his position amidst the guards, surrounded by
Rehnskjöld, Piper, Levenhaupt, and the other generals, who, wrapped in their mantles, lay or sat near

the King's litter. Immediately after midnight
Rehnskjöld gave the order to break up, and advance
nearer to the enemy's lines, and at dawn of day the
Swedes saw the Russian bastions straight in front
of them. The Swedish cavalry on the left wing was
commanded by General Creutz, and here the King
and Rehnskjöld were posted; the centre, consisting
of the infantry, was led by Levenhaupt, the cavalry
on the right wing by Schlippenbach, while Axel
Sparre and Carl Gustaf Roos were sent on in front
to clear the way by capturing the enemy's line of
field batteries. The Swedes, who had few cannons
and wretched powder, reckoned chiefly on their
swords; and at first things went well enough.
Sparre captured the field batteries on the left by a
gallant dash, and put the garrisons to the sword, and
had Roos only been properly supported till he had
captured the batteries on the right, the guns of all
the Russian batteries could have been turned against
the Russian intrenched camp, and, under cover of
the fire, the whole Swedish army might have made
a combined attack in perfect order. Unfortunately
Piper, who had followed the king, advised "striking
while the iron was hot," by making Creutz follow up
the advantage gained by Sparre, and the consequence
was that the whole of the cavalry on the left wing
advanced and scattered the Russian cavalry which
stood behind the captured-batteries, but at the same
time left General Roos, whose duty it was to capture
the batteries on the right, entirely unsupported.
The Tsar perceived the blunder, and at once sent
Menshikov with 10,000 Russians to cut off Roos

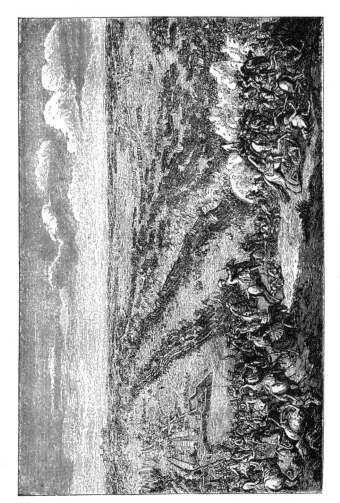

THE BATTLE OF PULTAWA.

FROM AN OLD PRINT.

who had already been thrice repulsed from the batteries in front of him, and was now completely
surrounded and ultimately compelled to surrender
after making an heroic resistance. Nevertheless the
issue of the battle was still doubtful, for Levenhaupt
with his infantry, although altogether without artillery, had captured two of the batteries in his way,
and was preparing to storm the southern side of the
enemy's intrenched camp, where it was weakest, at
the point of the bayonet, when he received an order
to halt. To this day it is not known who gave this
order, but circumstances seem to point to the King
as responsible for it, for when Rehnskjöld, astonished
and indignant that Levenhaupt should have stopped
short at the very moment when victory seemed
within his grasp, came rushing up and accused him
of not acting as " a loyal servant of the King," Levenhaupt replied that he was only obeying orders, and
at that moment Charles himself was borne to the
spot in his litter.   Then Rehnskjöld, turning towards
the King, exclaimed : " Is it your Majesty who ordered
Levenhaupt to halt in front of the foe?"   Charles
coloured up and answered, " No!" but in such a way
as to make most of those present believe that he
really had given the order. So at any rate Rehnskjöld took it, and he made no secret of his indignation. "Yes, sir," cried he, "that's what you are
always doing! I am never allowed to do what I
would. For God's sake, sir, leave me to manage."
Charles took the rebuke in perfect silence, and the
whole Swedish army was re-formed in front of the
hostile camp, which it was now to storm. But the

favourable moment had gone. Peter, after the first successes of Creutz and Sparre, had been on the point of flying, but on perceiving the ridiculous numerical inferiority of the foe, his courage revived and he brought up every available man and gun to the front for the final struggle. The Russian infantry numbered 40,000 men supported by 100 cannon, the Swedes had only 4000 infantry, exhausted by hunger and fatigue, with bad powder, no artillery, nay, not even cavalry to support them, for, to Levenhaupt's amazement, Rehnskjöld now posted his cavalry *behind* the infantry. Throughout the earlier part of the struggle Charles, sword in hand, had been carried through the lines, and done his utmost to encourage his men, utterly regardless of the rain of bullets that fell thickly around him. During the interval between the two engagements Charles rested a little, drank a glass of water, and had his foot re-bandaged, after which he was again carried to the front. And now the signal to attack was given, and the heroic 4000 rushed into certain death. The Russian fire was so terrible that before the Swedes could reach the intrenched camp, half their number already lay bleeding on the ground. With despair in their hearts, the remainder of the gallant little band rushed forward, and literally disappeared among the myriads of Russians who engulfed and overwhelmed them. Yet they sold their lives dearly, the guard in particular fighting with its usual doggedness, though it lost all its officers in a few moments. Charles, to encourage his "blue boys," had had himself carried into fire, but the litter on which he lay was now smashed by a cannon-ball, he fell heavily to the ground, and twenty-one out of his twenty-four bearers were shot dead by his side. "My lads," cried Rehn-skjöld, who perceived that all was now lost, "save the King!" then he himself plunged into the thickest of the fight, and was shortly afterwards made a prisoner. Charles himself meanwhile was in the most imminent danger; indeed he owed his life entirely to the devotion of a Major Wolffelt, who lifted him on to his own horse, and was immediately afterwards cut to pieces by the Cossacks. On this horse the King continued to ride about, with his wounded foot, which bled profusely, resting on the animal's neck. Presently he fell in with Levenhaupt. "What are we to do now?" enquired the King. "There is nothing for it but to try and collect the remains of our people in camp," replied the general. This they accordingly did, and the same evening what remained of the Swedish army quitted the field, the cavalry, which had suffered comparatively little, covering the retreat.

The Russians are said to have lost 1300 men at Pultawa, the Swedes 3000 killed and 2000 prisoners, among whom were one field-marshal, four major-generals, and five colonels. Count Piper, who had followed the King all day, and was separated from him in the final *melée*, made his way up to the gates of Pultawa, and there voluntarily surrendered. Peter had fully expected to capture the Swedish King also. "Where is my brother Charles?" he asked repeat-edly. He received the Swedish officers with respect and courtesy, but he asked Marshal Rehnskjöld how he had dared to invade a great Empire like the Russian with a mere handful of men. Rehnskjöld replied that the King had commanded it, and it was his first duty as a loyal subject to obey his Sovereign. "You are an honest fellow," replied the Tsar, "and for your loyalty I return you your sword."

Meanwhile, with banners flying and music playing, the Swedes had quitted Pultawa, and two days later reached Perewoloczna, an insignificant place on the Dnieper, situated on a narrow neck of land enclosed on three sides by that river and its confluents. Here Charles, who was utterly exhausted by pain and fatigue, was persuaded, though only by the most urgent entreaties,* to cross the Dnieper with some 1500 cavalry, including Gyllenkrook, Mazeppa, and Secretary Müllern, and take refuge in Turkish territory, leaving Levenhaupt in command of the thoroughly cowed and demoralised mob that only twelve months before had been the finest army in Europe. Two days later Levenhaupt surrendered with the whole of his army (nearly 14,000 men) to the Russian general, Menshikov, who had in the meanwhile reached Perewoloczna, and effectively closed every loophole of retreat. Under the circumstances it was the best, or rather the only thing the unfortunate general could do, but Charles XII. never forgave him for it. Thus Peter had triumphed at last. "The foundations of St. Petersburg are now firm and immovable!" he exclaimed when the struggle was over.

---

* Levenhaupt and Gyllenkrook went down on their knees before him, and besought him with tears in their eyes, to escape while there was yet time. Charles took with him his silver plate, and most of the treasure he had collected in Saxony.

CHAPTER X.

THE TURKISH EXILE.

1709–1715.

The flight to Oczakow—At Bender—Charles's serene optimism—
Death of his sister Hedwig Sophia—Pathetic references to her
loss in his correspondence—Hospitable reception of the Swedes
at Bender—Charles's mode of life there—The Turks' opinion of
Charles—His prodigality—Russia and Turkey—Charles's nego-
tiations with the Porte—Mehemet Baltadji Vizier—Outbreak of
the Russo-Turkish War—Peter in Moldavia—He is surrounded
and cut off from Russia by the Grand Vizier—His critical posi-
tion—Peace of the Pruth—Indignation of Charles—Fall of
Mehemet Baltadji—War declared against Russia a second time—
Counter intrigues of the Peace Party—Fall of the Vizier Jussuf
Pasha—War declared against Russia a third time—Grudzinski's
Polish raid—Charles requested to quit Turkey—He refuses—
The *Kalibalik* of Bender—Charles at Timurtash—Effect of the
Kalibalik on European opinion—Peace of Adrianople—Charles
at Demotika—His departure from Turkey.

FTER leaving the remains of his army
at Perewoloczna, Charles crossed the
Turkish border, hastening through
the steppes towards the fortress of
Oczakow on the Euxine. The little
army suffered much from the intense
heat and still more from hunger.
The Zaporogeans lived on the flesh of the horses
which they stole at night from their Swedish com-

rades, while the Swedes starved on black bread and wild cherries, and the King and his officers had nothing better than a little gruel and an occasional partridge, half-roasted on fires of dried horse-dung and grass. At Oczakow the Pasha detained them on the opposite bank of the Bug, while he haggled over the price of the boats which were to carry them across, insisting on the extortionate price of 16 ducats a head, till the King, growing impatient, commanded his men to seize the boats by force. The delay caused thereby cost Charles 800 men, for it enabled the Russians to overtake the Swedish rear-guard, and cut them off to a man: sick, famished, and utterly exhausted, the remaining 500 made the best of their way to Bender on the Dniester, the most important Turkish fortress in those parts.

It was at Bender, most probably, that Charles first learnt the death of his favourite sister, Hedwig Sophia, Duchess of Holstein, a calamity which, for the time, completely overcame him. Hitherto he had shown himself insensible to suffering and quite indifferent to misfortune. Throughout the long and weary retreat from Pultawa to Bender he had been imperturbably serene, and he playfully alluded to the intensely painful wound which crippled him for months to come, as a little "*faveur* in the foot." His sublime self-confidence made light of even such catastrophes as Pultawa and Perewoloczna, which, to friends and foes alike, seemed to be the beginning of the end. "Everything has gone well," he wrote home on reaching Bender. "Only towards the last, owing to a particular circumstance, the army had

HEDWIG SOPHIA, DUCHESS OF HOLSTEIN.

CHARLES XII'S SISTER.

FROM AN OLD PRINT.

the misfortune to suffer a loss, which will be righted
again in a short time, I hope."* In a subsequent
letter, twelve months later, he adds: "The difficulties which Sweden has now been in for some little
time will shortly, I hope, with God's help and
favour, completely disappear, if they in Sweden
only remain stout-hearted to the end." -Farther
than this optimism could not go. But when the
news of his favourite sister's death was broken to
him at last, † his stoicism gave way and he wept
like a child. "O my sister, my sister!" he exclaimed, and for many days afterwards he would
ride a little way apart from his soldiers, with his
mantle wrapped around his head to conceal his
agitation and his tears. Very pathetic are his
references to this, the one great grief of his life,
in his correspondence with his surviving sister, the
Princess Ulrica; one would scarcely have credited
the saturnine young hero with so much feeling.
Thus he writes to her from Bender, on June 12,
1709: "I must confess that since all my hope‡ in
this matter has gone . . . I have been so cast
down that it has been hard for me to write about,
or even mention, this grief which will never leave
me till those who are now parted shall meet together again. My only remaining wish is that our
Lord may uphold, comfort and preserve my heart's

---

* *Egenh. Bref*, No. 72.

† The account of her death reached the camp at Pultawa shortly
after Charles had been wounded. The tidings was kept from him
lest it should make him worse.

‡ He had refused to believe the truth of the report at first.

13

sister on whom all my hopes now hang." And again, more than eighteen months after the event: " My only hope is that my own heart's sister is well. May our Lord preserve her in good health, and give me, one day, the happiness of seeing my dear sister once more. This is now my only consolation since I have gone through the affliction which I never thought I should survive. But I would have cheerfully endured all things, if only I could have had the joy of being the first of us three to complete the allotted span. At any rate, I hope I shall not be so unfortunate as to be the last of us, but hope and trust that our Lord may allow me to be the next to go. It is my due by nature as being the eldest, so I trust my own heart's sister will not take it ill of me to wish as much." * His wish was gratified ; his younger sister both survived and succeeded him.

At Bender the Swedes rested at last from their long and painful journey, and enjoyed a comfort and luxury that they had not known for many years. Charles himself was received with every demonstration of respect and honour. The presence on Turkish soil of the most formidable antagonist of Turkey's mortal foe, Russia, was not displeasing to the Porte, and secret orders to treat the royal guest right royally seem to have been sent to the Seraskier of Bender, Jussuf Pasha, and the Tartar Khan, Devlet Gerai, who was also staying there at the time. And the wishes of the Khan and the Seraskier coincided with the commands of the Padishah. Both of them hated the Tsar, and both had a pro-

* *Egenh. Bref*, No. 76.

found admiration for the King of Sweden. Splendid
indeed was the hospitality which Charles now enjoyed. Sumptuous pavilions were provided for the
Swedes on their arrival, the King and his soldiers
were escorted to the town with great pomp and ceremony, and at the gate Jussuf presented to Charles
the keys of the fortress, on his knees. During the
summer the Swedes dwelt in tents near the Dneister,
but on the approach of winter the Turks built huts
and houses for them, while Charles ultimately erected
for himself a large stone mansion, the walls of which
were made several feet thick, so that it might serve
as a fortress in case of need. Here he lived, with a
court, a chancellery, a Janissary guard of honour, and
all the appurtenances of royalty. Everything was
conducted with military order and precision, even to
divine service, which, held every morning and evening and thrice on Sundays, was duly announced from
the royal balcony by a flourish of trumpets. Charles
spent his time in reviewing and exercising his little
army, transacting current business, playing chess,
reading or listening to French tragedies (especially
those of Corneille) and mediæval romances of chivalry, and taking long and violent rides in the neigh-
bourhood, generally exhausting a couple of horses a
day. At night he very often had fits of sleepless-
ness, and would then pay visits upon his officers and
secretaries, and sit talking by their bedsides for hours.
He gave them of his money without stint, but would
never come to their banquets, contenting himself
with looking through the windows at them when the
mirth was growing fast and furious. At other times

he would explore their rooms during their absence, ransack their drawers, and throw behind the fire all lace collars, embroidered vests and other frippery which did not correspond with his idea of soldierly simplicity in dress. On red-heeled shoes and slippers and fancy leather boots in particular he waged a relentless war. And here it should be remarked that the men Charles had about him at Bender were for the most part of subaltern rank or servile character, honest, devoted, laborious and loyal no doubt, but obsequious, reckless or unprincipled, obeying implicitly orders they frequently knew to be mischievous, and never venturing to injure their own prospects by giving unpalatable advice. After the capture of Gyllenkrook by the Russians while reconnoitring in southern Poland, and the death of Mazeppa (March 18, 1710), who was buried in the monastery of St. George at Galatz,* the only person of any real eminence, both as to dignity and character, was the Polish refugee Stanislaus Poniatowski, whose courage, address, brilliant gifts, large experience and *savoir faire* were chiefly employed on diplomatic missions to Stambul where, as we shall see, he rendered Charles some signal services. Of Charles's remaining satellites a few may be briefly mentioned. Hermelin's † successor as secretary and chief of the Chancellery was Von Müllern, a learned and industrious man, but with little will of his own and no political influence to speak of. The

---

* His tomb was rifled by the Tartars a few months later, and his bones scattered on the banks of the Danube.

† He had been captured at Pultawa.

most considerable among the surviving warriors were
Axel Sparre, valiant almost to foolhardiness, always
merry and occasionally tipsy, and Colonel Grothusen,
an extravagant *bon vivant*, who presided over the
household and threw away his master's money as if
it were dirt, though it is fair to add that he kept
none of it for himself. He was moreover a very
brave soldier, and his loyalty and devotion were
above suspicion. Finally, in the summer of 1710,
Charles was joined at Bender by the Holstein Minister Baron Ernest Fredrik de Fabrice, who remained
with him during the whole of his remaining stay in
Turkey, and was of great service by keeping the
King in diplomatic touch with his friends and allies
on the Continent.

To the Turks round about, Charles was an object
of the deepest interest. The rumour of his exploits
had spread throughout the Ottoman Empire, and
thousands of inquisitive Mussulmans flocked every
day to Bender to gaze upon the Northern Paladin.
They were much impressed by the calm courage with
which he endured his reverses, and quite delighted
with the truly Oriental prodigality with which he
scattered his ducats among them. But when it was
observed that neither wine nor women had the
slightest charm or temptation for the young hero,
that, although a King, he despised all pomp and
splendour, and that no orthodox Mussulman could
be more scrupulously regular in his devotions, the
admiration of the Turks became something like veneration and worship, and they began to regard Charles
as an almost supernatural being, above and beyond

the ordinary infirmities of humanity. " If only Allah
would give us such a ruler," many of them were
heard to say, " we should conquer the whole world."

Charles's expenses during his residence in Turkey
were very considerable. In his adversity he considered it a point of honour to maintain a far grander
household than he had ever had in prosperity, and,
unlike his father, he was a very bad manager and
never understood the value of money. The Jews,
Armenians and Wallachs, who supplied his camp
with provisions, made large fortunes out of him ; but
when his Turkish friends advised him to examine his
accounts, as he was being charged at least 50 per cent.
above the market value of the wares supplied, he
only laughed contemptuously as if it were beneath
the dignity of a Prince to descend to such petty
huckstering. Many of his own servants also helped
to fleece him, though others again, it is fair to add,
ruined themselves by contracting loans for their
master which were never repaid. No wonder then
if the King of Sweden speedily ran through the large
amount of treasure which had been saved from the
wreck of Pultawa ; when it had gone he was content
to live upon the bounty of the Sultan. And Achmed
III. certainly extended a magnificent hospitality to
his uninvited guest. To say nothing of frequent and
costly gifts of carriages, horses and arms, the Porte
allowed Charles for his maintenance from £125 to
£150 a day, and the Swedish and Polish refugees who
flocked to the Danubian provinces during Charles's
stay there also richly enjoyed the Imperial largesse.
Indeed, so great at last did their numbers grow, that

they became not only a burden, but even a danger to the Turkish Empire.

Since the publication of Charles's correspondence two years ago, it has become pretty plain that he had no intention, as has so often been imagined, of making a prolonged stay * in Turkey. It is highly probable that he meant to depart as soon as his wound (which again became very dangerous during the earlier part of his residence at Bender) had healed, and he was able to mount his horse again. He comforts his sister and his anxious friends at home by repeated assurances that he will speedily come nearer to the frontier, and bids them keep a stout heart in the meantime. In September, 1709, he was able to ride again, but by the end of the same year he had come to the conclusion that he could serve his country much better by staying where he was than by returning to her at once as originally intended. And certainly during the course of 1710 the clouds that had obscured his star lifted a little; Fortune seemed inclined to befriend him once more; and an extraordinary series of favourable circumstances seemed to place his great antagonist Peter absolutely at his mercy.

Charles's saving opportunity was the outbreak of the Russo-Turkish War, of which he was not only the predisposing cause, but the actual promoter. Ever since the conclusion of the thirty years' truce of Constantinople (3d July, 1700) whereby the Porte had ceded Azov to Russia, the attitude of the two Empires towards each other had been one of watch-

* *Egenh. Bref*, Nos. 74, 75 and 76.

ful suspicion : another war between them was inevitable, but each shrank from striking the first blow.
The Russians in Azov were as much of a menace to
Stambul as the Russians in St. Petersburg were to
Stockholm ; both the Turkish army and the Turkish
capital were eager for a war of revenge ; and at the
outbreak of the Great Northern war Peter trembled
lest Charles XII. and Achmed III. should join hands
against him.   There is indeed no more striking proof
of Charles's recklessness than his utter neglect of
such a powerful contingent ally as Turkey.   It was
only after the collapse of Pultawa, when he was
already a fugitive on his way to Oczakow, that he
proposed through Captain Thomas Funck, his envoy
at Constantinople, a Swedo-Turkish alliance against
the Tsar.   The Divan was inclined to listen to the
proposal ; but the Grand Vizier was in the pay * of
the Russian Ambassador, Count Tolstoy, who played
his cards so well that, as late as November, 1709, an
agreement was entered into between Russia and the
Porte, whereby Charles, whose presence in Turkey
seriously disturbed Peter, was to be escorted to the
Turkish frontier by Turkish troops, and from thence,
by Russian troops, to the Swedish frontier.   Behind
this open agreement there appears to have been a
secret conspiracy on the part of Michael Rakovitsa,
Prince of Moldavia, (unknown to the Porte) to hand
Charles over to his enemies ; but the King heard of
it in time, and skilfully used it as a means of inciting
Turkey anew against Russia.   Funck was reinforced
by two fresh envoys, Martin von Neugebauer, and

---

* It is said that he received 40,000 ducats a month from Russia.

the Pole Poniatowski; Charles himself wrote a letter
to the Sultan, accusing the Grand Vizier of treachery
and corruption ; and this letter, translated into Turkish through the agency of the French Ambassador
at Stambul, was delivered to Achmed III. while on
his way to the Mosque of Sophia. The result was
the fall of the Grand Vizier (June, 1710) who
was succeeded by Numan Köprili generally supposed to be devoted to Charles's interests ; but,
proving lukewarm, he also was overthrown in a few
months' time through the skilful intrigues of Poniatowski * supported by the war party in the Divan
headed by the Tartar Khan,† and a third vizier, Mehemet Baltadji, was appointed for the express purpose of declaring war against Russia. The ultimatum
of the Porte demanded the surrender of Azov, the
evacuation of Poland and the restitution of all the
provinces captured from Sweden. Peter returned a
defiant reply, whereupon war against him was formally declared (November 20, 1710) and Count Tolstoy was thrown into the Seven Towers. A few
months later hostilities actually began. At the commencement of 1711 the Tartar hordes ravaged the
Ukraine and South Russia with fire and sword as far
as Kharkov, but failed to take the fortress of Voro-

---

* He exhibited documents he had got by bribery from a high official
at Moscow, showing that the Tsar had serious designs upon the Crimea.

† Devlet Gherai was for a long time a particular friend of Charles's,
who thus describes him to his sister : " He is a little old man, whose
beard is already touched with grey, but sprightly withal, and very
talkative, and well informed. As a rule there are very few Turks or
Tartars who know of anything outside their own land."—*Egenh.*
Bref, No. 74.

nets, while the Grand Vizier set out for the frontier
at the head of 100,000 Turks and Tartars, confidently
declaring that he would carve a way home for the
King of Sweden in whichever direction he liked best.
But Peter was equally confident. So confident
indeed was he that he left the best and largest portions of his troops at home, resolved to trust rather
to the ambiguous promises of notoriously corrupt
and fickle allies. These were Constantine Brancovanu, Hospodar of Wallachia, and Demetrius
Cantemir, Hospodar of Moldavia, who had long been
chafing beneath the suzerainty of the Sultan and
were anxious to strengthen their unstable thrones by
making them hereditary. Brancovanu offered to
provision the Russian army during its stay in the
Danubian provinces, and place 30,000 men at the
Tsar's disposal, while Cantemir concluded a definite
alliance with Peter at Jaroslaw, 13th April, 1711.*
Accordingly a Russian army under Krapotkin appeared at Jassy, at the beginning of June, to support
the Moldavians, while Sheremetev, with the main
army, estimated at some 60,000 men, arrived almost
simultaneously at Çuçora on the Pruth where Peter
joined it towards the end of the same month. At
Jassy, the capital of Moldavia, he was received with
imperial pomp, regaled by the Hospodar at a
grand banquet, when the Russians tasted absinthe
and the wine of Cotnar for the first time,† and

---

* I here follow the Roumanian Chronicles published by Kogalni-
ceanu.

† Peter returned the compliment by making his guests drunk at
another banquet when he introduced them to the wines of France.

the Metropolitan of Moldavia celebrated the anniversary of the victory of Pultawa by singing a
Te Deum in the cathedral.   These festivities and
rejoicings proved a trifle premature.   While the
Russians and Moldavians were carousing together,
the Grand Vizier, Mehemet Baltadji, with an army
of at least 200,000 men, was advancing rapidly to the
Pruth, with a plan of campaign, drawn up by Charles
XII.'s own hand, in his pocket.   The Turks had
been anxious to treat at first through the mediation
of the Hospodar of Wallachia : but Peter refused to
listen to them, and, in an access of arrogance, even
detached a division of his army to seize Braila
one of the fortresses of Brancovanu.   That Prince,
already incensed by Peter's masterful tone, was now
completely alienated, and not only withheld the
promised provisions, but went over to the Grand
Vizier with all his forces.   The consequences of this
defection were very soon apparent in the Russian
camp.   A want which soon rose to the intensity of
famine began to be felt there, and the Turks, informed by their spies of the existing state of things,
pressed the Muscovites more and more.   By the 9th
July, Peter, who now lay between Husi and Stân-
derci on the Pruth, was completely cut off from his
own land, and at night the Russians could see the
camp fires of the Turks and Tartars sparkling among
the low-lying hills on both sides of the Pruth, as far
as the eye could reach.   The Tsar would have run
away if he could and left his army to shift for itself,
as he had done at Narva, and meant to do at Pultawa, but John Neculec, the Moldavian general,

whom he privately consulted on the subject, would not at any price take the responsibility of saddling himself with so illustrious a fugitive. Peter now frankly confessed that he had made the same mistake as his brother Charles, the mistake of venturing too far into an enemy's country. He had set out with the intention of marching upon Constantinople across the Danube and the Balkans, but it now seemed more than probable that if he ever saw that city at all it would be as a captive in the train of the triumphant Grand Vizier. The fruits of twenty years of incessant toil seemed about to be dissipated by a single blunder, for it is certain that had Mehemet Baltadji, with his five-fold odds, now attacked the Tsar, the doom of the Russians would have been sealed. So desperate indeed did the position of the Russian army seem to its own commander-in-chief, Sheremetev, that when Peter proposed to send an envoy to the Vizier with a bribe and an offer of peace, his general bluntly remarked that only a madman would think of making, and only a madder than mad would think of listening to, such an offer. Nevertheless at the instigation of the Tsarina Catherine, as some say, Peter sent the diplomatist Shafirov to the Grand Vizier with an offer of peace, proposing to surrender Azov, dismantle Taganrog, restore Livonia and Esthonia to Sweden, allow Charles to return to his own kingdom unmolested, and cease interfering with Polish affairs. The conqueror of Pultawa must indeed have been in evil case to offer such humiliating terms, which ought, moreover, to have opened the Grand Vizier's eyes to the fact that the arch-enemy of Islam was absolutely in his power. But Mehemet Baltadji was no hero; his distrust of his own troops was only equalled by his respect for the Russians, and the sight of the wagon-loads of money that Peter sent into the Turkish camp was too much for his cupidity. So he opened his hand, and let his prey escape, for by the Peace of the Pruth, July 11, 1711, Baltadji accepted Peter's terms, and the famished Russians were supplied with food and permitted to return to their own country.

A couple of hours before the Russian army broke up, Charles XII. himself suddenly arrived on the banks of the Pruth. He had been informed by Poniatowski (who was with the Grand Vizier's army) of the desperate position of Peter, and riding night and day he hastened to the spot in order to see that the *coup-de-grâce* was properly administered. Instead of that he received from a couple of Pashas who had been sent to meet him, the unwelcome news that peace had been concluded. Without saying a word, he made straight for the pavilion of the Grand Vizier (whom he passed on his way without saluting) and, arriving there, flung himself down on a divan close beside the sacred green banner of the Prophet. Mehemet Baltadji hastened after him with his suite, and sat down on another divan opposite to the King. Charles opened the conversation by insisting that everyone present should withdraw, whereupon he said: "You have a fine army assembled here!" "It is God's gift," replied the Vizier meekly. "Then it is a pity you did not make a better use of it," continued Charles, and with that he reproached Baltadji for disobeying his master, and neglecting his (Charles's) interests. The Vizier began to feebly defend himself on moral and religious grounds, but Charles interrupted him by rising and exclaiming : "There is still time to make good your fault. Give me *carte blanche.* I will be personally responsible to the Sultan for everything that occurs, and it shall not cost you a single man, for I know well enough where to find people to follow me." " No," replied the Vizier, " 't is now too late, and I must abide by the peace I have signed." He then arose under the pretext of consulting the Tartar Khan, and early next morning Charles returned to Bender. From that moment the King and the Grand Vizier became mortal foes and each did his utmost to rid himself of the other. Immediately after the Peace of the Pruth was signed, Baltadji sent Charles 300 horses, 900 wagons and an escort of 6000 men, to enable him to depart at once, and on his refusing to stir, deprived him of his Janissary Guard of Honour, stopped his daily allowance, forbade the country folk to supply him with provisions and intercepted his correspondence. Charles retaliated with energy and effect. He informed the Sultan through his envoys, Celsing and Funck, of the treachery and corruption of the Grand Vizier ; and the delay of Peter to fulfil the conditions of the peace by surrendering Azov, and withdrawing his troops from Poland, enabled the War Party in the Divan, assisted by the French Ambassador, to gain the upper hand once more. On November 10, 1711, Mehemet Baltadji was deposed, and banished

to the Isle of Lemnos, and the Janissary Aga,
Jussuf Pasha, was appointed Grand Vizier in his
stead. Shortly afterwards war was declared
against Russia a second time. Charles now sent
Poniatowski again to Stambul, to act in concert
with his ordinary envoy, and the French Ambassador the Marquis des Alleurs. The English and
Dutch Ministers at Constantinople had protested
against the breach of the Peace of the Pruth, fearing
that a new war might re-act prejudicially on their
interests in the West, and they laboured energetically, and not unsuccessfully, to persuade the Porte
that Charles was now a useless and mischievous ally
who should be sent about his business as soon as
possible. Nay, they even gained over the Grand
Vizier, and the Peace of the Pruth was actually confirmed (April 16, 1712). The Sultan himself now
wrote an autograph letter to Charles, advising him to
depart, and offering to place either an army-corps
or a fleet at his disposal for the purpose, while
Poniatowski advised compliance, and pointed out
the danger of resistance. But Charles remained immovable. He thanked the Sultan indeed for his
courtesy, but reminded him at the same time of a
former promise to assist him to recover his lost
provinces, and demanded a larger escort and 600,000
rix dollars (£13,500) for travelling expenses. At the
same time he instructed his envoy Funck to use all
possible means to bring about the overthrow of the
new Grand Vizier, "insinuating in the Seraglio, by
secret ways, that the Sultan's own person is in constant danger and insecurity so long as this Grand

Vizier is suffered and upheld at Court."* Funck
was also materially assisted by the French Ambassador who incessantly reminded the Porte that the
Tsar still withheld Azov and occupied Poland and
finally (November 1, 1712) Jussuf Pasha was also overthrown; Soliman Pasha succeeded him as Grand
Vizier, and war was declared against Russia for the
third time.

Meanwhile Charles himself was improving the
opportunity by himself waging war on a small scale.
In May, 1712, Magnus Stenbock had landed in Pomerania † with the last army that the utterly depleted
Swedish State could bring together, and Charles sent
all the refugees about him, under Grudzinski, into
Poland to join hands and co-operate with Stenbock.
At first Grudzinski's success was astonishing. He
penetrated into the very heart of the Republic, and
his little band of adventurers soon swelled into a
conquering host of 15,000 men; but neither Stenbock nor Stanislaus could render him any assistance,
and he was finally surrounded by the combined
Polish, Saxon and Russian forces under Sienia-
wiecki and utterly routed at Posen. Those of his
followers who escaped returned to the Danubian
Principalities, where they soon became a menace to
public order, levying contributions and maltreating
the inhabitants who bitterly complained to the
Porte through their Hospodars, and at last a fulmi-

---

* See *Egenh. Bref*, No. 274. See also Nos. 272, 273 and 275-8,
which contain the despatches drawn up or dictated by Charles XII. to
his envoys at Stambul from 1711-1713

† See following chapter for details.

nating decree came from Stambul ordering them to be driven out of the country, or massacred *en masse.* Charles was not responsible for the excesses of his followers, and did all that he could to prevent them, but so long as he remained at Bender, Polish and Swedish refugees continued to flock to Moldavia, and the local authorities hesitated to take stringent measures against them for fear of provoking a Prince who had already overthrown five Grand Viziers. But the Sultan himself was now growing tired of his troublesome guest, especially when matters were still further complicated by the sudden arrival of the fugitive King Stanislaus at Jassy, * and at last he was driven to take vigorous measures to rid himself of Charles, although up to the very last he strove to avoid extremities. In December, 1712, 10,000 Turks and Tartars were collected round Bender, under the Tartar Khan and the Seraskier, to escort Charles home through Poland (a free pass having previously been obtained for him from Augustus): £10,000 were to be handed to him at the moment of his departure, but not before, lest he should use the money for bribing purposes. Nevertheless Grothusen succeeded in wheedling this money out of the Seraskier by giving a solemn promise, unknown to Charles, that his master should depart immediately afterwards; but Charles spent the money in paying his debts, and then coolly declared that he would not budge till he had received £8,000 more. This fresh demand filled both the Khan and the Pasha of

---

* He had come to beg Charles's permission to abdicate, but Charles would not hear of such a thing.

14

Bender with absolute terror. They had disobeyed
their master by parting with the £10,000, and, as
they now reminded Charles, their own heads would
be in danger if he did not go. But Charles remained
deaf alike to their arguments and entreaties, and
when, at last, the Khan declared that he would be
reluctantly compelled to hasten on the King of
Sweden's departure, Charles replied that he would
never suffer himself and his followers to be driven
away like a herd of cattle, and would meet force by
force. After this the Khan and the Seraskier had
nothing for it but to send a full report of the case to
Stambul. The Sultan was highly incensed. At a
meeting of the Divan at which he himself presided
(a most unusual occurrence) he solemnly declared
that the King of Sweden's conduct was a bad and
ungrateful abuse of hospitality ; that, as he would
not depart as a friend, it was necessary to drive him
away as a foe, and express orders were sent to the
Khan and the Seraskier to seize Charles by force if
he still refused to go, and convey him, alive or dead,
to Adrianople, whither the Sultan himself was about
to proceed. Early in January, 1713, the Sultan's
mandate was brought to Bender by a special Kapuji
Pasha. Charles who was duly informed of the fact
replied that he would not depart for ten Kapuji
Pashas, and at once set about entrenching and pro-
visioning his little camp, the friendly Janissaries
allowing stores and food to be brought in under
their very eyes. His ostensible reason for remaining
was the affected apprehension that the Khan and
the Seraskier meant to deliver him up to his ene-

mies,* his real reason, according to the Holstein
minister Fabrice and his own loyal servant Grothusen (and there is no reason whatever to doubt
their testimony), was the secret but consuming
desire to perform an exploit so extraordinary that
posterity would hardly believe it to be possible. So
during the remainder of January Charles was busy
completing his preparations. To all remonstrances
he was either deaf or rude. When the clergy protested against needless blood-shedding, he bade them
go and preach elsewhere as he meant to fight. When
even his own soldiers implored him not to stain the
honour of the Swedish name by drawing his sword
against friends and benefactors, he roughly replied :
" Hold your tongues and obey orders! " When the
Janissaries, alarmed for his life, entreated him to place
himself in their hands, and they would take care that
not a hair of his head was rumpled, he thanked them
for their good will, but assured them at the same
time that he was well able to take care of himself.
The attack upon the improvised Swedish camp had
been fixed for the 31st January, but when the signal
to advance was given, the Janissaries threw down
their arms, declared the Sultan's letter to be a
forgery, and vowed that nothing should make them
fight against " Iron Head," as they called Charles,
whereupon the whole Turkish army broke up in confusion. But the Seraskier, now seriously alarmed,
took the promptest measures to restore discipline.

---

* Compare his autograph memorandum drawn up in December,
1712, at Bender justifying his conduct (*Egenh. Bref*, No. 276), and
his correspondence with Maurice Vellingk.

Thirty of the mutinous Janissaries were seized, and drowned in the Dniester the same evening. The rest were summoned to the Seraskier's tent; convinced that the Sultan's mandate was genuine, and allowed to make a last attempt to bring the King of Sweden to his senses. On February 1, fifty of them, unarmed, with white staves in their hands and headed by Charles's favourite dragoman, proceeded to the Swedish camp to persuade "Iron Head" to trust himself in their hands, promising in that case to convey him whithersoever he chose to go. But Charles, who had made up his mind for a tussle and was impatient of any further parleyings, refused to see them, and even sent back the insulting message that he would singe their beards if they did not depart instantly. Then even the Janissaries gave him up: "Oh, Iron Head, Allah hath driven thee mad!" they cried as they returned to the Seraskier, convinced at last that force was the only remedy.

And now on February 1, 1713, began that extraordinary struggle which is generally known as the *Kalibalik** of Bender, a struggle only comparable with the extravagant exploits recorded by the mediæval romances of chivalry, for there is certainly nothing else quite like it in sober history. It was on a Sunday, and Charles, who was now ready for anything, was listening to divine service in his house when the sermon was suddenly interrupted by the thunder of cannon and loud cries of "Allah! Allah!" whereupon the Swedes, rushing to the windows, per-

* From two Turkish words meaning the hunting down of difficult game.

ceived the Turks and Tartars charging the camp at full tilt. Charles instantly threw himself on horseback, and, followed by his officers, hastened to drive back the foe, but, to his rage and astonishment, all the Swedish and Polish soldiers, convinced that resistance was hopeless, laid down their arms *en masse* at the first summons. Turning to those about him, some twenty in number, he exclaimed in a loud voice: "All who have still a spark of loyalty in their breasts, follow me!" and cutting his way through the ranks of the Turks, two of whom he killed with his own hand, he regained the threshold of his house. Just as he was dismounting from his horse, a powerful Janissary caught him round the waist to carry him away bodily, while another fired a pistol at him point-blank, which singed off his eyebrows and carried away the tip of his left ear; only with the utmost difficulty did his officers rescue him and drag him indoors by force. They found every room of the house full of Janissaries in search of loot who had already broken open the strong-box containing the King's plate. To drive them out was now Charles's first object, and after mustering in the vestibule his little band (six officers and thirty-four soldiers in all), he bade them fight like brave fellows, and then opening the door of the nearest saloon, rushed in sword in hand. The saloon was crowded with Turks and Tartars, but in a few moments the King and his men had cut down most of them, while the remainder leaped out of the windows. Thence Charles proceeded to the grand saloon where were no less than two hundred Janissaries. A terrific struggle

now ensued. In a few moments the room was so darkened with smoke that the combatants could scarcely
distinguish each other. Charles, at the very outset,
was separated from his followers by three gigantic
Janissaries who attempted to take him alive. Two
of them he immediately ran through the body, the
third aimed a tremendous blow with his scimitar at
the King's head, but Charles parried the blow with
his left hand (losing part of his thumb and forefinger
in the attempt), and felled his antagonist to the
ground with his right. The next instant another
Turk caught him tightly round the body, pinned
him against the wall and called loudly to the others
to help him. But Charles, perceiving Axel Sparre's
cook standing close by with a pistol, beckoned him
with his hand to shoot the Janissary. He did so
forthwith and the King, rejoining his comrades,
succeeded at last in driving all the Turks and Tartars
out of the grand saloon also. Charles's own bedroom
was next cleared. He led the way as usual, and
seeing two Turks, one behind the other, with loaded
pistols in their hands, he rushed upon them furiously,
and spitted the pair of them with his long sword.
A third Turk he dragged from under the bed, and
was about to dispatch him also, when the man threw
away his scimitar, and embracing the King's knees,
begged for mercy. Charles at once spared him, and
after exacting a promise from him that he would tell
the Khan and Pasha what he had seen, helped him
out of the window. By two o'clock in the afternoon
the house was completely cleared, but the floors of
the rooms were strewn with corpses, and Charles him-

self had lost eight of his gallant little band. The
remainder he distributed among the doors and windows, telling them to hold out till four o'clock next
morning, when they would be able to dictate their
own terms besides filling the whole world with amazement at their valour. A determined attempt by the
whole Turkish army to carry the house by storm was
then made, but was repulsed with heavy loss to the
Moslems after three hours' stubborn fighting. Then
the Khan and Pasha, as a last resource, resolved to
burn the besieged out ; arrows and faggots covered
with tar, and ignited, were discharged at the timber
roof, and in a few moments the whole house was in a
blaze. Charles himself clambered on the roof to
help to extinguish the fire, with a hail of bullets rat-
tling about his ears ; but the flames soon gained the
upper hand, and the heat grew so intense that the
King and his followers, with their mantles wrapped
round their heads, had to take refuge in a room on the
ground-floor where Charles, exhausted by fatigue and
parched with thirst, was persuaded to drink a glass
of wine, a beverage he had not tasted for many
years. Presently the roof fell into the top rooms,
and the whole of the upper portion of the house resembled a flaming furnace, yet, to the amazement of
the Turks, the Swedes still remained inside it. "Allah ! Allah ! " they cried, " will Swedish Charles allow
himself and all his men to be consumed ? Or can
they live in the midst of flames like salamanders ? "
And now the roof above the heads of the Swedes
was beginning to burn, and portions of it even fell
into the room where they had taken refuge. Still

Charles refused to budge. When one of his soldiers suggested that it would be better to quit a place that could no longer be defended, and that it was cruel and unjust to allow his men to be burnt to death, he only replied that it was preferable to die where they were than surrender, and at any rate there was no danger till their *"clothes began to burn."* Fortunately Captain Roos suggested that it better became brave men to die sword in hand, face to face with the foe, and he reminded the King that the Chancellery, still unscathed, was only fifty paces off, and that they might manage to force their way into it if they used their weapons properly. " Well said!" cried Charles. " My lads," added he, turning to his soldiers, " let us out and fight 'em, and let us fight till they capture us alive or dead." With that he rushed forth in advance of the others, but the same instant tripped over his spurs, and fell heavily to the ground. Immediately a whole heap of Janissaries threw themselves upon him, wrenched his sword from his hand and made him a prisoner, whereupon all the Swedes at once surrendered. For eight hours Charles with only 40 men had defended his mansion against 12,000 Turks and Tartars with 12 cannons. Two hundred Turks had fallen, 10 of them slain by the King's own hand, while the Swedes had lost only 15 men ; but it should never be forgotten that the Janissaries used unexampled forbearance towards " Iron Head " whom they might easily have killed several times during the day. Had Charles fallen into the hands of the

Tartars, he would, undoubtedly, have been massacred on the spot.

The captive King was conveyed at once to the pavilion of the Seraskier, and on his arrival there gave a handful of ducats to his Janissary escort to drink his health. The Pasha expressed his satisfaction at the King's escape, apologising at the same time for the violent means adopted to capture him. Charles, on the other hand, begged the Pasha to forgive the Swedes for not defending themselves better, " for," added he, " had they all behaved themselves as I and my little band did, the game would have had a very different ending." " The game has been quite severe enough already " returned the Pasha, " for it has cost the Sultan 200 men." Charles himself was a pitiable object. His clothes were ragged and blood-stained, and his face was so covered with dirt, blood and powder, as to be almost unrecognisable ; but he was imperturbably serene as ever ; spoke as calmly as if nothing out of the way had happened, and gazed at the Seraskier with such haughty defiance, that the Turk cast down his eyes in confusion.

The *Kalibalik* naturally caused a sensation throughout Europe, but proved, on the whole, rather prejudicial to Charles than otherwise. There were many indeed, both in Sweden and out of it, who regarded it as the *ne plus ultra* of heroism, and looked up to the young King ever afterwards as a sort of demigod. He was compared indiscriminately to Alcibiades, Alexander, Achilles and Hercules. A

medal was struck representing him as a lion tearing
in pieces a whole herd of Turks and Tartars. Another medal of a more pious type exhibited him in a
prayerful attitude, with the inscription : "I will not
be afraid of ten thousands of people that have set
themselves against me round about."* Yet in the
opinion of the more moderate or less enthusiastic,
Charles had committed a grave blunder in thus re-
quiting the hospitality of the Sultan, and his enemies were naturally delighted thereat. When Peter
heard of it he exclaimed : "I now perceive that God
has quite abandoned my brother Charles, inasmuch
as he has taken it upon him to attack and irritate
his only friend and ally." Augustus of Saxony even
gave the messenger who brought the news to him
200 ducats. Many of the Turks began to consider
too that "Iron Head" had gone mad, and this opinion was largely shared by the German Lutherans and
the Scotch Calvinists, who had hitherto regarded
Charles as a sort of Maccabæus. France was the
only country that protested against violent hands
being laid on a crowned head. England, Holland and
Prussia, on the contrary, began to look askance at
a monarch who so little understood his own interests and so recklessly threw away his chances.
Hitherto they had been willing to be his allies, from
henceforth they only waited for a decent pretext for
joining his foes.

A week after the *Kalibalik*, Charles, who now
feigned sickness, was conveyed not, as he expected,
to Adrianople to meet the Sultan, but to Timur-

* Psalms, iii., 6.

tash, a stately and well-appointed old castle near the
Pruth. He was accompanied by some scores of
friendly Poles and Swedes whom the Sultan had
ransomed and restored to their master. Indeed, for
an instant, it seemed as if, even now, war would be
once more declared against Russia. For Peter still
obstinately refused to part with Azov, and the news
of Stenbock's astounding victory at Gadebusch* had
reached Constantinople, and there excited the hope
that Sweden might still make head against her
numerous enemies. Once more therefore Charles
became high in favour at Stambul. The Tartar Khan
and the Seraskier were arrested and disgraced for
having laid hands upon him, and the hostile Grand
Vizier, Soliman Pasha, who had succeeded Jussuf,
was superseded by Ibrahim Pasha, an ex-bandit of
great energy who at once set out for the frontier.
Charles's hopes revived, but only to be as speedily
dashed. The surrender of Stenbock at Tönning
cooled the ardour of Turkey for the Swedish alliance,
the Peace of Utrecht threatened to let loose hostile
Austria upon her, and at the eleventh hour the Tsar,
thoroughly alarmed at the menacing tone of the
Porte, gave way on all points, accepted the mediation of England and Holland, and the Peace of
Adrianople (June 24, 1713) put an end at last to
the differences between the two Powers.

Charles was now utterly abandoned, but still he
refused to quit Turkish soil. After a short stay at
Timurtash, he had been removed (for he still feigned

---

* See next chapter.

illness) to Demotika, a little Turkish town a few miles south of Adrianople, where he lay in bed for nearly eleven months, " for a particular reason," as he told his sister * (though what that reason was nobody has yet been able to discover †), passing his time in playing chess, reading romances, and dictating despatches. Not till New Year's Day, 1714, did he resume his clothes and his old active habits. In the following March a special envoy from Stockholm, the able, amiable and experienced Henrik Lieven, arrived at Demotika with orders from the Senate to bring Charles back at any cost. For by this time the condition of the kingless kingdom was absolutely desperate. Her resources were utterly exhausted, the last vestiges of her continental empire, except Stralsund and Wismar, had been swept away, and the people, believing Charles to be either mad or dead, clamoured for a new sovereign. Some were for the Princess Ulrica, others for the young Duke of Holstein, so that a civil war seemed likely to complete the ruin of Sweden, and was only prevented by the intervention of Arvid Horn, now Chancellor.‡ All these reasons were adroitly but energetically represented to the King by Lieven, and after weeks and months of obstinate counter arguments, Charles at length gave way. On

---

* *Egenh. Bref*, No. 83.

† Some have put it down to the desire of absolute privacy, others to a wish to conceal his poverty, others again (and this seems most likely) to a fear lest the Turks might otherwise seize and carry him off.

‡ For details, see Chap. XII.

September 20, 1714, he quitted Demotika, travelling with his usual rapidity through Wallachia, Transylvania, Hungary and Austria, and thence, making a long detour, via Vienna, Regensburg, Nuremberg, Hanau and Cassel, to avoid the domains of the Elector of Saxony. Charles, who travelled under the name of Captain Peter Frisk, was accompanied by only two adjutants,* and, after encountering innumerable and incredible dangers and adventures, arrived at midnight on November 11, 1714, at the gates of Stralsund. It was fifteen years since he had last trodden Swedish soil.

Whether Charles XII.'s sojourn in Turkey was wise or foolish, is a question which has been long and fiercely debated between his critics and his apologists. The former maintain that it was his first duty after the collapse of Pultawa, to hasten home as quickly as possible, in order to save what still remained to him, instead of burying himself in a distant land, and allowing everything to be lost in his absence. The latter reply that never did Charles show himself so great and so patriotic as when, in default of forces of his own, he bent his efforts to arm the forces of the Ottoman Empire against his country's mortal foe. They point to the Russo-Turkish war as a signal triumph of his diplomacy, and insist that but for the venality of the Grand Vizier, a contingency impossible to foresee, Peter must have had his Pultawa also, and the King of

---

* The rank and file of his followers, some 500 in number, could not keep up with their master, and returned by another route.

Sweden would have been able to dictate his own terms to the captive Tsar. There is certainly much force in the latter contention. Even if Charles had hastened back to Sweden in 1709, he would have been obliged to remain on the defensive till he had raised another army strong enough to contend with his numerous enemies, and must in the meantime have been obliged to sacrifice either his Baltic or his German possessions, whereas he had everything to gain and nothing to lose by making the Sultan's armies fight his battles. It was therefore his truest policy to trust in the Turk so long as the Turk was trustworthy. Unfortunately that obstinate tenacity with which Charles always clung to his pet projects long after the original conditions had changed and favourable opportunities had gone, ruined everything. After the *Kalibalik* of Bender it must have been quite plain to him that the Turkish alliance project was dead and buried, and that honour and duty, to say nothing of self-interest, imperatively demanded his return home. Yet he chose to remain where he was nearly two years longer, though even so late as 1713 his presence in Sweden or Pomerania would have completely changed the face of things, for England and Holland were still friendly disposed towards him, while Prussia was ready to become his ally. When he *did* return, at the end of 1714, he had to reckon with all three of these Powers as antagonists.

And now, before following Charles through the final stadia of his extraordinary career, it will be necessary to go back six years, and see what Sweden underwent during and in consequence of his prolonged absence from her. It is a sad but also an inspiriting story, for it tells of a depth of devotion and a heroism of self-surrendering endurance on the part of the nation almost unexampled in history.

CHAPTER XI.

SWEDEN AND EUROPE FROM THE BATTLE OF PUL-
TAWA TO THE BATTLE OF GADEBUSCH.

1709–1711.

Pultawa not an irreparable disaster—Anomalous position of Sweden
in 1709—The Danes invade Scania—Stenbock defeats them at
the battle of Helsingborg—Total loss of Sweden's Baltic provinces—Neutrality Compact of The Hague—Charles repudiates
it—The Russo-Turkish war—The King and the Senate—Arvid
Bernhard Horn—Growing differences—Charles's reproaches—
Dire distress of the nation—Financial shifts—Stenbock sent
to Germany with a fresh army—Capture of Rostock— Desperate
position of Stenbock—King Stanislaus departs for Bender—
Battle of Gadebusch.

THE Pultawa catastrophe was not, as has
so often been supposed, a mortal, it
need not even have been an irreparable injury to Sweden. Nay more, terrible as it undoubtedly was, it did her
far less immediate damage than the
trumpery reverse of Fehrbellin some
forty years before. The reason of this apparent
anomaly is that the astonishing victories of Charles
XII. had restored to his country her ancient prestige
which she had done so much to forfeit during the

minority of Charles XI., and prestige is in politics,
what credit is in finance, a means of recovery which
operates chiefly by concealing, and thereby minimis-
ing disaster. On the other hand, prestige, like credit,
is so essentially sensitive and elusive that it can only
be preserved by the constant exercise of the nicest, the
most watchful tact and prudence. The hands of the
statesman who holds it must be equally strong and
supple if he is to keep possession of it. The obstinacy
which refuses to recognise facts, and the irresolution
which hesitates to take advantage of circumstances,
are equally fatal to it. Now it was the peculiar misfortune of Sweden that at the very moment when
she had most need of a strong and stable executive
with the power and will to swiftly and decisively
grapple with the multitudinous and enormous difficulties of the situation, one by one, as they arose, it
was her peculiar misfortune, I say, that she should
find herself in the unnatural position of being gov-
erned absolutely by a monarch so far away from his
realm that months must elapse before his orders
could arrive, by which time the circumstances which
originally dictated them had, in nine cases out of ten,
completely changed. The Senate at Stockholm had
no independent authority whatever, and if the stress
of circumstances frequently compelled it to take
prompt preservative measures on its own responsibility, it was always with the paralysing apprehension that a royal mandate from Bender might arrive
any moment to undo all that had already been done
after the most anxious deliberation. It is true, as
we shall see, that Charles had a definite policy of his
15

own which at one time promised the most brilliant results and that this policy was diametrically opposite to that of the Senate ; but even admitting the intrinsic superiority of the King's plan, inasmuch as he was seven hundred miles away at the other end of Europe, he could not possibly be as good a judge of the state of affairs as the statesmen who were actually on the spot, while the fatal obstinacy with which he clung to his projects, long after they had become demonstrably impracticable, was more fatal to his country than half-a-dozen Pultawas might have been.

The immediate result of that catastrophe was to bring to light again the ill-concealed hostility of Sweden's numerous foes,* and she suddenly found herself involved in a war with as many adversaries as at the beginning of the century, at the very moment when her original resources had been reduced by at least one half. Augustus of Saxony lost no time in repudiating the Peace of Alt-Ranstadt, while Denmark refused to be bound any longer by the Peace of Travendal. The Senate thereupon demanded from England and Holland the fulfilment of their guarantees of those treaties ; but instead of sending a fleet to the Baltic, as required, the Maritime Powers would only try remonstrances, and the consequence was that in the beginning of November, 1709, 16,000

---

* As my authorities for this chapter, I mainly depend upon : Carlson, *Om Fredsunderhandlingarne aren,* 1709–1718 ; Svedelius, *Minne af Kansli-Presidenten Grefve Arvid Bernhard Horn ;* Lilliestrale, *Magnus Stenbock och slaget vid Helsingborg ;* and Charles XII.'s *Egenhandiga Bref.*

Danes crossed the Sound, established themselves in
the Swedish province of Scania, and after investing
Malmö and Lund, proceeded in January, 1710,
against the fortress of Christianstadt. Fortunately
for Sweden, the Governor-General of Scania at this
time was Magnus Stenbock, the most popular and
valiant of all the great Caroline captains. At first
indeed, with only three cavalry regiments at his disposal, he could offer no resistance to the invader, and
therefore fell back upon Carlscrona, to defend as
best he could the navy which was lying in dock at
the great arsenal, but by the end of February, 1710,
he had, by the most strenuous exertions, got together an army almost as large as the Danish
(though most of his men were raw recruits in goat-
skins and wooden shoes) and at once marched
against the foe who retreated before him to Helsingborg. Here, on the 28th February, after a bloody
contest of two hours, " the Buck * and his goat-
boys," as the splendidly dressed and equipped Danish
soldiers derisively dubbed Stenbock and his hap-
hazard host, routed the invaders, capturing 3000 of
them (with thirty cannons and their baggage) and
slaying 3000 more. The remainder of the Danish
army took refuge within the walls of Helsingborg,
and a few days later evacuated Sweden altogether.
This great victory was totally unexpected and caused
a considerable stir throughout Europe. Stenbock's
return journey to Stockholm resembled a triumphal
progress : he received letters of congratulation from
all manner of celebrities, including the Duke of

* Stenbock—wild goat.

.Marlborough, and on the special recommendation of the Home Government was created a Senator by the King, although, oddly enough, Charles withheld the Marshal's bâton which, in the opinion of the Senate, Stenbock had also richly deserved. Not for three years, not till after he had won a still more signal victory, would Charles raise his most brilliant general to the rank of a Field-Marshal.* The victory of Helsingborg did much to revive the drooping courage of the Swedes, and kept the Danes quiet for some time; but it was but a momentary gleam of comfort, and everywhere else disaster followed hard upon disaster. In the summer of the same year Riga was surrendered by Count Stromberg, after an heroic defence of many months which cost the Russians no less than 40,000 men; Dunamünde, Pernau and Reval quickly shared the same fate, and before the end of the year the whole of Sweden's Baltic provinces were in the possession of the Tsar, who invaded Finland also and captured the fortresses of Keksholm and Viborg, the latter of which had never before fallen into an enemy's hand. The one remaining standing army Sweden now possessed was

---

* Up to 1704 Stenbock had been a prime favourite with the King; after that date, for some inscrutable reason, he ceased to be so. Yet the following anecdote shows that Charles respected him even after he had ceased to like him. Lagercrona, one of the King's hangers-on, knowing his master's dislike of wine and wine-bibbers, told him on one occasion that Stenbock had greatly exceeded at a banquet, and been very noisy and incoherent, thinking to curry favour thereby. But Charles sternly bade him be silent, adding : You only mean to blacken Stenbock, but let me tell you that Stenbock drunk is more capable of giving orders than Lagercrona sober."

Krassau's, which Charles had left in Poland to co-
operate with him ; but it was now compelled to
evacuate that country, and fall back upon Swedish
Pomerania, bringing along with it King Stanislaus,
henceforth a pensioner of Charles XII.'s.

Fortunately for Sweden her enemies, especially
after the battle of Helsingborg, believed her to be
very much stronger than she really was, and the sudden appearance of Krassau's army in Pomerania so
alarmed the Emperor and the Maritime Powers, that
they made a serious attempt to localise the Great
Northern war, lest it should prejudicially affect
their gains in the war of the Spanish Succession, in
which, after the bloody battle of Malplaquet (September 11, 1709), they had at last got the upper
hand of France. For it was feared that if Sweden
invaded Holstein from Pomerania, Russia and Poland would fall upon the Saxon Circle, over which
Sweden had joint jurisdiction with the Kaiser, in
which case the Allied Powers would be compelled to
send troops to the assistance of the threatened German provinces, and thus weaken their own armies in
Flanders. To prevent such a contingency, England
and Holland entered into the Neutrality Compact of
The Hague (March 20, 1710), whereby they engaged
to guarantee the neutrality of Sweden's German
possessions, on condition that Krassau's army should
neither invade Jutland nor return to Poland through
German territory, and they invited Sweden, Denmark and Saxony to accede thereto without delay.
The Swedish Senate was inclined, on the whole, to
become a party to this Neutrality Compact. It is

true that it would seriously hamper Sweden's strategy in the future, and unfairly shield Denmark
who had been the aggressor, while the alacrity with
which it had been accepted by Sweden's enemies
was of itself a somewhat suspicious circumstance.
It might also be fairly argued that the elusive
guarantors of the Peace of Travendal and the Peace
of Alt-Ranstadt were no longer to be trusted ; but, on
the other hand, the Neutrality Compact promised to
give Sweden breathing time, besides protecting from
attack her German possessions which she herself was
just then quite powerless to defend. But what principally moved the Senate to view it with favour, was
the private assurance of Marshal Gyllenstjerna, who
had taken over the command of the Pomeranian
army, that the Swedish forces were really not strong
enough even to invade Jutland. Under the circumstances therefore the Neutrality Compact offered
Sweden very real and distinct advantages, and, what
is more, offered them gratis. But Charles XII.
could not be brought to look upon matters in this
light. To him the Neutrality Compact was neither
more nor less than an attempt to bind his hands; he
described it as "useless and senseless," and refused
to entertain the idea. He would not even connive
at it till he had the opportunity of safely repudiating
it. Instead of that he demanded the active assistance of his allies, the Maritime Powers, unconditionally, and it seemed to him the most natural
thing in the world that they should keep the promises made to him years before, although they
themselves were actually engaged in a costly war,

and circumstances had completely changed. Accordingly in a manifesto issued from Bender (November 30, 1710) he formally repudiated the Neutrality Compact, declaring that, trusting to God and the righteousness of his cause, he was determined to have his hands free, so as to use, whensoever and wheresoever the exigencies of war might demand it, all the means and powers that God had given him. His alternative plan was a Swedo-Turkish alliance against the Tsar, which, after the Porte's first declaration of war against Russia, seemed about to become an absolute fact. Now it is quite indisputable that immediately after that event Sweden's prospects improved immensely. One of its first fruits was an offer of peace from Denmark, through the Holstein Minister, Baron Georg Heinrich von Görtz, on the basis of the Treaty of Travendal, which Charles was inclined to listen to, and pacific overtures from Augustus of Poland, which he summarily rejected. The Maritime Powers also took the trouble of sending a special envoy to Bender, to beg for Charles's adhesion to the Neutrality Compact, and for permission to trade with the Baltic ports, now in the possession of Russia, but on both these points they found the King of Sweden as haughtily inexorable as if he had not lost a single inch of territory. It is from this time forth that a growing coolness between Charles and the Maritime Powers, and a corresponding *rapprochement* between Sweden and France, her historical ally, and certainly the one Power that had given her any active assistance, becomes observable.

Meanwhile all Europe awaited the issue of the

Russo-Turkish war, with the most anxious suspense. It was well known that Charles had provided the Grand Vizier with an elaborate plan of campaign, that, properly carried out, must have ended in the total ruin of the Russian army, which event was momentarily expected, so that the Peace of the Pruth proved almost as great a surprise as the battle of Pultawa. Its effect upon Sweden's fortunes was naturally disastrous. The Danes, once more seeing their way to make conquests with little risk to themselves, invaded and occupied (1712) the whole of the Duchy of Bremen, and Krassau's army was dissipated by the Russians, Poles and Saxons without the neutral Powers raising a finger to save it. Nevertheless, black as the prospect now looked, there was always a chance (though a very remote one) that the Turks might change their minds again, and it was to bring this about that Charles now exerted all the strength of his unconquerable will. And in December, 1711, to the amazement of friends and foes alike, he again won his object: the Porte declared war against Russia a second time. It was part of Charles's plan of campaign to effect a diversion on the Swedish side. The Turks had laid great stress upon his active assistance, and from the beginning of 1711 onwards, the King began commanding the Senate to send an army through Germany into Poland, to co-operate there with the forces he meant to bring with him from Turkey. But here he met with an unexpected and irritating obstacle in the inability of the Senate to obey such commands, and this leads us to examine more closely the peculiar relations between a King who could not conceive the possibility of the ultimate failure of his plans, and a Senate that had the most convincing proofs before its very eyes that the realm, for whose defence it was responsible, stood on the verge of absolute destruction.

The Caroline apologists have always led the world to suppose that the Swedish Senate during 1709–1714 was a self-seeking coterie of ambitious politicians secretly bent upon undermining the King's power by deliberately thwarting all his projects, and only prevented by fear from downright rebellion. Such an accusation is not merely false, it is absurd. Charles XII.'s Senate was composed of ardent royalists, headed by a man who, whatever his hopes and misgivings, was, at least, during the lifetime of his master, that master's most devoted servant. Arvid Bernhard Horn had been conspicuous among the heroes who surrounded the heroic Charles XII., but his martial exploits were as nothing compared to the courage and energy with which, as Chancellor of Sweden, he now supported cares and anxieties under which an inferior man must inevitably have succumbed. Horn was a man of exceptional, even extraordinary abilities, but it was his bitter fate to be only one of the many instruments of a will far stronger than his own, and the displeasure of his royal master was presently to be superadded to his other troubles. It never seems to have occurred to Charles XII. that his exhausted people might be utterly crushed beneath the weight of their heavy burdens. The proud thought of saving *everything* left no room in his breast for the wise thought of saving what might have been saved. But the Senate, on the spot, with every means of rightly judging the state of things, thought differently. So serious did the situation seem to them, even after the victory of Helsingborg, that they not only wrote to the King that, so far as human foresight could perceive, Sweden had only a few months longer to live ; but they took the bold step, in 1710, of convening, without the consent of the King, a sort of national assembly to which they might give an account of their stewardship. This assembly, which sat from April to June, was of the most informal kind. Its members were carefully selected beforehand ; it was kept well in hand throughout its short session, the slightest symptom of independence was sternly suppressed as criminal, and Horn was careful to exhort its members to show that the King was "lord not only of their possessions, but of their hearts also." His only object in convening this consultative assembly at all was to convince the nation that the Senate could not have done otherwise than it had done, and, if possible, to get a little extra money out of the people for current expenses. Yet informal, circumscribed, inoffensive, as this phantasm of a parliament actually was, to convene it at all was such an infringement upon the royal prerogative, that Horn and his colleagues thought it necessary to justify themselves to the King for so doing on the plea of dire necessity. Charles's reply was very gracious. He approved of the good intentions of the Senate, though opining

at the same time that a Riksdag was quite unnecessary, and after thanking God for the victory of
Helsingborg, he warmly praised his Ministers for the
zeal and assiduity they had displayed in his service.
Indeed up to the autumn of 1711 the relations between the King and the Senate were excellent, but
after that period differences multiplied, and the Government at home had to listen to reproaches instead
of praise. The first cause of contention was the
Neutrality Compact of The Hague, already alluded
to. Another quarrel, arising out of it, was the agreement actually entered into by the Senate for lending
the Maritime Powers Krassau's army to fight their
battles in the Netherlands, in exchange for a sum of
money and a fleet, which would have been of ines-
timable advantage to Sweden. The bargain seemed
all the more profitable to the Government at Stockholm, as the army in question was lying quite idle
in Pomerania, while its maintenance was a serious
burden to the impoverished exchequer. Charles,
however, indignantly repudiated the arrangement,
declaring that he would never consent to sell the
flesh and blood of his subjects to foreign potentates
whatever the political advantages of it might be. In
this noble sentiment one cannot but sympathise
with him, but his high displeasure on the occasion
prompted him to a step most prejudicial to his own
interests. Not content with upbraiding the Senate
for its conduct, he issued from Bender a circular to
all his ambassadors abroad, strictly enjoining them
to take no orders save from himself, and declaring at
the same time that the Senate had no authority what-

ever to treat with foreign Powers direct. This hasty and injudicious measure had, of course, the effect of weakening still further the hands of the Government at home, which had henceforth nothing whatever to do with diplomatic affairs, Charles transacting all such business himself through Baron Maurice Vellingk (one of the most experienced of his father's diplomatists, whom he now made Governor-General of Bremen) and the Holstein Minister Baron de Fabrice who was with him in Turkey.

But what irritated the King against the Senate most of all was its perpetual supplication for peace. Pathetic indeed are the despatches which the Government at Stockholm addressed from time to time to the Government at Bender. As early as the autumn of 1710, they complain that the realm " in all its parts and powers " is utterly weakened, exhausted and helpless. The pestilence which carried off thousands in Stockholm alone had now been added to famine and bankruptcy, and the intolerable wretchedness of the people inclined them to the most desperate expedients. Then the Senate reminds the King that he keeps it for months at a time without a reply to its letters, and implores him to come to terms with his foes by all " possible and conceivable means." No peace, it urges, can be hoped for unless *something* be surrendered. Charles's reply betrays considerable though restrained anger, and a very unusual hardness. He begs his Senators not to trouble him any more with the old and oft-repeated tale of suffering and distress. It will henceforth be quite sufficient if they briefly report that

things are " either as they were or worse." The unhappy condition of the realm, he goes on to say, can
only be cured by an honourable and advantageous
peace, yet such a peace is not to be won by faint-
hearted wailing, but by strenuous and unflinching
vigour intelligently applied. He will never consent
to anything so shameful as the cession of a
province, whatever the conjunctures may be. In
March, 1711, Charles still further afflicted the
Senate by desiring it to despatch another army to
Germany to co-operate with him. The Senate re-
plies that their present distress renders such a
thing impossible, whereupon, in the autumn of the
same year, the King imperiously insists upon his
commands being instantly obeyed, at the same
time accusing the Senate of slackness and wilful
procrastination. They have thereby, he adds,
prejudicially affected his Turkish policy, and he
cannot return home unless an army be sent to
meet him. The Senate was in despair. It was
anxious to obey the King's commands, but saw
no way of doing so. Admiral-General Wachtmeister had already informed them that not a
ship could be put to sea till he had received
£15,000, but where the money was to come from
nobody could tell. Horn was only expressing the
opinion of all his colleagues when he said in the
Senate: "It behoves us to judge what may best
serve his Majesty's interests, and what is prejudicial thereto. If his Majesty commanded me to
send regiments to a fortress already in the hands of
the enemy, it would be impossible for me to obey

His Majesty's commands, in view of altered circumstances." All that could be done to raise money he did. He gave up a quarter of his salary, placed all the cash he had in the bank at the disposal of the Crown; offered to sell his house and yacht for the same purpose, and literally begged for money from door to door. Everyone else showed an equal readiness to make all imaginable sacrifices. The old Queen gave up her priceless silver for the melting-pot, the Princess Ulrica abandoned all her jewels * ; the members of the Senate voluntarily contributed 14,000 silver dollars (£1500) between them, and the merchants of Stockholm and Gothenburg were equally liberal and patriotic. By a special decree, which met with general approval, all official salaries between £25 and £125 were reduced one-half, and all above £125, three-fourths. By means of these desperate shifts, Horn was able to scrape together £3825 to begin with, and thus by the end of August, 1712, the King's command could at last be obeyed, and Admiral Wachtmeister quitted Carlscrona for Pomerania with the fleet, having on board an army of some 9000 men under the command of the gallant Stenbock.

The Swedes reached the Isle of Rugen in the middle of September, though not without loss, for the Danish admiral, Gyldenlöve, who followed them all the way, dexterously separated Wachtmeister from

---

* Charles, however, would not accept these sacrifices, and ordered most of the jewels and silver to be returned to his grandmother and sister.

his transport vessels, most of which he then destroyed with a very considerable quantity of provisions and stores.   It had been Charles XII.'s original plan that Stenbock should invade Poland from
the north, while Grudzinski attacked her from the
south, thus making a powerful diversion in favour
of the Turks, who had been moved by the tidings of
the landing of a Swedish army in Germany to declare war against the Russians for the third time.
Unfortunately, by the time that Stenbock was able
to set foot in Pomerania, any such combined plan of
attack had become perfectly impracticable.   Grudzinski's army, as already explained,* had been
routed and dispersed; King Stanislaus had taken
refuge in Pomerania, and was given the nominal
command of the Swedish army, while a strong
Russo-Saxon army under Peter and Augustus was
closely investing Stralsund.   Stenbock therefore
found himself completely isolated.   He was not
strong enough, even after his army had been raised
by reinforcements to 17,000 men, to relieve Stralsund ;
he durst not invade Poland, unsupported, especially
after the King of Prussia had formally notified that
he would consider any such invasion as a *casus belli*,
and, more than that, the Swedish forces had already
begun to suffer severely from want of provisions.
Stenbock therefore decided to invade Mecklenburg, a
rich and hitherto undevastated land, and thus well
able to support his army for some time, besides af-
fording him the advantage of a central position from
which he could easily attack either Denmark or

---

* Chapter X.

Poland in case of need. Into Mecklenburg, therefore, he marched forthwith, and occupied Rostock,
but his difficulties increased at every step, so that on
being offered an armistice by the Saxon Minister,
Fleming, he was easily persuaded by King Stanislaus to accept it. As for the unfortunate Stanislaus,
he was by this time weary of war and anxious to lay
down a crown that had brought him nothing but
misery and disaster. His pride, too, revolted against
being a pensioner of Sweden, and, at a council of
war held in Stenbock's tent, he announced his intention of proceeding direct to Bender, to resign his
crown into the hands of the man who had given it
to him. "I must go to your King," said he to Stenbock, "to put an end to this shedding of blood, for
I have resolved to sacrifice myself for Poland and
Sweden." So to Bender he went accordingly, and
arrived there shortly after the *Kalibalik*. But his
journey came to nothing. Charles absolutely refused to accept his friend's abdication, and the crest-
fallen Stanislaus was obliged to return to Sweden,
and submit to the humiliation of being supported by
a nation that pinched and starved in order to maintain him in regal style. With Stenbock Charles was
still more indignant. As soon as the King heard of
the truce his general had made, he sent him one of
the most severe letters he ever wrote, asking him
how he dared to commit such an unheard-of and indefensible act of weakness, and ordering him to make
good his fault by instantly proceeding to action.
Stenbock apologised abjectly, and obeyed. And
certainly it was high time he did something. The

King of Denmark had been almost as displeased with
the armistice as Charles XII. himself. " We must,"
he wrote to his allies, " we must unite all our forces
to crush' Stenbock and his 18,000 men, which is the
one remaining staff the haughtiness of Sweden has
to lean upon." Stenbock's position had now become highly critical. A large Danish army, commanded by King Frederick in person, was approaching him from the west, the Russians and Saxons were
advancing from the east, and intercepted letters
told him that it was their intention to drive him into
Wismar or Rostock, and there invest him with a
threefold odds. Stenbock's resolution was immediately taken. He determined to attack the Danes
before they joined the Russians and Saxons, and
deal with the latter afterwards. Breaking down all
the bridges behind him, and mounting his infantry
behind his cavalry for the sake of speed, he turned
westwards. The Russians and Saxons imagined at
first that he was about to seek refuge in the fortress·
of Wismar, but when he passed it by they guessed his
design and hastened after him as rapidly as possible.
But Stenbock was too quick for them. By dint of
forced marches he came so suddenly upon the Danish
camp at Gadebusch that King Frederick had only an
hour's warning of his approach. Stenbock found the
Danes very strongly posted, and it is said they outnumbered him by at least ten thousand men ; but as
the Saxons and Russians were following hard upon
his heels, there was nothing for it but to fight there
and then, and he fell upon the enemy without a
moment's delay. The battle lasted only two hours,

16

but it was most stubbornly contested. The Swedish artillery was superior to the Danish, and, admirably handled by the great engineer, Carl Cronstedt,* wrought fearful havoc. At the first discharge, it is said, the whole of the Danish front line was "reduced to rags and tatters." But the Danes had numbers on their side, and they fought so well under the eye of their King, that for a long time the issue of the struggle was very doubtful. Many of the Swedish regiments lost all their officers, and but for the cheering presence of the ubiquitous Stenbock, who, although suffering so severely from stone that he could scarcely keep his saddle, led the van in person, the battle might have been a repetition of Pultawa. Finally victory declared itself for the Swedes, and the Danes, utterly routed, retreated towards Holstein, leaving 3000 killed and wounded on the field, and 4000 prisoners, 13 cannons, and all their baggage in the hands of the victors. It was Stenbock's crowning exploit, and Charles no longer refused him his Marshal's bâton; but, with characteristic modesty, Magnus attributed his success partly to Cronstedt's skill, and partly to the extraordinary valour of his troops. "Such soldiers and such subjects," he wrote, "are not to be found the wide world over except in Sweden. Never have I

---

* Carl Cronstedt, the one great artillery officer Charles XII. produced, learnt the art of war entirely under that heroic monarch, and followed first him and then Stenbock through their principal campaigns especially distinguishing himself at Helsingborg, Gadebusch and the siege of Stralsund. He is said to have been the first to invent special carriages for artillery, which before his time had been carried on wagons.

seen such a combination of uncontrollable dash and
perfectly controlled discipline." Similar testimony
from the other side is given by Maurice of Saxony,
the future victor of Fontenoy, who describes the
bravery of the Swedish infantry at Gadebusch as
absolutely astounding.

CHAPTER XII.

SWEDEN AND EUROPE, FROM THE BATTLE OF GADEBUSCH TO THE FALL OF STRALSUND.

1712–1715.

Necessity for Sweden to surrender something—Obstinacy of Charles —Rejects the mediation of England—And the offer of the alliance of Prussia—Movements of Stenbock after Gadebusch— The burning of Altona—Surrender of the Swedes at Tönning— Last sufferings and death of Stenbock—Desperate position of Sweden—Finland lost—Stettin occupied—Charles refuses the mediation of Louis XIV.—Despair of the Swedish Senate—A Riksdag summoned—Condition of the finances—Dissatisfaction of the Estates—Their revolutionary projects—Ambiguous conduct of the Princess Ulrica—Energetic intervention of Chancellor Horn—Return of Charles XII.—Enthusiasm in Sweden— Fresh complications—Prussia and Hanover declare war against Charles—The siege of Stralsund—Engagement of Stresow— Fruitless heroism of the King—Fall of Stralsund.

HE battle of Gadebusch materially improved the position of Sweden, at least for a time, and indeed during the whole course of 1712 she had several opportunities of coming to terms with her numerous foes on relatively favourable conditions, considering her really desperate position. But by this time it had become evident to her wisest and most patriotic statesmen

that something must be sacrificed. After a century
of almost unbroken triumphs and conquests, Sweden
found herself face to face with the painful necessity
of surrendering part of her dominions in order to
save the rest. She had to choose between an indispensable peace that could only be purchased by a
cession of territory, and a ruinous war with the
prospect of still greater losses. It was manifestly
impossible that she could stand much longer against
a European coalition. Even Maurice Vellingk, the
most adroit and audacious of Charles XII.'s diplomatists, felt in duty bound to urge his royal master
to give way. "I am not courtier enough," wrote he,
"to flatter myself with the assurance that we can
raise ourselves up again by our own might, and
compel our enemies (and all the world besides) to
respect the treaties and compacts dictated to them
by us during our former victories." But Charles remained immovable. It was characteristic of his
policy that it remained the same in prosperity and
adversity, and he was determined, even now, to
resist to the death rather than make the slightest
concession. "It becomes us," he wrote,* "religiously
to keep the solemn vow we made never to relinquish
or surrender any portion of those territories and
lordships which our forefathers, the Kings of Sweden, have given into our hand." Amidst the universal confusion and despair, the imperturbable
young monarch still dared to hope. The poets and
historians of a later generation have marvelled at
and magnified the sublime self-confidence which

* Letter to Vellingk of May 18, 1713.

refused to yield even to Fate; but it must have been with bleeding hearts that Charles's contemporaries watched their master throw away one chance after another, and plunge his country into apparently irreparable ruin.

For thrice during the year 1712 did Sweden receive advantageous offers of mediation or alliance. The first of these offers came from the Maritime Powers. At the beginning of 1712 the great peace Congress of Utrecht had assembled for the purpose of putting an end to the war of the Spanish Succession, and as England and Holland were desirous, in their own interests, that the Great Northern war should also terminate as soon as possible, they proposed to mediate between Sweden and her enemies. England, in particular, was very favourably disposed towards Charles, and Queen Anne expressly declared herself bound by her former promises to assist him with troops, if necessary. But Charles had lost all confidence in the promises of England and her allies, and not without reason. They had plotted against him at Constantinople; they had traded with the Baltic ports against his prohibition; they had not upheld the treaties of Traventhal and Alt-Ranstadt, of which they were the guarantors, and they had allowed Krassau's army to be dispersed without making a single effort to save it. He therefore not only rejected their pacific overtures, but even alienated them by entering into direct negotiations for an offensive and defensive alliance with France.

But now two fresh offers of alliance reached Charles from another quarter.

The astonishing progress and the unprecedented successes of Russia had seriously alarmed Peter's neighbours Poland and Prussia, and both those Powers naturally turned to Sweden as the historical adversary and the proper counterpoise of Muscovy. In the course of 1712 Augustus went the length of proposing a partition of Poland between himself and Stanislaus as the easiest method of adjusting matters; but Charles summarily rejected the proposal on the double ground of its immorality and its impracticability. Besides, he had now less confidence than ever in the professions of Augustus. A much more weighty and promising affair was the alliance offered by the King of Prussia.

In the course of 1712, Frederick I. sent a special envoy, Baron Johann Friedrich Eosander, to Bender, with a definite offer of alliance, whereby six thousand Prussians were to be placed at Charles's disposal for the purpose of recovering his lost Baltic provinces, on condition that Charles returned home at once to lead this host in person. All that Prussia asked in return was the town of Elbing, and the bishopric of Ermeland for herself, and a stipulation that Stanislaus should resign the throne of Poland to Augustus. That such an offer should have been made to Sweden, even at the eleventh hour, says much for her prestige, but it was certainly more than she had any right to expect. It was indeed her last chance of saving the bulk of her possessions. A combined Prusso-Saxo-Swedish army under Charles XII. was the one possible means left of recovering Livonia and Esthonia, and keeping Rus-

sia within due limits; the mere contracting of such an
alliance would have had the effect of securing Sweden's German provinces from attack, and, had she
accepted it, she might still have emerged from the
Great Northern war, a power of the first magnitude.
And all Charles was required to do in return was to
give up Stanislaus, who, already a penniless fugitive,
was himself willing, and even eager, to resign the
burdensome crown that he had been forced to wear!
But this Charles would not do. In vain all his
ministers and diplomatists seriously assured him
that he could hope for no improvement in his affairs
till he had abandoned Stanislaus; in vain Stanislaus
himself hastened to Turkey to persuade Charles to
accept his abdication; in vain the Prussian envoy
Eosander lingered two months at Bender, in the
hope of persuading the King to listen to his terms;
Charles refused to accept Prussia's conditions. What
he desiderated was absolutely gratuitous, uncon-
ditional assistance, and failing to obtain that, he was
content to do without any assistance whatever, and
calmly abide the issue of events. What seemingly
confirmed him in this suicidal obstinacy, was Stenbock's victory at Gadebusch, which he regarded as
a fresh proof of the inherent invincibility of the
Swedish arms. But within a few months of Charles's
rejection of Prussia's advantageous offer, Stenbock's
army, the last army Sweden possessed, had ceased
to exist.

The position of the unfortunate Stenbock, after
his brilliant but useless victory, was almost as desperate as before it. He and his 12,000 men were

surrounded by some 36,000 Danes, Russians and
Saxons, who durst not attack him, but were quite
determined not to lose sight of him. He was much
too weak to make his way back to Pomerania and
clear that province of the invading Russians, Saxons,
Poles and Prussians, as Charles expected him to do,
while to shut himself up in the fortress of Wismar
would simply have meant slow starvation. Finally,
after anxious consultation with Maurice Vellingk at
Hamburg, he adopted that diplomatist's urgent advice to invade Holstein, and destroy the Danish city
of Altona, partly out of revenge for the burning of
the Swedish town of Stade by the Danes in the
earlier part of the year, and partly because the
destruction of the valuable magazines of stores collected at Altona would seriously cripple the fighting
capacity of the Danish Government. Accordingly,
after sending all his sick and wounded to Wismar,
Stenbock continued his march westwards, crossed
the Trave, and fixed his headquarters in and about
Oldeslohe, while the Russians and Saxons, led by
the Tsar in person, followed him into Holstein, to
help the Danes, who continued to retreat before
him. All this time Vellingk kept urging him to
destroy Altona, but for a long time unsuccessfully.
Stenbock was naturally a kind-hearted man, and he
had always endeavoured, as far as he could, to wage
war humanely. Besides, the case of Altona was
different to that of Stade. The latter was a fortress.
It had been reduced to ashes indeed, but only after a
stubborn siege, and in the ordinary course of warfare.
Altona, on the other hand was an open, defenceless

city that could do no harm, and had given no offence.
But Vellingk continued to insist, and even to
threaten, and at last Stenbock, whose firmness was
never equal to his valour, gave way, and he sent
word to Altona that if the city did not pay
him a ransom of £22,500 it should be burnt to
the ground.   The terrified inhabitants sent a
deputation to the Swedish General, offering half
the amount, which was as much as they could
scrape together; but Stenbock was inexorable, and
after all the women and children had been removed,
and strict orders had been issued that nothing
should be plundered, the city was set on fire at twelve
o'clock on Sunday night, December 28th, and by
three o'clock next morning it was in full blaze.   The
conflagration lasted all day, till at last only a hundred
of the poorest houses and three churches remained,
and 10,000 people were rendered homeless.   Vellingk is said to have given a banquet to some burgesses of the rival city of Hamburg in honour of the
event, and, taking them after dinner to the city
walls, pointed gleefully at the flames which lit up
the sky, and said :   "That is a spectacle for which
Hamburg ought to be grateful to me."   Stenbock,
however, had sufficient grace to be ashamed of his
own barbarous deed.   "From that hour," he mourn-
fully confesses, "the blessing of the Lord departed
from me."   At any rate he never prospered afterwards.   On the same day that Altona had begged
Stenbock for mercy, the Swedish fleet that had put
to sea to rescue him and his army, sighted the German coast; but on the very day that Altona was set

on fire the wind suddenly shifted, and drove Stenbock's expected reinforcements back to Sweden
again. His sole hope was now in a hard winter
which might enable him to cross to Funen over the
Belt, or at any rate make his way to the Scaw,
whence the Gothenburg squadron might convey him
and his troops back to their native land ; but the
weather suddenly became so exceptionally mild
and rainy, that he had to abandon both these projects, and, his numerous enemies pressing hard upon
him from every side, he was driven to take refuge in
the narrow peninsula of Eiderstadt in the south-
western corner of Sleswick, where, protected by the
rivers Eider and Treene, he hoped to hold out till
the following summer. But at the end of January
and beginning of February, the Russians, Danes and
Saxons crossed the Treene in force and drove Stenbock back into the extreme western corner of the
peninsula, closing every avenue of escape. After an
ineffectual attempt to break through the enemy's
lines, Stenbock shut himself up in the fortress of
Tönning which, in consequence of a secret conven-
tion with the Holstein-Gottorp Government, opened
its gates to him, and there, for the next three
months, he was closely invested by the allies, till his
provisions failed, and he surrendered (May 16, 1713)
to King Frederick IV. with his whole army, 11,000
strong. Extremely melancholy were the last days
of this gallant officer. He was conducted to Copenhagen where, at first, things were made as comfortable for him as possible ; but, when it was discovered
that he was in secret correspondence with his friends

abroad, he was removed to the fortress of Fredrik-
shavn, where he was treated with inhuman rigour.
His dungeon was over a swamp the pestilential
vapours from which penetrated through the thin
floor of his room which he was never allowed to
leave even for exercise or fresh air. Nobody, not
even a doctor or a clergyman, was permitted to visit
him, except at very rare intervals. The servants who
waited upon him were allowed and even encouraged
to insult their helpless prisoner. He lingered on till
March 6, 1717, when death put an end to his misery.

The news of the capitulation of Tönning became
generally known in Western Europe about the same
time as the *Kalibalik*, and the immediate effect of
these two events was to complete the ruin of the
Swedish Empire. England and Holland, who, after
the battle of Gadebusch, had been inclined to aid
Sweden, now drew back. The King of Prussia occupied Stettin, on the pretext of saving it from
Charles's enemies. The Russians threw all their
forces upon Finland, captured Helsingfors and Åbo
with their galley-fleets, and routed the gallant Carl
Gustaf Armfelt at the bloody battle of Storkyro,
where the raw Swedish and Finnish levies fought
heroically for three hours against a threefold odds
and lost all their officers but ten, so that by the end
of 1714 the whole of the Grand Duchy was in the
power of the Tsar. And this desperate state of
things was accentuated by the absence and the
obstinacy of the King. His diplomatists and statesmen, notably Vellingk and Horn, put forth all their
exceptional abilities to save something from the

wreck only to find themselves thwarted at every step by their master. The former had attempted to save Stettin by an ingenious arrangement whereby it was to be garrisoned by neutral troops (Prussians and Holsteiners) and handed back to Sweden after the war was over. Charles would not hear of any such arrangement. Horn had entered into negotiations with Russia, in order to separate her from her allies, with a fair prospect of success. Charles peremptorily commanded the Senate to cease all such negotiations. Charles's own counter-offer of alliance to the Court of Berlin was so preposterous, that the King of Prussia laughed in the face of the Swedish envoy, remarking at the same time that he was not so simple as to make such sacrifices for the sake of advantages he already possessed. Even Louis XIV., Charles's one remaining disinterested ally, ably counselled surrender in the strongest terms. In February, 1714, Prussia had laid before the Court of Versailles a fresh project for helping Sweden to recover her lost provinces on the basis of a peace with Augustus, whereby Russia was to be isolated, while Prussia obtained for her good offices Stettin and Pomerania as far as the Peene. Louis XIV. approved of this plan, and communicated with Charles on the subject. The old King adjured the young one to now add the prudence of a statesman to the valour of a hero by making some reasonable concession, and reminded him that it was his first duty as a ruler to look after the true interests of his realm. But Charles declared he would rather lose all Pomerania than give up Stettin, whereupon Prussia made secret terms of her own with Russia whereby each Power guaranteed to the other the conquests it had made at the expense of Sweden. With equal obstinacy Charles refused the mediation of the Emperor, whom he offended besides by refusing him the honorary title of King of Spain, so that when peace was finally concluded between France and the Empire at the Congress of Baden, 1714, Swedish affairs were, by common consent, left out of consideration altogether.

Meanwhile the condition of Sweden herself was truly piteous. Abandoned by everyone, even by her own monarch, she seemed to be lost beyond the possibility of recovery. The distracted Senate began to fear that by the time the King thought of coming back to his realm there would be no realm left to come back to. Three years before, things had seemed as bad as they could be, but now they were infinitely worse. Then at any rate the Danes had been driven out of the land by Stenbock's army, a second army, under Krassau, in Germany, still excited the fears or the hopes of Sweden's friends and foes, while it was confidently expected that the King was on his way back from Turkey with a third. But now Stenbock's and Krassau's armies had been annihilated; the last fragments of Sweden's continental possessions, except Wismar and Stralsund, were lost; the victorious Russians were preparing to invade Sweden from the east, and the Danes from the west. Nay more, there were dangerous symptoms of disaffection in Sweden itself. There was a very general belief among the common people that the King

was either dead or mad and that the Senate was
bent upon hiding the fact from sinister motives. So
far had things already gone that it was not so much
a question of governing successfully as of governing
at all. The very bonds of society seemed to be
loosening. " This realm," as the Senate emphatically
phrased it, " can only be compared to a human body
most of whose sinews have been cut through and
out of whose veins the greater part of its blood has
already run, inasmuch as things have come to such a
pass that those of us who still survive see only the
respite of a few months between them and total
ruin." In its dire extremity the Senate felt that it
was not strong enough to bear, alone, the burden of
government under such overwhelming circumstances,
so, by the advice of Chancellor Horn, a Riksdag was
summoned in the autumn of 1713, although the
King had expressly forbidden any such step as unnecessary in itself and encroaching on his prerogatives. Previous to taking this momentous step, the
Senate attempted to strengthen its position by in-
viting the Princess Ulrica to take her seat in the
Council, as a member of the administration, an in-
vitation with which Her Royal Highness promptly
complied.

The Estates met together at Stockholm on December 14, 1713. Their first act was, on the motion
of the aged Archbishop Spegel, himself an ardent
royalist, to draw up a document to be forwarded to
the King, in which they pathetically described the
intense distress of the nation, and implored him to
return home and make peace. This document

drawn up in the name of the four Estates, although
couched in the most submissive and dutiful language, drew a terrible picture of the hopeless state
of the realm, and was ultimately taken to Demotika
by Major-General Henrik von Lieven, together
with letters from the Princess and the Senate to the
same effect, and a short note from the venerable
Queen Dowager, now in her 77th year, in which she
begged her grandson to hasten home that she might
embrace him once more before she died. * The Estates next proceeded to the consideration of the
finances which were in a truly appalling condition.
The estimated revenue for the year 1714, including the extraordinary war taxes, was about
£675,000 of our money, while the expenditure
came to £1,755,000, thus leaving a deficit of
no less than £1,080,000 which there were no
means whatever of meeting, for Sweden was already over-taxed, while all foreign powers regarded her as a bankrupt gambler who could
not be trusted with loans. Nevertheless, a Committee of Ways and Means was formed to take
the matter into consideration, but after the most
extraordinary proposals were adopted, such, for
instance, as the mortgaging of the town of Wismar and the island of Gotland ; the selling of all
the church bells ; the coining of the cannons and
other trophies captured during the war ; the sequestration of tithes, etc., supplemented by loans of land
and money from all who still had anything to lend,
only a fourth part of the deficit could be covered,

---

* She died, however, before his arrival.

and, with the menace of a simultaneous invasion
from the east and west, there was scarce money
enough to keep on foot the inadequate little army
of 23,000 men actually employed in guarding the
frontiers, to say nothing of raising the 50,000 which
military experts declared to be the absolutely indispensable minimum for purely defensive purposes.
No wonder, then, if a feeling of indignation against
the absent King, who seemed disposed to allow his
realm to perish utterly rather than purchase peace
by the slightest concession, began to make itself felt
among the Estates, especially when they had listened to letters recently received from Charles,
wherein he forbade the Senate to enter into any negotiations with foreign Powers, or diminish the crushing war taxes; commanded them to dismiss the
Estates immediately in case they had already assembled, and take prompt measures to send 20,000 more
men to Pomerania. Such commands, at such a
time, seemed to show an utter indifference to the
terrible sufferings of the exhausted nation, and filled
the minds of the deputies, especially those of the
first and fourth Estates, with bitterness, and an
intense longing to save themselves as best they
could. "If," wrote the French Ambassador at
Stockholm, "if the Princess, the Senate, and the
Estates were only resolute and unanimous, the King
might very easily be deposed." It was this feeling
of despair and dereliction which now induced the
Estates to make an attempt to take the Government
into their own hands. If, they argued, the King
cannot conclude peace because of his enemies, the

17

Estates of the Realm ought to do so for him. On
January 18, 1714, the day after the arrival of the
King's disturbing despatches, the burgher deputy
Hylten proposed in the Secret Committee that the
Princess, the Senate and the Estates should appeal
to England, France and Austria to mediate a peace
for them. The proposal found favour with the
members of the first and fourth Estates (the latter
going so far as to say they would transact no business till peace had been actually concluded), and it
finally took the form of a memorandum, presented
by the Secret Committee, to the Senate, in which,
while admitting in the abstract that the King alone
had the right to conclude peace, the signatories declared that, in view of his Majesty's absence and
helplessness, and the dire need of the Kingdom, they
considered it unpardonable of the Government to
continue waging "an obstinate and impotent war,
thereby still further jeopardising both king and
country," and concluded by urging the Senate to
petition the King for leave to open peace negotiations. Nay, the Riksdag proceeded still further. It
was on the 8th March that the Secret Committee
was informed by the Senate of the purport of the
King's last despatches in which he forbade all peace
negotiations through mediators and arbitrators. Two
days later the Secret Committee declared that, at
that rate, peace would never be obtained at all, and
they therefore insisted that the Princess Ulrica,
"with the authority due to her as the King's sister,
and nearest heir to the throne, should in conjunction
with the Senate and the Estates, take such measures

COUNT ARVID HORN AS MARSHAL OF THE SWEDISH DIET.

for bringing about a peace as might be deemed best."
The Senate was now thoroughly alarmed. It perceived well enough that a peace concluded without
the King's knowledge or consent, would be a fla-
grant breach of the constitution, in fact an act of
rebellion, which would probably lead to a civil war,
while the attempt to make the Princess Regent in
her brother's lifetime was an unheard of audacity on
the part of the Estates, amounting to leze-majesty,
at the very least. For a few days the country tot-
tered on the verge of a revolution, for the majority
of the first and fourth Estates had voted for both
the peace and the regency proposals, while the second and third Estates could not make up their minds
either way. Fortunately for Sweden, at this crisis,
she possessed in Arvid Horn a statesman capable of
browbeating even a mutinous parliament when the
interests of his country demanded it. Yet Horn's
position was a most difficult one. He had to defend
his master's authority when he could not defend his
master's conduct. Openly, and before the world, he
spoke the language of autocracy, but in secret he
nourished liberal views, and really sympathised with
the Estates. He was convinced that a parliamentary government was the only government that Sweden would tolerate in the future ; but he was equally
convinced that that future could not begin till
Charles XII. was no more. The ambiguous conduct
of the Princess Ulrica was another source of embarrassment to him. That Princess was both ambitious
and vindictive and for her brother she seems to have
had but little love. It is true that he had always

treated her with a chivalrous courtesy and regard which is rarely to be found among even the most affectionate brothers and sisters; but the liking he had for his younger sister, genuine as it was, seemed coldness itself when compared with the excessive love that he had lavished upon his elder sister Hedwig Sophia, the late Duchess of Holstein. Ulrica had secretly but most bitterly resented the preference thus given to her elder sister, and in that sister's infant son, Charles Frederick, Duke of Holstein, she saw not so much a nephew who had a claim upon her affections, as a rival who stood between her and the throne she hoped to inherit. The revolt of the Estates, therefore, was not altogether unwelcome to her, and she was suspected by the Senate, not without some reason, of currying favour with them. But, on the other hand, Ulrica had neither the courage nor the talent to play the part of a usurper successfully, and Horn, well aware that his one defensible course of action was to maintain the King's prerogatives at all hazards, proceeded, with characteristic energy, to stamp out the smouldering discontent before it blazed up into open rebellion. On March 15th he convened the Senate, and, the Princess also being present, declared that it had come to his knowledge that the Estates, misled by certain persons, had trespassed upon his Majesty's rights. "If," continued he, "we look through our fingers any longer at such behaviour, there is not a King in the world who would forgive us, and I, for my part, demand that the unruly be at once sent up hither, and severely reprimanded, and that the Estates there-

upon be ordered to disperse." Ulrica feebly attempted to defend the deputies, and would have
withdrawn while they were being reprimanded, but
Horn, courteously but firmly, insisted upon her
countenancing his proceedings by remaining where
she was, and in her presence he forthwith proceeded
to rebuke, in no measured terms, the ringleaders of
the opposition in the first and fourth Estates for
their insubordination, though he acquitted them of
any malevolent intentions. Thus, by his firmness
and presence of mind, the Chancellor, in all proba-
bility, saved the country from the dangers of a
revolution.

The proceedings of the Riksdag of 1714 were
thus abortive enough, yet they had one good effect
—they brought the King home at last. It now became quite clear to Charles XII. that any longer
sojourn in Turkey might bring about the total loss
of his power, perhaps even of his crown. So in the
autumn of the same year, he quitted Demotika, and
at midnight, on November 11, 1714, as already mentioned, arrived before the gates of the fortress of
Stralsund, which, excepting the city of Wismar, was
now all that remained to him of his continental
possessions.

Indescribable was the enthusiasm excited by the
tidings of the arrival of Charles XII. at Stralsund.
The whole Swedish nation ran wild with joy; all
their losses, the calamities of the last five terrible
years, all actually existing hardships and burdens
were forgotten in an instant; even the more sober-
minded began to entertain the most extravagant

hopes. After a separation of fourteen years the
King had come back again to his people, and the
people were ready to welcome him with every mark
of affection and veneration. Nothing seemed impossible to such a monarch as Charles XII. It was
loudly proclaimed that "the most righteous and heroic of princes" was about to utterly crush his
presumptuous enemies, recover his lost possessions, give to his people the long-desired blessings
of peace, and, as his father had done before him, re-
establish order and prosperity throughout his
realm. "Ye doubting prophets! ye self-wise statesmen!" cried one popular writer, "ye who declared before the whole world that Bender was the
coffin in which the world-renowned Charles was shut
up after Pultawa . . . and ye faithless ones who assured us that he would never return to us . . . nay
that he no longer existed . . . can ye now for very
shame pronounce a single word in your defence!
But unto thee, O loyal Swedish nation, I say . . .
Behold thy King cometh! go thou forth to meet
him!" But the enthusiasm that was so sanguine in
the winter of 1714, had, by the autumn of 1715,
given way to a blank despair. Instead of returning
home, the King remained at Stralsund, and ordered
20,000 more men to be sent from Sweden to join
him there. Instead of the peace she pined for, the
nation had once more to prepare for a still more
hopeless war, and two fresh foes now joined the
coalition that was compassing her destruction. No
doubt Charles's haughty obstinacy in rejecting all
terms of peace that did not include complete resti-

tution of whatever he had lost, was partly responsible for this new imbroglio, yet it should never be forgotten that, throughout this terrible period, he was acting strictly on the defensive, fighting simply to keep his own, and he might even have held his own but for the greed and rapacity of the very two Powers who claimed to be his allies and from whom he had a right to expect assistance. These Powers were Prussia and England. Prussia had all along been playing a waiting game. So long as Charles had been victorious, she had been quite willing to fight his battles for him, for a consideration; but when his ruin seemed irretrievable, and the Swedish Empire began to crumble to pieces, she made haste to enlarge her own domains out of its ruins. The so-called sequestration of Stettin was the first step in this land-grabbing policy, and upon Charles very naturally refusing to sanction such a barefaced act of robbery, the new King of Prussia took the still further step of occupying the town of Wolgast and the adjacent islands. Charles, without a moment's hesitation, drove the Prussians out again. " The King of Prussia," he exclaimed, " has not the slightest right to hold possessions on ground belonging to the Swedish Crown." This act of hostility gave Frederick William I. the pretext he wanted for breaking definitely with Sweden, and in the spring of 1715 he declared war against her. Still more disreputable, if possible, was the conduct of England-Hanover, for the Elector of Hanover had now become King of England, and the English Ministers, however reluctantly, felt bound to support the foreign policy of the monarch of their choice. In the beginning of 1715, the Elector of Hanover was readily persuaded by Russia, Prussia and Denmark, to join the confederacy for the partition of Sweden's continental possessions, and a compact was made between them whereby Wolgast, Stettin and district were to fall to the share of Prussia, Rügen and Pomerania north of the Peene to Denmark, and the Duchies of Bremen and Verden to Hanover, who was to pay Denmark, their present holder,* 600,000 rix dalers (about £135,000) for the possession of them. Charles indignantly protested against this iniquitous traffic in stolen property of which he was the real owner, whereupon Hanover also declared war against him (October, 1715).† Thus by the middle of 1715, Sweden, now at the last stage of exhaustion, and bleeding at every pore, was at open war with Russia, Prussia, Poland, Saxony, Hanover and Denmark.

Yet, even in this extremity, Charles's courage did not forsake him. On the contrary it is plain from his correspondence that his confidence in his ultimate success was as unbounded as ever, nay all the treachery and rapacity of his numerous enemies is not sufficient to draw from him a single hasty or violent expression. The tranquillity with which he alludes to events which filled all Sweden with terror

---

* It will be remembered that Denmark had wrested them from Sweden in the course of 1712.

† England was nominally at peace with him, yet eight English men-of-war were now sent to the Baltic to co-operate with the Danes against him, under the pretext of protecting English trade from the Swedish privateers.

is astounding. "The Brandenburger is also beginning to be surly and seek a quarrel with us," * he
writes to his sister, apropos of the breach with Prussia. "He thinks he will win since his opportunity
seems to have come, and he may give us a little
trouble, but I hope that in the end he will be somewhat out in his reckoning." In the same letter he
talks of compelling his little brother " † to restore the
lands of the Duchy of Holstein which Denmark had
seized after the surrender of Tönning, and he laughs
at the idea of the allies being able to do him any
serious harm for at least twelve months to come.
Yet at this very time Sweden was completely
isolated. Charles had succeeded indeed in obtaining subsidies from Louis XIV., to the amount
of about £135,000 a year, but France declined
to make a diversion in his favour by invading
Rhenish Prussia ; all attempts to raise troops in
Germany failed, and, excepting 4000 men placed at
his disposal by the Administrators of Holstein-Gottorp, he had nothing but his own meagre resources to
depend upon. By the most strenuous exertions,
however, he contrived to collect some 17,000 men in
and about Stralsund, which he now prepared to
defend to the uttermost against the banded might
of Europe. So long as the Swedes held the adjacent
island of Rügen, it was difficult for the allies to completely invest the fortress. Charles had ordered the
Senate to send reinforcements to Rügen, but contrary winds drove the fleet back to Carlscrona, where-

---

* *Egenh. Bref*, No. 85.
† *I. e.*, the King of Denmark.

upon Charles himself was obliged to hasten to the
island from Stralsund, with 6000 men, but was unable to prevent 17,000 Prussians under Leopold of
Anhalt-Dessau from landing, and strongly intrench-
ing themselves at Stresow. The King gallantly
attacked this threefold odds, but, after performing
prodigies of valour, was beaten off with terrible loss,
severely injured, and carried back stunned and half
senseless to Stralsund. In the beginning of July,
that fortress was completely invested, in September
the siege artillery arrived, in October the trenches
were opened, and, after the destruction of the little
Swedish flotilla on the Peene, all communications
with Sweden were cut off. Yet for nearly two months
longer the garrison offered the most heroic resistance, the presence of the King seeming to inspire
them with superhuman courage. Every inch of
ground was stubbornly contested, and, though the
issue could not be doubtful for a moment, every
fresh advance cost the besiegers hundreds of men.
Charles seems to have excelled himself on this occasion, and his extraordinary fortitude filled friends
and foes alike with astonishment. Throughout the
siege he chose the most dangerous positions, took
his frugal meals within range of the enemy's guns,
and from September 8th to December 9th slept every
night, wrapped in his mantle on the bare ground
with a stone for his pillow. Some of his exploits
during the siege border on the fabulous. On one
occasion as he stood in the market-place, in the midst
of a group of officers, a bomb plumped down amongst
them. All the officers instantly scattered, but Charles

coolly kicked the bomb into an adjacent ditch, where
it exploded without doing any harm. And he could
be as kindly as he was courageous. An old colonel
named Reichel, wearied out by the fatigues of the
day, had laid himself down on a bench for a brief
rest, when he was suddenly aroused to go on duty
again. Grumbling and swearing at the hard necessity of turning out in the middle of his slumbers, the
old man rose to go, but Charles, who happened to be
close by and heard him, approached with a smile
and said: "You are tired I see, my dear Reichel,
but I have rested. Lie down on my mantle and
take a little nap, and I meanwhile will do duty for
you, and wake you if you should be wanted." The
veteran, full of shame and confusion, vainly remonstrated. Charles wrapped him up in his own mantle,
and silenced his protests by commanding him to
obey. Such little traits go far to explain the intense
affection with which the Swedish nation, as a whole,
and especially the Swedish soldiers, regarded their
King and comrade to the last. But the utmost
prowess could not save Stralsund. On December
12, 1715, the fortress, or rather what remained of it,
for it was now little more than a rubbish heap, capitulated. The day before, Charles XII., perceiving
he could do no more, quitted Pomerania in a little
boat, and on the 13th, after a dangerous passage
during which he narrowly escaped falling into the
hands of the Danish cruisers, landed in Sweden
which he had not seen for fifteen years.

CHAPTER XIII.

"GRAND VIZIER" GÖRTZ.

1715–1718.

Poverty of Sweden—Charles invades Norway—Capture of Christiania and attack on Fredrikshald—Retreat of Charles—League of the Powers for the invasion of Sweden—Departure of the combined fleets from Copenhagen—Russian troops conveyed to Denmark—Defensive measures of Charles—The Tsar postpones the whole enterprise—Jealousies and dissensions among Charles's enemies—Baron George Henry von Görtz—His true character—Early career—Becomes Charles XII.'s "Grand Vizier"—His plan for negotiating with all Sweden's enemies Simultaneously—Görtz meets the Tsar at The Hague—Alarm of George I.—Alleged Jacobite plot—Görtz arrested—Peace negotiations opened with Russia in the Aland Islands—Dexterous diplomacy of Görtz—Russia's favourable offer—Obstinacy of Charles—Despair of Görtz—His extreme danger—Terrible condition of Sweden—Görtz's warnings—Intrigues of the Holstein and Hessian factions in the matter of the succession —Count Horn and the parliamentary party.

IT was generally anticipated by the enemies of Charles that the loss of Stralsund would break even his spirit, or, at least, would so far humble his pride as to make him amenable to reason. Many of them had even confidently hoped that he would either perish or fall into their hands during the siege, for, in either case, so it was argued, the

war must come to an end of its own accord. But when, escaping, as by a miracle, across the sea, the " Lion of the North " succeeded in regaining his own realm it was not long before the allies felt his heavy hand once more, and it became quite clear to them that nothing short of a life-and-death struggle in the heart of Sweden itself could bring the vanquished hero to acquiesce in the wholesale spoliation of his continental possessions. Charles himself was well aware of the designs of his enemies, and determined, so far as he was able, to circumvent them. He knew right well that his best, or, rather, his only, policy was now one of audacity. It would never have done to let the foes of Sweden suspect how exhausted she really was. The more imposing her armaments, the more menacing her attitude, the more likely she would be to command respect and obtain favourable terms of peace. But her resources were now so meagre, and the state of the country so deplorable, that he soon found he could only partially carry out his great designs. Things had, by this time, come to such a pass * that the Senate had not sufficient money to pay for official sealing-wax and writing paper ; the revenue of the year 1716 had been largely anticipated ; the taxes could only be collected with the utmost difficulty ; the peasants fled by hundreds into the forests, and even mutilated themselves to avoid conscription ; in some places the gentry resisted the enrolling of soldiers from

---

* See Lagermark : *Karl XIIs Krig i Norge.* Ups. Univ. Års., 1883.

among their tenantry by force of arms, and there
was such a dearth of sailors that the ships had to be
manned by soldiers. On returning from Germany,
Charles had proceeded first of all to the southern
post of Ystad, to organise an expedition for the relief of the fortress of Wismar, his last remaining
German possession, which was now closely invested
by an army of 30,000 Danes, Hanoverians and Prussians. But the Swedish Admiralty was too poor to
repair the ships actually lying in dock, much less set
a fresh fleet afloat, so that Wismar had to be left to
its fate. But now a sudden opportunity seemed to
present itself of striking a blow at Sweden's nearest
and most obstinate foe, Denmark. In the beginning
of January, 1716, there was such a severe frost that
the Sound was frozen, and Charles prepared to cross
over to Zealand forthwith, at the head of 12,000
men. This projected *coup-de-main* caused a panic at
Copenhagen, which happened just then to be almost
defenceless, but a violent storm, which raged incessantly from the 9th to the 11th of January, suddenly
broke up all the ice, and the Danish capital was
saved. Charles next turned his arms against Norway. Ever since 1709 Sweden had been exposed to
an invasion from that quarter, though hitherto hostilities had been mostly confined to border raids.
In the beginning of 1716, circumstances seemed to
favour an attack upon Norway. The country was
ill-governed by an incompetent Governor-General,
and a Council of War, who were constantly at vari-
ance, the treasury was empty, the magazines and
store-houses ill-stocked, and the Danish Government

had barely 20,000 men wherewith to defend a frontier extending over many hundreds of miles. It is true there were also great obstacles in the way. The numerous mountain passes and deep rapid rivers made a defence comparatively easy, the frontier rock-built fortresses were almost impregnable, the hardy peasantry was animated by a fanatical hostility against the Swedes, and it would be a matter of great difficulty for an invading army to find provisions among the barren and sparsely populated fells. On the other hand the intense cold had, for the present, frozen all the watercourses, and the Norwegian Government did not anticipate an invasion. These last two reasons were sufficient to decide Charles XII. At the end of February he crossed the border with only a few hundred men, and, after some successful skirmishes, occupied Christiania (March 10th). Here he remained with his little army for more than a month, awaiting reinforcements from Sweden, but the cowardice and incompetence of General Aschenberg, whose business it was to observe the fortresses of Fredrikshald and Fredrikstad, which Charles had left behind him, enabled the Danes to cut off a large Swedish detachment lying at Moss; want of money prevented the Swedish fleet from running out during the spring, and when, in April, the Danish Admiral Gabel arrived in Norway with a fleet and an army corps, the position of Charles had become so insecure that he was compelled to retreat. But now even a retreat seemed impossible. The deep and dangerous river Glommen barred the way in front, while two army corps, each twice as numerous as Charles's little host, were converging upon him simultaneously from the east and west. By the time he had reached the Glommen, the enemy was only two hours' march behind him, and he had no boats in which to cross the river. But his courage, his good fortune, and the terror he inspired saved him from what threatened to be a repetition of Pultawa. The Swedes contrived to cross the Glommen on hastily-constructed rafts and prahms, and fixed their headquarters at Svinesund on the Dynekilden creek in Norwegian territory, where they were presently joined by the Gothenburg squadron, which brought them ammunition and reinforcements. On June 23d, Charles once more assumed the offensive by making a daring attack on the frontier town and fortress of Fredrikshald. He succeeded in capturing the town, after some very severe fighting, but while he was preparing to make it a basis of operations against the citadel, the inhabitants defeated his project by patriotically burning the place to the ground, and four days later the Danish Admiral, Peter Tordenskjold, audaciously made his way up the narrow Dynekilden, in the teeth of the hostile batteries, and almost totally destroyed the Swedish fleet and transports lying there, thus entirely cutting off Charles's communications with Sweden by sea, and compelling him to evacuate Norway immediately. A fresh invasion of that country was, for the present, out of the question, for Sweden herself was now threatened by a combined attack from all her enemies together, which compelled her to use every

ship and every soldier she possessed in a struggle
for very existence.

After the fall of Wismar (April 8, 1716) the league
that had been formed to despoil Sweden of her con_
tinental possessions had got everything it coveted,
except Charles's sanction of the spoliation, and
this it also hoped to obtain by force of arms.
Prussia and Denmark held Pomerania : George I.,
Bremen and Verden ; Russia, Finland and the Baltic provinces; Wismar was garrisoned conjointly by
Hanover, Prussia and Denmark. Pacific overtures
had been made to Sweden, but to no purpose.
Charles disdained to haggle with his despoilers, and,
for six months after the fall of Stralsund, all negotiations between Sweden and foreign Powers were
broken off. Then the allies proceeded to try what
pressure could do, and Russia who had most to gain
and Denmark who had most to fear, from Sweden,
led the way.* On June 3, 1716, the two Powers engaged by the Treaty of Altona to make a combined
descent upon Scania, the southernmost province of
Sweden, and Prussia promised, for a consideration,
to supply most of the necessary transports to convey 20,000 Russian troops from Mecklenburg to
Zealand, where they were to unite with the Danish
forces lying there, while England sent a fleet of 22
liners to the Sound, under Admiral Norris, to cover
the landing, and help to blockade the Swedish fleet
in Carlscrona. The descent was to have been made

---

* By far the best monograph on the subject is the Danish historian,
E. Holm's *Studier til den store nordiska Krigs Historie.* Hist.
Tidsk., Række v., Bd. 3.

at the end of June, but countless delays, owing to the greed of Prussia, the poverty of Denmark and the mutual jealousies and suspicions of all the allies (of which more anon) retarded the expedition for months, so that it was not till late in the summer that everything was ready, and the combined navies could proceed to sweep the Baltic clear, so as to enable the Russian army, lying in Mecklenburg, to be transported to Denmark. On August 16th, the Tsar, who since July had been the unwelcome guest of the Danish Court, hoisted his flag on board the *Ingria*, as Grand Admiral of the Russo-Danish fleet, and, accompanied by the English fleet under Norris who was to act in concert but independently, quitted the Sound, and proceded to the Isle of Bornholm. It was the mightiest fleet * that had ever appeared in the northern waters, and the Swedish admiral prudently retreated before it towards Carlscrona. Norris would have followed him up and forced on a battle and Peter supported him, but the Danish Admiral Gyldenlöve, partly out of jealousy of the Tsar, and partly owing to secret instructions from his government to spare his fleet as much as possible, refused to lend himself to any such adventure, so the combined fleets were constrained to remain at Bornholm, and be content with the mastery of the Baltic. Meanwhile the Tsar's soldiers had been safely conveyed over to Zealand by Tordenskjold, and, by the middle of September, a

---

* There were 19 English, 14 Russian and about 23 Danish liners, to say nothing of smaller vessels. The Dutch also sent a fleet to the Sound, but refused to co-operate in the descent.

combined force of 53,000 Russians and Danes were ready to cross over from Copenhagen to Sweden. All Europe now awaited, with the most intense expectation, the life-and-death struggle that was expected to ensue. Charles XII. had made the most of his six weeks' respite, and done wonders with his scanty resources. All the Scanian fortresses were well garrisoned and provisioned ; all the inland towns had been converted into military depots ; batteries had been built along the coast and an immense park of artillery had been got together at Carlscrona, ready to be conveyed wherever it was most wanted. Masses of infantry and cavalry were quartered where the attack was anticipated to fall first, and the King directed all the operations in person from a central position at the city of Lund.* It is true that, despite all his exertions, he had only been able to raise 20,000 men to meet 53,000, but every man of that 20,000 was willing to shed the last drop of his blood for his King and country, and, in the opinion of his enemies, Charles himself was worth 10,000 more. The descent had been fixed for the 21st September, but four days previous to that date the Tsar suddenly issued a " categorical resolution," whereby he declared that the season was now too far advanced for the projected descent, and it must therefore be postponed till the following year. In vain both England and Denmark indignantly protested, the Tsar remained immovable, and as the Danish Gov-

---

* He was prepared, in case of need, to raze all the southern towns of Sweden to the ground and burn all the villages so as to leave a wilderness behind him if a retreat became advisable.

ernment durst not attack Sweden single-handed, the whole project fell to the ground, for England, although quite willing to facilitate the descent, would take no active part in it.

Peter's extraordinary conduct on this occasion was due partly to a real fear of Charles XII., whose valour and ability he always rather overrated than under-rated, but chiefly to a deeply rooted and ever increasing distrust of his allies—England and Den-mark. From the very beginning, indeed, Peter, George I. and Frederick IV. had been singularly suspicious of each other's intentions, though each had solemnly and repeatedly guaranteed to the others their prospective conquests. Stress of circum-stances had held the three confederates together for a time, but with the fall of Wismar, their dissensions broke forth unmistakably. Both Prussia and Han-over had been very anxious to prevent Russia from taking any part in the siege of that fortress. They both considered that there were already far too many Russian troops in north Germany, and Peter's openly declared intention of marrying his niece, Catherine Ivanovna, to the Philo-Swedish Charles Leopold, Duke of Mecklenburg, seemed to them to point to the ultimate absorption of the Duchy by Russia. George I. was particularly energetic in the matter, even going the length of refusing to admit a Russian garrison into the captured city along with the Han-overians and Danes, a slight the Tsar never forgave him, although hostile activities were avoided. Peter's sudden abandonment of the Swedish expedition naturally did not tend to mend matters. His double-

dealing now appeared more than manifest both to
Denmark and England, the latter power even
thought of forming a league against him, to prevent
him from entirely dominating the Baltic. Peter, who
had in the meantime (under pressure it is true) withdrawn his troops from Mecklenburg, endeavoured to
strengthen his position by drawing closer to Frederick William of Prussia, who was also apprehensive
of Hanover, and, by the compact of Havelberg,
Russia and Prussia contracted a fresh offensive and
defensive alliance. Yet, for all this, the Tsar did not
absolutely break with his other allies, and negotiations were proceeding throughout the winter of
1716-1717 between Russia, Denmark and England-
Hanover with the sole result of widening still
farther the breach between the three Powers.

Thus, when he least expected it, Charles XII. saw
a last chance presented to him of retrieving his well-
nigh desperate fortunes by making capital out of
the dissensions of his enemies. This, it is true, could
only be done by diplomatic methods, and he himself
was no diplomatist ; but Fortune now singularly be-
friended him by placing by his side a man who was
a past master in all those subtle devices and dexterous
arts which he himself neglected or despised, a man
who seemed made by nature to be the right hand of
a hero in extremities, I mean, of course, the much
maligned and ill-fated Baron George Henry von
Görtz, whose judicial murder is one of the foulest
blots on Swedish history.

Few names have gone down to posterity more
blackened by calumny than the name of Görtz.

According to the Swedes, there was no vice to which he was not addicted, no crime of which he was not capable. But the Swedes had too many good reasons for detesting this extraordinary man to be able to do him justice. Anyhow, although no saint, Görtz was very far from being a mere scamp, and his character, if always more or less of an enigma, is, so far as it is intelligible at all, rather attractive than otherwise. He seems to have been an audacious adventurer with a perfect passion for intrigue on a vast scale ; not over-scrupulous, perhaps, as to his means and methods, but intent rather on glory than gain, and quite capable of the most enthusiastic, the most self-sacrificing devotion. No really bad man could have idealised Charles XII. so completely, no mere poltroon could have braved the wrath of a whole nation as nonchalantly and met death on the scaffold as gallantly as he did. As to his abilities, nobody, not even his bitterest enemies, ever dared to deny them, indeed, it was the dread even more than the hatred of him, that ultimately brought him to the block. He was a man of brilliant parts, wide culture, fascinating often irresistible address, equally ready with his pen and his tongue, and with a marvellous knowledge of human nature, especially the seamy side of it. A perfect master of finesse, and inexhaustibly rich in projects and expedients, his supple, versatile intellect could work a dozen divergent, even contradictory, schemes simultaneously, to the utter mystification of less adroit politicians. He was, in fact, a born diplomatist who did twenty times as much as Talleyrand or Metternich, with not a twentieth part of their resources.

BARON GÖRTZ.
FROM AN OLD ENGRAVING.

Nothing is known for certain of Görtz till his thirtieth year, except that he was born in 1668 of a noble Franconian stock, that he studied at Jena, and had one eye knocked out there. He first comes prominently before the world about the year 1700, when we find him high in the favour and confidence of the Duke of Holstein-Gottorp. But the little Duchy was much too narrow a field for a man of Görtz's abilities, and he looked abroad for more congenial employment. He seems always to have had an intense admiration for Charles XII., and this feeling, together with the bold ambition of helping the King out of his manifold difficulties, induced him to enter the Swedish service at the very time when Sweden's fortunes were at their lowest ebb. On Charles's arrival at Stralsund, Görtz hastened to meet him, solicited and obtained an audience, although he well knew that his numerous enemies had already done their utmost to prejudice Charles against him, and succeeded in a single interview in completely winning the King's favour. From that moment till Charles's death, Görtz was indispensable. Although still, nominally, only in the service of the young Duke of Holstein, he became, in reality, Charles's "Grand Vizier," as the Swedish Ministers, naturally indignant at seeing themselves set aside to make room for a foreign adventurer, preferred to call him. He had the absolute control of the finances and of all the great departments of state thrust upon him at the same time, and was entrusted besides with the Herculean task of making the best terms he could with Sweden's enemies. This he was eminently qualified to do, and his plan was, at bottom, an ex-

tremely simple one. Clearly perceiving that the
rupture between Sweden's most dangerous antagonists, Russia and England, was mainly due to the personal hatred between George I. and the Tsar, he
proposed, in the first instance, to open negotiations
with each of them simultaneously, adroitly work
upon their mutual jealousy to make them bid against
each other for the support of Sweden, and so, ultimately, obtain better terms from both. In pursuance of this plan, Görtz, on June 16, 1716, quitted
Sweden for The Hague, where he met and sounded
the Tsar whom he found inclined for peace, nay
Peter even promised that Sweden should obtain from
him much better terms than she expected, if only
she opened negotiations with him direct. The
tidings of this interview flashed like an electric shock
through Europe, and suddenly produced a complete
change in the aspect of affairs. All Sweden's enemies now showed a commendable desire to come to
terms with her, and George I. transmitted to Stockholm, through Count Gyllenborg, the Swedish Minister at London, a message to the effect that if the
King of Sweden were willing to forget the past, and
cede Bremen and Verden to Hanover, his Britannic
Majesty was ready to unite with him to drive the
Russians clean out of the Baltic. But Charles, justly
suspicious of the benevolent intentions of Hanover,
received the proposition coldly, and presently fresh
complications arose between the two Powers. At
the beginning of 1717, Gyllenborg in London, and
Görtz in Holland, were simultaneously arrested, by
order of the English Government, for alleged com-

plicity in a suspected Jacobite plot, of which Charles himself was believed to be the promoter. It appears that Jacobite emissaries had, in the course of 1715, secretly sounded Gyllenborg as to the possibility of conveying 6000 Swedes from Gothenburg to Scotland. Gyllenborg had reported the scheme to Charles at Stralsund and been snubbed for his pains. Another similar Jacobite project was submitted to Erik Sparre, the Swedish Ambassador at Paris, accompanied by a bribe of 50,000 rixdalers, and General Dillon actually brought about an interview between the Pretender and Sparre in the Bois de Boulogne; but Charles had peremptorily forbidden Sparre to dally any more with the Jacobites, and ordered the money to be returned. On the arrival of Görtz in Holland, however, the hopes of the Jacobites revived, and they began to negotiate with him. Görtz listened to them, not with any intention of helping them, which he knew to be useless, but in hopes of getting some money out of them, and he actually did obtain 80,000 rixdalers, which he spent in purchasing six vessels for his master. But he was very careful not to commit himself in any way, so that when he was arrested, and his papers were examined, nothing could be found to incriminate him, and he was therefore speedily released. He then reopened the question with the English Ministers, and even held out hopes of the cession of a part of the Duchy of Bremen and Verden, if Great Britain would guarantee Norway and Bornholm to Sweden. The English Ministers drew back, considering such counter claims excessive, whereupon Sweden drew still nearer to

Russia, and formal negotiations were opened between
the two Powers at Lofö, one of the Aland Islands
(May 23, 1718), to the chagrin of England and the
utter discomfiture of Denmark, Görtz and Carl Gyllenborg being the Swedish commissioners, and the
Russian Vice-Chancellor, Ostermann, acting with
General Bruce on behalf of the Tsar.

And now the eyes of all Europe were anxiously
fixed upon this rocky islet in the Gulf of Bothnia,
where the peace of the North was about to be decided. The star of Sweden seemed, thanks mainly
to Görtz's adroitness and audacity, to be once more
in the ascendant. The real extent of her weakness
was little suspected, but her heroic King, with a
powerful army behind him, and the wiliest diplomatist in Europe by his side, was a fact patent to all the
world, and the belief began gradually to gain ground
that even now Sweden might emerge triumphantly
from her difficulties. Thus in 1718 her position was
distinctly better than it had been any time since the
catastrophe of Pultawa. Even Prussia began to sue
for peace, while George I., thoroughly alarmed, sent
a special envoy to Lund, offering Charles XII. a
million rix-dalers, and England's friendly mediation,
if only he would part with Bremen and Verden ; but
the utmost that Charles would do was to pledge that
Duchy, or part of it, to Hanover, till the purchase
money given for it to Denmark by George I. had
been refunded by Sweden, yet only on condition
that England would, at the same time, place twelve
line-of-battle ships at Sweden's absolute disposal. To
this counter proposal George I. declined to listen.

Meanwhile Görtz pursued his negotiations at Lofö with consummate skill. Though all his far-reaching plans absolutely depended on the speedy conclusion of peace with Russia, though failure meant ruin, perhaps death, to him, he completely hoodwinked the Russian envoys by an affectation of nonchalance and superiority, which increased their eagerness to come to a settlement. He appeared at the rendezvous with princely pomp, kept Ostermann waiting a whole week, and affected to listen to his terms only as a matter of favour. He also skilfully insinuated that the negotiations with England were now approaching completion, and, by these and similar devices, finally extorted from the Russian commissioners incredibly favourable conditions of peace. For Ostermann, on the Tsar's behalf, actually offered to restore to Sweden, Finland, Livonia and Esthonia, provided that Ingria with Narva, Petersburg and part of Carelia, were ceded to him, or, as an alternative, promised to give back Finland, and assist Charles to conquer Norway and recover his German possessions, to which the Duchy of Mecklenburg was to be added, if only he ceded Ingria, Livonia and Esthonia. Görtz hastened off to Gothenburg to communicate these terms to his master, but Charles, more than ever suspicious of the Tsar, rejected his terms as "too high-flying," and sent Görtz back again to negotiate anew. Görtz himself had no great faith in Peter's promises, and quite expected him to break them the moment he had got what he wanted ; but he had built fresh plans on the hypothesis of even such a contingency

as this, arguing that in any case Finland would be
recovered, Russia separated from her allies, and
Sweden afforded a brief respite to look about her,
while it would always be open to Charles to recover
his losses from Russia when he had settled with his
other foes. He had, besides, another audacious
scheme for counteracting the Quadruple Alliance
recently formed by England, France, Holland and
the Emperor, against the ambitious designs of Spain
under Cardinal Alberoni, by forming a Quintuple
Alliance in support of that adventurous statesman.
But peace with Russia was his trump card, and he
was back again in his "enchanted island," as he
humorously called Lofö, at the end of July. The
Russian negotiators were growing uneasy at his
prolonged absence, but he adroitly succeeded in
disarming their suspicions and concluding a definite
treaty which was actually accepted and signed by
Peter, on August 26th, at Åbo. By this treaty, in
consideration of the cession of the Baltic provinces,
the Tsar solemnly engaged, with all his might, to
assist Sweden to compensate herself at the expense
of both Hanover and Denmark, and he had a special clause inserted in the treaty to the effect that
Charles should in future not expose his person to
danger, as the success of the whole plan depended
on his being able to lead it. Görtz was jubilant at
his triumph, but his joy was short-lived, for Charles's
inveterate obstinacy now ruined everything. With
as imperturbable a serenity as if he had suffered not
the slightest loss and Sweden was perfectly secure,
Charles immediately rejected all the Tsar's terms, on

the ground that the compensation offered him for the
cession of the Baltic provinces was uncertain and illusory, and the proffered alliance rather a hindrance
than a help. In vain did Görtz point out that it was
no longer a question whether the terms offered were
good, but whether, under the circumstances, any
better could be obtained ; Charles remained inflexi-
ble, and Görtz was sent back to Lofö for the third
time. It was with a sinking heart that the unfortunate Minister departed on what was to be his last
mission. Only by the most incredible exertions,
the most arbitrary measures, the most unscrupulous
devices, had he contrived during the last two years,
I will not say to uphold the State, but to prevent it
from collapsing altogether, but now he found himself absolutely at the end of his resources. When
there was no more money to be had, he had supplied
an artificial credit by issuing a vast quantity of metal
tokens,* and introducing a paper currency which had
relieved Charles XII. of his more pressing difficulties
for a time, enabled him to raise his army to nearly
70,000 men, rebuild numerous warships, and establish granaries and store-houses all over the kingdom ;
but this had only been done at the cost of fearful
suffering to the population, and on the assumption
that peace would shortly be concluded either with
Russia or England, or with both at once. For it

---

* In justice to him, however, it should be added that he limited
the issue of the token money to 2,000,000 rixdollars, providing for its
ultimate redemption ; but he found on his return from Holland that
the King, during his absence, had issued 13,000,000 more, which
upset all his calculations.

can never be repeated too often that Görtz's whole
plan for the rehabilitation of Sweden had been based
entirely on the prospect of a speedy and honourable
peace. If the King were to die in the meantime,
he, Görtz, was lost, and he knew it. The murderous
hatred with which the whole Swedish nation, high
and low, now regarded him, was irrational perhaps,
but perfectly intelligible. He, an alien, had become
not merely the supplanter but the ruler of all the
native statesmen. Even the Senate was insignificant beside him. He had only accepted office on
the express stipulation that he should be responsible
to the King alone, and Charles had given him *carte-
blanche* to employ and dismiss whomsoever he
would, and take whatsoever measures he chose, so
long as he could furnish the sinews of war. He had
used to the uttermost his enormous powers,* and
hitherto done all and more than all he had promised,
but he now foresaw that a crash was coming and he
trembled for the consequences. The country in fact
could literally bear no more. Two thirds of the
best land had ceased to be cultivated because there
were no labourers. Most of the fisheries had been
abandoned because the fishermen had been taken
for sailors. Foreign trade, owing to the blockade
of the Swedish ports, had been almost ruined, the
rate of marine assurance between Holland and
Gothenburg had risen to 25 per cent. of the value of

---

* Perfectly disinterestedly however. He took no reward or salary
for his services, and spent his private means, to the last penny, in the
service of the Crown.

the cargo. In the capital the utmost misery prevailed. Home baking and brewing was strictly forbidden, lest the Government bakeries and breweries should suffer. There was an indescribable dearth of meat, butter, salt and tallow. Artisans had to leave off work in the winter time for want of candles. Many even of the gentry were obliged to lie in bed for twelve or eighteen hours in the dark, for the same reason. By the end of 1718, the Government had just enough money left to go on with for another fortnight and no more. Görtz himself had already compared the state of the finances to a tottering tower threatening every moment to crush the whole political edifice beneath its massive weight, and he now frankly informed the King that he could do no more. "We cannot go on beyond the end of the year," he said, "and we shall be plunged into a greater chaos than has ever been seen in any other country, unless, before that time, we are quit of at least one of our enemies." Then he begged, as he had so often done before, to be released from his duties ; but Charles could not spare him, and accordingly he set out again for the Åland Islands, full of the gloomiest forebodings. He declared to his friends that in the event of " a certain unlucky conjuncture," by which he evidently meant the King's death, he saw only the wheel and the stake before him, and he advised his ward, the young Duke of Holstein, in case of accidents, to send his jewels to the residence of the French Ambassador at Stockholm instead of to his, Görtz's, house, which might any day be plundered by the mob.

Yet, in the eyes of many, Görtz's dynastic sympathies were a far greater offence than his alleged oppression of the people, and he himself knew full well that the blow which was to bring him down would come rather from above him than from below. For though, in point of fact, Charles's "Grand Vizier," it should be borne in mind that Görtz had no legal status whatever in Sweden, and was only known there, officially, as the chief minister and counsellor of the young Duke of Holstein. Now the young Prince was the nearest heir to the throne. He had had a formidable competitor in his aunt the Princess Ulrica; but she, by common consent, had forfeited whatever claim she might once have possessed by marrying, without obtaining the previous consent of the Estates, an alien in religion, Prince Frederick of Hesse. Charles evidently thought so too, for when the news of the ball following the espousals was brought to him at Stralsund, he said with a smile: "My good sister is dancing away the crown of Sweden!" On the other hand, by one of the laws of Charles XI., the reigning monarch had the sole right of appointing his successor, and the Princess now bent all her efforts to obtain from her brother a declaration in her favour. But Görtz, with equal pertinacity, was also striving for a similar declaration on behalf of his ward the Duke of Holstein, and thus there went on around the King, in the last years of his reign, a stealthy but ceaseless struggle for the succession, all the more venomous because these mortal antagonists were compelled to meet and even to work together as friends. Both

the Hessian and the Holstein factions did their best
to circumvent and traduce each other, as far as they
dared; but Charles, though he saw and heard everything, treated them both with a mystifying im-
partiality, which made it impossible to say to which
side he really leaned. On the one hand he appointed
his brother-in-law, the Prince of Hesse, his generalissimo, and confided to him his military projects, but
on the other hand he would allow of no interference
with Görtz, and he invariably treated both his sister
and his nephew, on the very rare occasions when he
met them, with equal politeness, but also with equal
reserve. The truth seems to be that Charles saw
much farther ahead than any of the schemers who
beleaguered him, and already recognised the utter
futility of attempting to anticipate the future.
"What is the use of *my* fixing the succession?" he
said on one occasion. "It is as much as I can do to
make these Swedes of mine obey me while I am still
alive, how then can I expect them to obey me when
I am dead."

And there was a third Party, which, though it kept
discreetly in the background and gave no visible sign
of life, embraced within it the most thoughtful and
prudent statesmen in the realm, and was in the
end to prevail. This was the Party of Freedom
and Parliamentary Government, and its leader
was the Chancellor Count Arvid Bernhard Horn.
We have seen what a difficult part Horn had
had to play between inclination and duty during
the King's absence; but he had, on the whole,
acquitted himself well, and when Charles landed

at last on Swedish soil, Horn felt that he could
face his sovereign with a good conscience, and
straightway set out to meet him, taking along with
him his ward the Duke of Holstein. Charles received his nephew kindly, but, turning to the Chancellor, first measured him from head to foot, and then
exclaimed: "Count Horn, Count Horn, methinks
you have grown a head taller since last we met!"—
and with that he turned his back upon him without
another word. Horn rightly took this to be a sign
of disgrace, and retired forthwith to his country seat
at Ekebyholm. He perceived that the King had no
further need of his services, and indeed what fellow-
ship could there be between a monarch who was prepared to perish sword in hand for an idea, and a
minister who desired peace instantly and at any price?
Görtz presently succeeded Horn as Governor of the
Duke of Holstein, and when, shortly afterwards, the
University of Upsala honoured the Count by electing
him its Chancellor, the King, who had the right of
veto, refused to either sanction or annul Horn's
nomination. Henceforth the Party of Freedom was
constrained to look on while Charles XII. drained
away the very life blood of the nation in the prose-
cution of what seemed to men of Horn's stamp a
useless and hopeless war. Interference on their part,
during the King's lifetime, was out of the question.
The common people, though they murmured loudly,
still looked up to their King as almost a superior
being, while even the Magnates, who knew him
better, were fascinated, in spite of themselves, by

CHARLES X.I.

FROM AN ENGRAVING OF A PORTRAIT BY ENGBERG.

his nobler qualities and his heroic virtues. But now a sudden yet not altogether unlooked for catastrophe occurred which shattered the monarchy, and enabled the people to re-fashion what remained of their ancient liberties out of the ruins.

CHAPTER XIV.

THE LAST VENTURE.

1718–1719.

Charles XII. at Lund—Meeting with his sister Ulrica—Invades Nor-
way a second time—Siege of Fredriksten—The King shot dead
in the trenches—Arrest and judicial murder of Baron Görtz—
Charles's death a benefit to Sweden—Heroic endurance of the
Swedish nation during his reign—Agriculture—Trade—Finance
—Population—Character of Charles XII.

E have seen that at the end of August,
1716, Charles XII. hastened from Nor-
way to defend the south of his realm
against the threatening Russo-Danish
invasion, fixing his headquarters at
the old university city of Lund.
Here, excepting two rapid tours of
inspection to the Norwegian frontier, he remained
till June, 1718, or nearly two years, lodging at
the house of Master Martin Hegardt, professor
of theology at the university, whose wife and
children the King ennobled as a reward for their
attention to him. He also stood godfather to a
baby who was born during his stay at the house.

From a military point of view Lund was, under existing circumstances, perhaps the most convenient place of residence Charles could have chosen both for attack and defence, besides being more in touch with the rest of Europe than the comparatively remote capital which the King was never to see again, although, in his letters to his sister, he expresses the hope of re-visiting it one day. His mode of life in these latter years was even more austere than usual. He rose at three o'clock in the morning, giving audiences or working with his secretaries till seven. Then, whatever the weather, he would mount his horse and take violent exercise till two. His meals were, as usual, very short and simple, home-made marmalade, of which he was very fond, being the only delicacy he allowed himself, and this was regularly supplied to him by his sister Ulrica.* The royal table reflected too the poverty of the land. The silver and even the zinc plate had long since disappeared ; all the dishes were now of pewter. At nine or ten the King retired to rest, sleeping generally on nothing but a straw mattress, with his mantle spread over him. On Sundays he always went to church, morning and evening, he also attended special service, every Friday, and observed his daily devotions with the most scrupulous regularity. Occasionally he would amuse himself by disputing with the university professors or listening

---

* After acknowledging the receipt of one such consignment, he adds politely : " I am sure it will taste all the better from being *mon cœur's* own handiwork." Then in a postscript, " I have since eaten *mon cœur's* health in it."—*Egh. Bref,* No. 100.

to their disputations on the most abstruse philosophical or mathematical subjects, and the heads of
one such argument drawn up by his own hand, and
entitled " *Anthropologia physica*," has come down to
us.* Twice during his stay at Lund he fell ill, the
second time seriously, the hard life he led having
affected his chest, and re-opened the wound in his
foot. On August 30, 1716, Charles met his " sister
Ulla," whom he had not seen for sixteen years.
There is reason to believe that the relations between
them were now somewhat strained, for, although
the Princess had pressed for an interview again and
again in the most urgent 'terms, Charles could not
find the time to go and see her for nearly nine
months after his arrival in Sweden, and when he did
go, it was only for a few hours, for he rode back
direct to Lund the following day. After that they
did not see each other again for twelve months,
although the Princess insisted again and again on
another interview, would not accept her brother's
excuses† and apologies, and even humorously
threatened to invade his camp if he did not visit
her bower. Some historians have seen in this pro-

---

* The document itself, with an interesting account of its genesis,
is in the Appendix to the *Egh. Bref*.

† They were mostly pleas of want of time and opportunity. Thus
on Sept. 17, 1717, he wrote : " I much regret that I must still postpone personally visiting my best of all sisters. I protest that my
dearest and only desire is to have that pleasure again, nay that my
desire thereof is so great that it cannot be greater. But necessity has
demanded, and still demands, that for the sake of various circumstances and opportunities I should remain on the borders of Scania."
—*Egh. Bref*, No. 108.

crastination on Charles's part a symptom of coolness
and estrangement which they attribute to his secret
displeasure at his sister's unauthorised interference
in state affairs during his absence. It may be so,
but it is pure conjecture; and, on the other hand,
there are many facts which point to the opposite
conclusion, such, for instance, as the increase the
King made to his sister's already ample allowance,
the frequent gifts he gave her, the favour he showed
to her husband and the kindly almost sportive tone
of his letters to her. It should also be remembered
that, during these last three years, Charles was
literally overwhelmned with cares and anxieties,
negotiating constantly with all or nearly all the
Powers of Europe, and expecting a fresh invasion of
his domains every day. Finally, however, on March
21st, he did find the time to visit his sister at Kris-
tinehamn, where the whole royal family, including
the Prince of Hesse and the Duke of Holstein, had
assembled to meet him. He stayed with them till
April 2d, or nearly twelve days, when the Princess
returned to Stockholm, and the King, after escorting her part of the way, repaired to the Norwegian
frontier, where for the next six weeks he carefully
inspected all the Swedish outposts from Eda in
Vermland to Stromstad.

For Charles had now determined upon a second
invasion of Norway. He himself, at the head of
the main army, was to advance upon Christiania,
General Armfelt, with a subsidiary force, upon
Trondhjem. The boundary fortresses were to be
captured and demolished; the various Norse coun-

ties converted into Swedish provinces under Swedish laws in order of conquest, and Swedish governors
and officials substituted for Norwegian wholesale.
Accordingly, in August, Armfelt set out with 14,000
men, and, favoured by an unusually dry season,
made his way, without meeting with any serious
opposition, up to the very walls of Trondhjem.
But the city was too strong to be taken by
assault, and throughout the autumn the Swedish army gradually wasted away in the fruitless
attempt to blockade it. Meanwhile the King had
assembled another army of 22,000 men, with which,
towards the end of October, he invaded southern
Norway. The season was late, the weather rainy,
the roads were difficult, the rivers in flood. But, with
Charles at their head, the Swedes defied every obstacle, waded, or swam through the floods, scaled the
mountains, and drove the Danes before them over
the Glommen. But the troops soon began to suffer
terribly from stress of weather, exposure, bad water,
want of food and extreme fatigue. It is said that,
before the end of November, 2000 of the younger
men had sickened and died. But the example of the
King made it a point of honour with the soldiers to
endure the most terrible hardships silently and even
cheerfully, and throughout this, his last campaign,
Charles fared worse than the meanest of his warriors, frequently returning from long rides soaking
wet, and throwing himself, just as he was, on a
wooden bench in some wretched hovel, or even sleeping on the coldest night in the open air, with his
weary head resting on a soldier's knee. The first

THE FORTRESS OF FREDRICKSHALD.

FROM AN OLD PRINT.

operations of the Swedes were directed against the frontier fortress of Fredriksten near Fredrikshald. On November 27th an outlying bastion, called Gyllenlöw, was stormed by 200 grenadiers led by the King in person, who helped to place the storming ladders against the walls, and was the second to enter the breach, and immediately afterwards trenches were opened against the fortress itself. Charles had his headquarters at Tistedal, a little place north of the river on which the fortress lay, but, in order to be constantly at hand to hasten on the operations and share the dangers of his soldiers, he had built for him a little wooden hut closer to the fortress, where, for the most part, he slept and had his meals. On November 30th, which happened to be the first Sunday in Advent, the King rode over to his headquarters at Tistedal, changed his clothes, and sorted his papers, many of which he destroyed. It was noticed that he appeared ill at ease all day, but he gave his orders as usual, and attended divine service both in the morning and the afternoon. At four o'clock he rode out as usual to his little hut, and presently the soldiers, whose duty it was to work in the trenches, came marching up, and were allotted their respective positions. By this time the trenches had been carried within musket-shot of the fortress, and the soldiers were obliged to keep well behind their fascines, as they worked. At about eight o'clock the King had his supper, standing upright in the trench. He was now in a particularly good humour again, and playfully caressing his old pantler Huttman, raised him to the higher grade of chief-cook, and

ordered the certificate of appointment to be made
out at once. The trench in which the King now
stood was within range of the fortress, but the
dusk of evening made it difficult for the enemy
to sight objects properly. They therefore hung
out a number of burning pitch-wreaths on the walls,
and discharged fire-balls from time to time to light
up the country around. Observing this, Charles
began to suspect a coming sortie, and, in order to
see exactly what was going on, he climbed to the
top of the trench, and lay down along the inner
slope of its breastwork, with his head and arms
above its crest, so that he could observe both the
fortress in front of him, and his own soldiers working in the trenches below, but, at the same time,
exposing himself freely to the bullets that were flying about. " That is no fit place for your Majesty,"
observed one of the officers, a Frenchman, Maigret
by name, " musket-balls and cannon-balls have as little respect for a King as for a common soldier."
" Don't be afraid," replied Charles, and he remained
where he was. Maigret would have protested still
further, but some of the Swedish officers whispered :
" Let him be! The more you warn him, the more
he 'll expose himself ! " It was now about nine o'clock,
and the moon had just risen. The King still lay
along the slope, with his head above the crest of the
rampart, and his cheek resting on his left hand.
Quite close to him in the trench below were nearly
a dozen officers ; General Schwerin, with a few others,
stood a little distance off, and hundreds of soldiers
were busily working all around. The officers in the

trench began secretly deliberating among themselves
as to the best way of enticing the King down from
his dangerous point of vantage, when suddenly they
heard a dull thud like a large stone falling on damp
earth, and the same instant the King's head sank
down upon his mantle, while his left hand dropped
limply to his side, though his body remained in exactly the same position as before. " Lord Jesus!
The King is shot!" cried one of the officers close at
hand. General Schwerin was immediately sent for,
while Maigret and his comrades lowered the body into
the ditch, when it was found that a canister-shot had
pierced the King's left temple, close to the eye, and
come out again on the right side of the head, a little
lower down, leaving behind it a wound so large, that
three fingers could be thrust into it. Death must
have been instantaneous.*

The very day after Charles's fall, Baron Görtz was
arrested and imprisoned, in the King's name, by
order of his arch-enemy the Prince of Hesse. Görtz
had only just returned from the Aland Islands, and
was actually on his way to the royal camp, to advise
his master to at once open negotiations with England, so as to checkmate, if possible, a rumoured
rapprochement between George I. and the Tsar,
which threatened to ruin all Görtz's plans. For six
weeks he was kept in close custody, while articles of
impeachment were carefully drawn up against him

---

* The absurd legend as to the alleged assassination of Charles by
one of his own people was disposed of, once for all, by Paludan
Müller's *Er Kong Carl XII. falden ved Svigmord.* Compare,
too, Carlens's *Några blad om Carl XII.*

by an extra-judicial tribunal, against whose jurisdiction he vainly protested. Even at this distance of time, it is impossible to read, without a thrill of indignation, of the scandalous treatment this unfortunate man received at the hands of self-styled judges who were really his personal enemies. His plea that, as an alien, he was not amenable to a Swedish tribunal was rejected as *absurd*. His petition for legal assistance was refused as *unnecessary*. He was not allowed to call witnesses on his behalf, he was not permitted to compose his defence in writing. To prepare his reply he was only granted a day and a half, which did not even give him time to read through a fifth part of the voluminous evidence. Nay, a new crime, unheard of before, had to be invented for his destruction. He was accused of compassing the ruin of the realm, and seeking, by the most abominable means, to *set the King against his subjects*.* This so-called trial lasted from January 16 to February 9, 1719, when the tribunal unanimously condemned Görtz to be beheaded, and his remains to be buried beneath the gallows. He received the tidings of his sentence in prison with composure, but petitioned the Senate that his body might be spared the disgrace of interment by the common hangman. Count Cronhjelm had the humanity to advise compliance on the ground that it

---

* It had been intended to charge him with peculation, but a careful examination of his papers showed that the State was his debtor to a very large amount. This amount, with compound interest, was chivalrously paid over to Görtz's descendants by Gustavus III. more than sixty years afterwards.

DEATH MASK OF CHARLES XII.

was not right " to treat so shamefully the man whom
his late Majesty had honoured with his closest confidence." Many of Cronhjelm's fellow Senators
were inclined to support him; but the pious Chancellor Horn opined that "he who had turned the
whole realm upside down could not be punished too
severely," and the Queen (for Ulrica already wore
her brother's crown) put an end to the discussion by
grimly informing the Senate that she had already
instructed the high-sheriff to proceed with Görtz
according to the sentence of the commissioners.*
A few days after his execution, when all Stockholm
had flocked to the cathedral to witness Charles
XII.'s state funeral, one of Görtz's faithful servants
dug up his remains, and conveyed them to his friends
abroad.

Charles XII. died in the thirty-sixth year of his
age, and the twenty-first of his reign. His death
meant the speedy and complete extinction of Sweden's political greatness, but it was a distinct benefit
to the Swedish people. His life was the sole obstacle in the way of the peace for want of which the
nation was perishing, and everything tends to show
that he would never have accepted any peace that
was unaccompanied by complete restitution of all
that he had lost, or an ample equivalent in exchange

---

* Görtz died with great dignity and courage. He was carefully
dressed in black velvet when he mounted the scaffold. As he took
off his coat and collar he was heard to mutter : " Ye bloodthirsty
Swedes, take then the blood you have thirsted for so long." His last
words, as he laid his head on the block, were : " Lord, into Thy
hands I commend my spirit." His head fell at the first stroke.

for it, which amounts to the same thing.*   It is true
that the sufferings of the Swedes during the last
years of the reign, terrible as they were, have been
made too much of by historians of a strong anti-
monarchical bias, like Fryxell for instance, and it was
therefore a comparatively easy task for a dialectician
of Bernard von Beskow's adroitness to detect and
expose many of such blunders and exaggerations.
But that chivalrous apologist certainly went too far
the other way, and in his eagerness to exonerate his
hero, the lion-hearted King, frequently maligned and
calumniated the long-suffering nation.   Moreover,
both sides had only very doubtful or insufficient
data to go upon, and therefore were, for the most
part, working or, perhaps I should say, fighting in
the dark.   Only within the last seven years has a
severely scientific examination of the subject been
attempted.   I allude to Herr Axelson's exhaustive
summary † of the official documents relating to the
economical position of Sweden during the reign of
Charles XII., and I am convinced that whoever has
the courage to patiently master this formidable

---

* On the other hand, as Herr Carlson, the able editor of Charles's
autograph letters, points out, the often repeated statement that Charles
XII. would never consent to cede *an inch* of Swedish territory, rests
on a misunderstanding.   Charles's instructions to Maurice Vellingk
as to the negotiations to be conducted with the English envoy at
Cassel in 1717, prove that he was quite ready to give an inch or two
of Bremen and Verden to Hanover, if he were allowed to take a corresponding number of ells from Norway at Denmark's expense.—
Egenh. Bref, No. 292.

† *Bidrag till Kännedomen om Sveriges tillståndt på Carl XII.'s tid.*
Visby, 1888.

array of summarised statistics, can only arrive at one
conclusion, which is that from 1709 to 1719 Sweden
was rushing to ruin at an ever accelerating speed.
It would require a volume half as large again as the
present one to adequately deal with Herr Axelson's
facts and figures, but even the few particulars there-
from, that I shall now proceed to set out, will prove I
think, that I am guilty of no exaggeration.

Sweden, under the Carolines, was, as she still is,
mainly an agricultural country, and it was upon the
agricultural population, therefore, that the grievous
burden of feeding the war mainly rested. Wonderful, indeed, was the dogged endurance and the
persistent dutifulness of the bulk of the Swedish
peasantry during the trials of Charles's later years * ;
to posterity it seems almost superhuman. Even the
splendid valour of the Swedish soldier in the field
was as nothing compared with the heroic endeavour
of the Swedish yeoman † at home to respond to the
endless and ever increasing demands made upon
him by the Government. These demands were of
many kinds. First there was the obligation of
supplying the crown magazines with grain and
provender, including the still more onerous duty of
conveying the stores, so requisitioned, gratis, often
hundreds of miles. Enormous quantities of horses,

---

* Previously to 1709 the burden of supporting the war rested, for
the most part, on Sweden's enemies.

† The gentry and wealthier classes were much more backward.
The authorities frequently complain of their shifts for evading their
obligations, and the King bitterly contrasts their "sluggishness"
with the zeal of the peasants.

wagons and wagoners were required for such purposes, and the ultimate consequence was that many
farmers were so impoverished as not to have the
means of cultivating their own lands ; thus many of
the most fruitful districts were deserted, and became
savage wildernesses. Still more oppressive was the
obligation of providing for the maintenance of the
troops, which, especially during the latter part of the
reign, were quartered on the people all over the
country, though the southern province of Scania
(" the bread-basket " of Sweden, as it was called from
its great fertility), which lived in constant fear of invasion, and had to support the relatively immense
army assembled to defend it, suffered most of all.
From the battle of Helsingborg to the King's death,
a period of nearly nine years, during which there
were no less than five total failures of crops, every
farm in that unfortunate province had to maintain
from two to three soldiers. In 1712, from 9143 to
13,150 soldiers were supported by the peasantry
there, besides 10,416 horses, while by 1716 the
numbers had actually risen to 20,000. Nay more,
besides maintaining these unwelcome guests, the
farmers had to put up with their violence and
extortions, and supply them with luxuries in
the shape of tobacco and spirits, while they and
their children were half starving. Another vexa-
tious burden was the supplying of post horses to the
royal couriers and other messengers, gratis, the
maintenance of prisoners of war, of whom there
were many thousands, and the forced requisitions of
live-stock. The King, to do him justice, attempted

QUEEN ULRICA LEONORA II.
CHARLES XII'S YOUNGER SISTER.

to relieve the sufferings of the willing peasantry, by
compelling the backward gentry to bear an equal
share of the burdens, and by abolishing several of
the more oppressive measures that had been adopted
during his absence ; but the misery of the nation
was so general and so obvious, that foreigners, who
visited the land at this time, were appalled by the
sights they saw. Van Effen, a Dutchman, who
traversed south Sweden in 1719, was struck by the
almost total absence of young men in the rural districts. He tells us that, throughout his travels, his
drivers were either grey-haired men, girls or lads
between eleven and twelve. "I can assure you,"
he adds, "that in the whole of [south?] Sweden, I
have not seen a man between twenty and forty,
soldiers excepted."

And if agriculture was dwindling and pining, trade
and commerce bid fair to die out altogether. From
1709 onwards, the Sound, the Belts and the Cattegat
were practically closed to Swedish vessels by the
Danes, while Charles's blockade ordinance, forbidding all trade with the provinces captured by Russia,
ruined the Baltic trade likewise. Equally mischievous was his privateering regulation authorising the
city of Gothenburg to fit out privateers for the purpose of seizing all foreign vessels that dared to ply
to and from the Russian ports in spite of him. This
only led to the appearance of English, Dutch and
Danish warships in the northern seas, to protect their
merchantmen from the Gothenburg privateers and
retaliate upon the Swedish merchantmen, with the
natural result that navigation to and from Sweden

became almost impossible except in neutral bottoms. Thus the Swedish merchant marine, which at the death of Charles XI. numbered 775 sail, had sunk at the death of Charles XII. to 209 sail.* Most of the foreign trade that remained was carried on secretly through the Dutch, and in consequence of the rise of freights to 50 per cent., and of assurances to 25 per cent., of the value of the cargoes, there was soon such a scarcity of hemp, wool, hides and other raw materials, that manufactures in Sweden were completely paralysed.

The finances had been in an unsatisfactory state from the very beginning of the reign. It is true that Charles XI. had left behind him a surplus of £450,000, † but, within a couple of years, the extravagant young King had spent every penny of this hoard, while two years later there was a deficit of about £1,212,035. This was partially made up again by foreign subsidies, and, during the earlier triumphant campaigns, the war was, for the most part, self-supporting; but the loss of the Baltic provinces in 1709–1710 deprived Sweden of an annual revenue of £210,000, and, by 1716, the deficit had risen again to £705,000, not including the debt of the Crown to

---

* Gothenburg alone flourished. During these years, her 50 privateers captured 136 prizes of an estimated value of £170,000, every penny of which went into the pockets of the Gothenburg merchants.

† That is, of course, allowing for the difference in prices now and then.

the Bank of Sweden, which amounted in 1718 to
£1,267,200. Then came the period of desperate
expedients, such as the issue of metal tokens, and
incontrovertible paper money. Görtz would have
strictly limited the issue of such notes and tokens to
an amount easily redeemable in better times, but the
King, who was no financier, and did not look a day
beyond his urgent present needs, disregarded all his
Minister's counsels and warnings, and, at the time of
his death, paper money to the nominal amount of
£3,724,050 was actually in circulation.

But the most significant symptom of the national
exhaustion was the steady decrease in the population. At the death of Charles XI. in 1697, the population of Sweden was 1,376,000, at the death of Charles
XII. in 1718, it had sunk to 1,247,000, a decrease of
between 11 and 12 per cent.* It is only fair to add
that a considerable proportion of this diminution
was due to the pestilences and famines which visited
Sweden during Charles's reign, the province of Scania
alone losing 20,000 men from these causes, between
the years 1700 and 1713 ; but there can be no doubt
that the drain of the long war upon the population
was very serious, especially during the latter years
of the reign, when the mortality among the raw recruits, upon whom Charles then mainly depended,
was terrible. Calculations have been made as to the

* On the other hand, during the thirty years immediately following
Charles's death, the *increase* in population was 569,589 or 45 per
cent.

exact number of those who perished during the wars of Charles XII., but, for want of proper data, all such calculations must be regarded as very unreliable. In the opinion of competent judges, however, Beskow's estimate of 150,000 comes nearest to the truth, which would make more than one fourth of the entire male population.*

It remains for me to attempt to give some idea of Charles XII.'s personality, and, if possible, of his character also, for, as Gustavus III. has well remarked, his character is much more difficult to determine than is generally imagined. And first, as to his personal appearance. In figure he was tall, broad across the shoulders, slim across the loins, and with a bearing at once erect and easy. Those who approached him were impressed by his manly gravity and imperturbable calmness, yet his manner, especially towards subordinates, was always gracious and reassuring, though never familiar, and the slight but invariable smile that played upon his lips somewhat softened the natural severity of his expression. His features were not unpleasing. His forehead was high and broad, his eyes dark blue, and " full of martial fire," his nose large, his chin smooth and dimpled. In his early years he wore a large peruke after the French fashion, but during his warfare it was laid aside, and his dark-brown hair (it grew grey before he was thirty) was clipped short, and brushed upwards

---

* Or distributed proportionately over the eighteen years that the war lasted, about 8000 men per annum. This does not seem excessive considering all the circumstances of the case.

THE HILT OF CHARLES XII'S SWORD

all round, so that it looked like a crown, which prac-
tice, together with the growing baldness of later
years, makes the forehead of Charles XII., in his
portraits, seem so abnormally high and long. His
personal habits were simple in the extreme. Nobody would ever have taken him for a King from his
dress. He would not tolerate even the most insignificant ornament, and wore invariably a dark blue
coat with a high collar, yellow vest and trowsers,
large elkskin gauntlets, a broad unembroidered belt
of buffalo hide, and huge heavily spurred riding
boots which reached above the knee, with an ordinary cavalry mantle thrown over the whole. He
would never wear furs in the coldest weather, nor
armour to protect him from pikes and bullets. His
food was of the simplest kind, strong fat meats,
coarse vegetables, fruit, bread and a little water.
His dinner rarely lasted more than a quarter of an
hour, and he ate rapidly and in perfect silence. In
his earlier campaigns he made use of a mattress and
counterpane, but speedily rejected them in his later
years as " unnecessary comforts," and was wont to
throw himself down on a heap of straw, or a bare
plank, and snatch a hasty repose with his cloak
wrapped around him. He never slept longer than
five or six hours. Charles's manners were austere
but never rude. The pains his excellent mother had
taken with him in this respect had not been thrown
away, and he was remarkable for his courtesy to
those around him. Towards ladies, in particular, he
was always punctiliously polite, although their society was, generally speaking, embarrassing to him,

and he avoided them as much as possible.* Nevertheless Charles was far from being the stern and
saturnine young hero he is commonly supposed to
have been. On the contrary, he had inherited from
his father a strong sense of humour which constantly
asserted itself in all sorts of ways; even in the most
anxious and terrible times, he was always rather gay
than grave. † Another very widespread fallacy is
that Charles was a hard, stern and even cruel man.
On the contrary, he was of a very kindly nature.
Particularly strong were his domestic affections. In
his correspondence he is perpetually enquiring after
the health of his sisters and his grandmother; always
writes to them most often when he hears that they
are unwell; never forgets their birthdays, and tries,
to the utmost of his power, to comfort them in their
afflictions. It is thus, for instance, that he consoles
his favourite sister, Hedwig Sophia, for the loss of
her husband: " *Mon cœur* must by this time be as
well acquainted as we who are here, with the heavy
and terribly great calamity which has befallen us in
that we have lost our dear and beloved brother-in-
law the Duke [of Holstein] whom we can never
sufficiently mourn and lament, a loss that has turned

---

* His grandmother and sisters were much grieved at this, as they
desired him to marry, but he always declared that he was wedded to
his soldiers, and, at any rate, could not think of matrimony till he
was forty.

† See Krmann: *Historia Ablegationis ad regem Sveciæ Carolum
XII.*, 1708–9. Krmann had almost daily opportunities of seeing the
King during the trying march to the Ukraine, and the terrible Pultawa campaign, and was much impressed by his invariable cheerfulness and gaiety.

all our joy * into mourning. And yet it becomes us
to resign ourselves to the will of the Most High, and
patiently endure the well earned chastisement which
it has pleased Him to lay upon us, for He has taught
us that He lays no cross upon us so heavy that He
Himself cannot help us to bear it." † He was also
capable of warm friendships, ‡ and no elder brother
could have treated a younger brother more tenderly
than Charles treated the youthful Duke of Wurtemberg during their campaigns together. He was also
fond of animals, especially dogs and horses. His dog
Pompey used to sleep at the foot of his bed every
night till it died. For his soldiers Charles had a particular care. They always fared as well, and often better,
than he did himself, and he frequently stinted himself to add to their comforts. There are also innumerable instances of his kindness to individuals.
A little page generally slept in his antechamber, and
frequently when the cold was very severe, the King,
as he came in, would carefully spread his own mantle
over the sleeping lad's counterpane, then throw himself down on his own heap of straw or leaves, without
any covering at all. On the other hand it is quite
true that he exacted the most absolute obedience,
the most complete self-surrender from his soldiers
and his servants, and had no regard whatever for
the sufferings of a foe who threatened to be obstinate. We find him, for instance, directing his hesitat-

---

* At the victory of Klissov.

† *Egenh. Bref*, No. 49.

‡ *E. g.* for the Duke of Holstein, Stenbock and Horn in his earlier
years, and, at a later period, for the Prince of Hesse.

ing generals to " rather let the innocent suffer than
the guilty escape," * to " ravage, singe and burn all
round about, and reduce the whole district to a
wilderness," † to "make them sweat out contributions,"‡ and so on—certainly revolting commands
in the mouth of a youth of twenty! On the other
hand, none could be more generous to the vanquished, and he sternly suppressed every act of
license on the part of his own soldiers when fighting
had ceased. As to Charles's valour, modesty, self-
restraint § and piety, certainly his dominant qualities,
little need be added to what has already been said
in the course of this biography, yet I may here
remark that his religious views, during the latter
portion of his life, took a strong tinge of fatalism,
whereby he tried to explain, to his own satisfaction,
the undeserved failure of his righteous cause. As
the able editor of his letters, Herr Ernst Carlson, has
so well expressed it : " He seems to have gradually
elaborated a theory of alternating cycles of good and
bad luck, which he expresses in the words : ' In times
of war unlucky events must occasionally happen in
order that [future ?] luck may have freer course.' "
Such a theory naturally tended to encourage him

---

* *Egenh. Bref*, 160.
† *Ib.*, 162.
‡ *Ib.*, 201.
§ His self-restraint and his modesty are especially remarkable. In
all his correspondence, whether private or official, there is not a single
allusion to his own innumerable and extraordinary exploits although he
is always lavish in his praise of others, and however angry he may be
a hasty or violent expression never once escapes him.

THE BODY OF CHARLES XII. CARRIED BY HIS OFFICERS ACROSS THE NORWEGIAN FRONTIER.

FROM A PICTURE IN THE SWEDISH ACADEMY.

still further to defy danger and risk everything while patiently awaiting more fortunate conjunctures.

But it would be a great mistake to imagine that Charles XII. was nothing but a mere warrior, or even a mere hero. Intellectually he was very highly gifted, and had many of the qualities of a great ruler. Like his father, he was fond of hard work, and had an infinite capacity for taking pains. He had a quick comprehension, great acuteness, and a really marvellous memory, especially for figures. More than once during his Polish campaigns, when he had mislaid the key of his cipher correspondence, he not only read ciphered letters from Rehnskjöld and others, without it, but even composed such documents " out of my own head," as he expresses it, without making a single mistake. He could read, write and speak German and Latin as fluently as Swedish ; but his favourite study was mathe-matics, for which he had a strong natural bent. He used often to say that a man who did not know mathematics was only half a man, and once when the use of algebraical figures had been explained to him, he rejected them as unnecessary, and, to prove his contention, proceeded to work out with simpler symbols of his own devising some abstruse problems set him by the Lundian professors. Ab-stract philosophical discussions had also a great attraction for him. That he did not apply his mathematical genius more to warfare, was due partly, no doubt, to his inordinate love of adventure and his passion for deeds of prowess, but partly also to his contempt for his foes. It is true that no great general ever left more to chance than he did, and some military critics have even denied him the capacity of drawing up a complete and regular plan of campaign beforehand. But this is going too far. Klissov and Holowczyn are standing monuments of his generalship, and Sarauw * scornfully rejects the hypothesis that Charles was a mere knight-errant as " fundamentally false," and proves to demonstration that every one of his undertakings was based on a well thought out plan, " carried out with iron consistency."

Yet, after all, it is still a little premature to sum up Charles's character, but perhaps his great descendant, Gustavus III.'s, opinion of him comes nearest to the truth, and it is therefore with the words of that eloquent monarch that I will now conclude. " Charles XII.," he says, " was rather extraordinary than great. He certainly had not the true conquering temperament which simply aims at acquisition of territory. Charles took dominions with one hand only to give them away with the other. Superior to Alexander, with whom it were an injustice to compare him, he was as much inferior to his rival Peter in the qualities which make a great ruler, as he excelled him in those qualities which go to make a great hero."

---

* *Die Feldzüge Karl's XII.*

WATCH AND SEAL OF CHARLES XII.

FROM AN OLD ENGRAVING.

INDEX.

315